Portrait of Eli Farmer when he served as a Whig in the Indiana State Senate, 1843–45

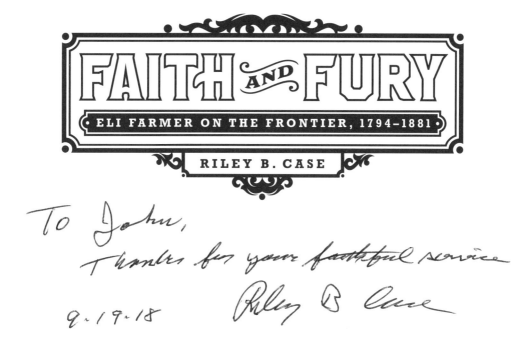

To John,
Thanks for your faithful service
Riley B Case
9-19-18

© 2018 Indiana Historical Society Press. All rights reserved.

This book is a publication of the
Indiana Historical Society Press
Eugene and Marilyn Glick Indiana History Center
450 West Ohio Street
Indianapolis, Indiana 46202-3269 USA
www.indianahistory.org
Telephone orders 1-800-447-1830
Fax orders 1-317-234-0562
Online orders @ shop.indianahistory.org

Library of Congress Cataloging-in-Publication Data

Names: Case, Riley B., author.
Title: Faith and fury : Eli Farmer on the frontier, 1794-1881 / Riley B. Case.
Description: Indianapolis : Indiana Historical Society Press, 2018. |
   Includes bibliographical references and index.
Identifiers: LCCN 2018014253 (print) | LCCN 2018033166 (ebook) | ISBN
   9780871954305 (epub) | ISBN 9780871954299 (cloth : alk. paper)
Subjects: LCSH: Farmer, Eli, 1794-1881. | Circuit riders—Indiana—Biography.
   | Methodist Episcopal Church—Indiana—Biography. | Itinerancy (Church
   polity)—Methodist Church.
Classification: LCC BX8495.F37 (ebook) | LCC BX8495.F37 C37 2018 (print) |
   DDC 287/.6092 [B] —dc23
LC record available at https://lccn.loc.gov/2018014253

The paper in this publication meets the minimum requirements of American National Standard for Information Sciences—Permanence of Paper for Printed Library Materials, ANSI Z39. 48–1984 ∞

No part of this publication may be reproduced, stored in or introduced into a retrieval system, or transmitted, in any form or by any means (electronic, mechanical, photocopying, recording, or otherwise) without the prior written permission of the copyright owner.

To the old circuit-riding-course-of-studies preachers (they missed seminary) of the former North Indiana Conference of the Methodist Church, who would gather in the 1950s and 1960s at the Love Feast at the annual conference to share their war stories. In Eli Farmer's language, they were not among the "authorities," but they did become the inspiration for my ministry.

Contents

Acknowledgments		ix
Introduction	*Religion in Post-Revolutionary America*	1
Chapter 1	*Eli Farmer's Family and Childhood, 1788 to 1813*	7
Chapter 2	*The Formative Years, 1814 to 1818*	17
Chapter 3	*Spiritual Searching and Conviction, 1817 to 1820*	31
Chapter 4	*Reclaimed, 1820 to 1822*	43
Chapter 5	*"God Has Given Me This Place," 1822 to 1826*	53
Chapter 6	*Officially Methodist, 1825 to 1826*	67
Chapter 7	*Good in Prayer and Singing, 1826 to 1827*	73
Chapter 8	*Taking on Lafayette, 1827 to 1828*	85
Chapter 9	*Sickness, Location, and Washington Circuit, 1828 to 1830*	93
Chapter 10	*Harvest Time, 1830 to 1832*	103
Chapter 11	*Greencastle, Location, and Brown County, 1833 to 1838*	117
Chapter 12	*Danville, Christian Union, and Sectarianism, 1838 to 1842*	129
Chapter 13	*Politics, 1830s to 1845*	141
Chapter 14	*The Trip South, 1846*	153
Chapter 15	*Nonsectarian Sectarianism, 1840s to 1853*	161
Chapter 16	*The* Bloomington Religious Times, *1853 to 1854*	169
Chapter 17	*Methodists Up-and-Coming without Farmer, 1850s*	179
Chapter 18	*The Civil War, 1861 to 1865*	185
Conclusion	*Christian Union at Last, 1863 to 1881*	193
Notes		197
Index		213

Acknowledgments

I wanted to write this book. It covers interests close to my heart: early Indiana, populist religion in the state, Methodism, revivalism, different understandings of the church, and good stories. I want to acknowledge and express appreciation for persons who guided me in writing the book and bringing it to publication. But I also want to recognize individuals, events, and influences that led to my desire to be a part of a book like this.

First, I want to thank my Aunt Gay Hughes, who even at age ninety-nine regaled me with stories passed down by grandparents and great-great uncles of life in Indiana long, long ago. Some of her stories went back to before the Civil War.

I am thankful for my parents, who took me to scores of different churches. Although we traveled a lot, our family never missed church meetings. It was an education in the multiplicity of religious expressions. One such expression was gained from my mother's eighty-three first cousins on her mother's side and other relatives among whom I lived as an Anabaptist Mennonite for five weeks each summer for many years in Berne, Indiana.

Taylor University, a school with a Methodist background in the Holiness tradition, was important to me. When I attended there, it seemed that on odd-numbered days we debated Calvinism in the dorm, and on even-numbered days we debated Holiness. It was there that I was called to the ministry.

Garrett Biblical Institute (now Garrett Evangelical Seminary) was also important in my education. I discovered early on there that the library had a complete set of *Methodist Quarterly Reviews* from 1818 on. This is where I was mentored by Doctor William Hordern, who actually understood fundamentalism. Hordern urged me to stay on for a second master's degree at Northwestern University, where I did my thesis on "Dispensationalism, Millennialism, and Sectarianism."

My education continued with my first three appointments in the ministry, all of them on circuits. The people of those circuit churches taught me about old-fashioned Methodism. Members of Union Chapel in Adams County, Indiana, introduced me to real Methodist revivalism and Holiness camp meetings.

I am grateful for my wife, Ruth, a true helpmate in many ways—especially when she proofreads my writings. Our nine grandchildren have been helpful, too. Whenever each of them completed third grade, we took them on an Indiana heritage grandparents trip, which lasted several days. This was partly for me, because it was fun and I always learned something new about Indiana. I also hoped they would impress their fourth grade Indiana history teachers with stories of James Whitcomb Riley, the Constitutional Elm, and the Reno brothers (Indiana train robbers).

I am grateful for the libraries of various Indiana communities where I have lived, particularly the genealogy departments in Marion and Kokomo, where sometimes, just for fun, I read county histories, the minutes of closed churches, and census reports. The Methodist archives at DePauw University have long drawn me in, thanks to archivist Wes Wilson and because I can go there to read the old *Western Christian Advocates* (from 1834).

Lilly Library, part of Indiana University Library and Archives in Bloomington, Indiana, and its staff are key. I very much appreciate their permission to grant publication of the Farmer manuscript as well as their support in many other ways.

I would also like to thank the many kindred spirits I have worked with at the Indiana United Methodist Commission on Archives and History and at the Indiana United Methodist Historical Society for their encouragement and for providing seed money for this book to be published. Another kindred spirit, Arlen Packard of the First United Methodist Church in Bloomington, was helpful in uncovering news stories of Eli Farmer from the church's archives.

I am grateful to Teresa Baer, managing editor of the Indiana Historical Society Press, for her suggestions and for guiding this book through to publication. And with her, appreciation goes to the IHS Press's graduate student intern for 2017–18, Patrick Hanlon, for research and editing help on the book, and to senior editor Ray E. Boomhower, editor Kathy Breen, and contract editor Natalie Burriss, who also helped to edit the book in various ways. I also thank Jennifer Harrison, consultant with the IHS, who spent much time with the Farmer story to help prepare it for an IHS You Are There exhibition.

Special recognition and appreciation goes to Robert Coolman, a building contractor from Valparaiso, Indiana, who is also a local pastor and coordinator of Operation Classroom, an Indiana missions project in Africa. One day I remarked to him that I wanted to write a book about Methodism in Indiana. He then told me about his great-great-great grandfather, a circuit rider named Eli Farmer, whose autobiography was languishing in the Lilly Library in Bloomington, unpublished and unappreciated. He procured a copy of the manuscript for me, and I soon forgot what else I had intended to write. Here were the stories, told firsthand, not only about Methodists on the frontier, but about camp meetings, revivals, republican forms of governance, populism in religion and politics, the Civil War, preaching to slaves in the South, fighting, business, Native Americans, poverty, and religious controversy. Farmer was on a first-name basis with such people as Sam Houston, Lorenzo Dow, and Andrew Wylie (first president of Indiana University). Furthermore, the stories pointed to bigger truths: the emergence of an American form of evangelicalism, how religion on the fringes became mainstream, the development of sectarianism in America, and the trajectory from camp meeting enthusiasm to religious expressions such as Pentecostalism.

Finally, and most of all, I thank Eli Farmer for a life well lived and his willingness to share it with us.

Map of Indiana showing the major cities and counties of Eli Farmer's Indiana life, 1820–81. The roughly shaped circles indicate the approximate areas of the circuits he rode and include the years that he served each circuit as an official traveling Methodist preacher. Major towns and settlements mentioned in Farmer's autobiography also appear on the map.

Introduction

Religion in Post-Revolutionary America

Most people enjoy a good story. Some like to tell stories. Old preachers are often known as storytellers. In Methodist language they were once referred to as "worn-out" preachers and sometimes as "croakers," a term applied because they often would grumble about how things were better in "the good old days."

One "worn-out" preacher who lived to a ripe old age was Eli Farmer (1794–1881). Farmer must have been telling his stories for years. In 1874, at the age of eighty, he began to put his stories together in an autobiography, which he introduced with these words: "I long have thought, I would give a sketch of my life and family, to have as a memento for my children, before I go hence to be no more, in this life. . . . In giving this sketch, I can but give an imperfect history but trust, a perusal of the events herein detailed, may instill the reader to higher aims in life, is the ardent wish of the Author."[1]

For most of his life Farmer owned property and a home in Monroe County, Indiana. In an early history of the county, he appears as a Bloomington businessman in the 1840s and as a founding member of the community's old settler's club in the 1850s. He was also a farmer, an editor, a Whig, a Republican, a soldier during the War of 1812, a self-appointed chaplain during the Civil War, a Freemason, and a state senator. If the manuscript is an indication of what he valued in his long life, however, Farmer remembered himself foremost as a preacher and evangelist. There is no mention of the Masonic lodge or the old settlers' club in his autobiography. He hardly mentions his life as an editor or his political philosophy as a state senator.[2]

Most of the manuscript is given to Farmer's life and adventures as a Methodist and as a Methodist preacher, and then it discusses his separation from the Methodist Church and his founding of a new denomination, the Christian Union Church. It is this material that will serve as the primary focus of this book. As a Methodist, Farmer was only officially a preacher for nine years, although a couple more years could be added when he was organizing Methodist circuits while not under appointment. He was not one of the Methodist "authorities," Farmer's own term for the Methodist leadership. But it is partly for this reason that Farmer's story is intriguing. Farmer writes as an "outsider," an independent spirit who—whether as a soldier, businessman, politician, editor, or preacher—did not easily conform to the expectations of others. At the height of his success as a Methodist preacher, when given the choice appointment of the Franklin circuit, which included Indianapolis, he is referred to as a "little" preacher, in contrast to others who had earned the reputation of "big" preachers.

Yet, in many respects, it was the little preachers, on the edges of the official system, who played a major role in developing what might be referred to as the frontier populist religious ethos, or guiding beliefs. This means, practically, that Farmer's description of frontier Methodism differs in a number of ways from the more accepted histories of western Methodism and Indiana Methodism and their interpretations of the developing frontier religious ethos.[3]

Some of these differences have been noted by historians. Nathan O. Hatch's excellent study *The Democratization of American Christianity* refers to the first half of the nineteenth century (the same period being covered in this book) as the most significant time in America's religious history.[4] Historians of American religion label this period the Second Great Awakening, or the Western Revival. During this era, according to Hatch, religious authority shifted from ecclesiastical superiors to uneducated preachers. New ideas, new movements, and new ways of expressing and working out religious faith served egalitarian purposes. As will be seen, Farmer is a prime example of Hatch's thesis.

Two different accounts of frontier Methodism illustrate portions of this thesis. In 1916 William Warren Sweet published *Circuit Rider Days in Indiana*, a history of Indiana Methodism from 1800 to 1844. While Sweet mentioned revivals and camp meetings generally, he did not identify any camp meeting specifically. Instead, he concentrated on the gatherings of annual conferences over the forty-four-year period, reporting on bishops and changing conference lines, the establishment of institutions, statistics, decisions made by the annual conferences, and the progress of the church. By way of contrast, A. H. Redford wrote *Western Cavaliers: Embracing the History of the Methodist Episcopal Church in Kentucky from 1832 to 1844*. While making mention of annual conferences and book concerns, Redford's book is essentially an account of ninety-one separate revivals that took place at camp meetings and in Kentucky churches during a twelve-year period.[5]

In another work, Hatch explores what he calls the "puzzle of American Methodism," questioning whether historians have adequately explained the spectacular growth of Methodism in the period leading up to the Civil War.[6] He suggests that the Second Great Awakening terminated the Puritan era, characterized by the Calvinist belief in a set of people chosen by God and led by elites, and inaugurated the pietist or evangelical age of American church history, characterized by a belief in one's personal experience with God and understanding of the Bible. He also argues that Methodist historians, almost always drawn from academia, have had reason to want to sanitize the rougher elements of this history. Yet, these rougher elements are a big part of what led to Methodism's spectacular success. In addition, according to Hatch, mainstream Protestant historians have wanted to emphasize Christianity's role in taming the western frontier toward the goal of a common Protestant value system and Church unity.

It is understandable that historians are interested in the themes of the civilizing nature of religion and the development of mainstream cultural values, but these themes do not explain the spectacular growth of the frontier churches, or how such growth was accomplished not by religious consensus and cooperation but by religious conflict and confusion and a growth in sectarianism—a splintering into numerous denominations. In its earliest years on the western frontier, Methodism developed customs, strategies, and an ethos that were, if not in conflict, at least in tension with the common Calvinist values of the day. Methodism was counter-cultural. It was during this time, basically from 1820 to 1840, that Methodism experienced its most spectacular growth in Indiana. And then, when Methodism began to mature on its way to becoming an American mainstream religion, a subset of Methodism resisted the change in defense of Methodism's original vision. Farmer was one of those who belonged to the subset. It was a subset that lived easily with camp meetings, revivals, altars, spirituals and the gospel chorus, egalitarian forms of church governance, controversy, and the multiplication of sects.

Farmer's story will introduce some themes that will give a different perspective on the significance of the Western Revival in Indiana history, the place of Indiana in that revival, and a few of the reasons for sectarianism and the development of an evangelical ethos in Indiana and elsewhere on the western frontier. One of the themes in Farmer's story is the prevalence of camp meetings, their place in the larger picture of revivalism, and their contribution not only to the spectacular growth of Methodism but also in the development of a new religious culture that is known today as American evangelicalism.

The camp meeting was an American phenomenon created on the western frontier and closely associated with the Second Great Awakening. America's first camp meeting is generally identified as Cane Ridge in Bourbon County, Kentucky, in August 1801. There were antecedents to Cane Ridge—sacramental outdoor meetings, Methodist massed quarterly meetings, and "revival" events in various forms—but Cane Ridge was different.

In April 1801 a revival had broken out in Logan County, Kentucky, at a gathering planned jointly by Presbyterians and Methodists. It generated such religious excitement that the meetings were extended, many more people came, and the crowds moved outdoors. Barton A. Stone, a Presbyterian minister from Cane Ridge, attended the revival and reported: "'The whole country appeared to be in motion to the place, and multitudes of all denominations attended. All seemed heartily to unite in the work and in Christian love. . . . A true description of this meeting . . . would border on the marvelous. It continued five days and nights without ceasing. Many . . . will through eternity remember it with thanksgiving and praise.'"[7]

Stone then announced a similar outdoor gathering in Bourbon County to last for several days. People would make their own provisions for eating and camping. There are several accounts of what happened at Cane Ridge. One is by James Finley of Ohio, whose father had been the Presbyterian minister preceding Stone at Cane Ridge. In his autobiography, he wrote:

> A vast crowd, supposed by some to have amounted to twenty-five thousand, was collected together. . . . [and] seemed to be agitated as if by a storm. I counted seven ministers, all preaching at one time, some on stumps, others in wagons. . . . At one time I saw at least five hundred swept down in a moment, as if a battery of a thousand guns had been opened upon them, and then immediately followed shrieks and shouts that rent the very heavens. My hair rose up on my head, my whole frame trembled, the blood ran cold in my veins, and I fled for the woods.[8]

Finley was converted at Cane Ridge and later became a well-known Methodist circuit rider, traveling often to Indiana, as well as a missionary to the Wyandotte Indians.

Peter Cartwright, another early Methodist frontier preacher, also described Cane Ridge in his autobiography, and then commented: "From this camp meeting followed 'a blessed revival of religion' spread through almost the entire inhabited parts of the west. Presbyterians and Methodists united in the earliest camp meetings but Presbyterians eventually pulled back" because of the "extravagancies that were hard to control." When

Presbyterians became reluctant to promote camp meetings the field was left open for Methodists and Baptists. Writing in the 1850s, Cartwright stated that camp meetings were held every year after Cane Ridge.[9]

Within weeks what had happened at Cane Ridge was reported and duplicated in many parts of the country, particularly among Methodists. Nathan Bangs, an early Methodist historian writing in 1830, stated that camp meetings "were introduced into various parts of the country" that year. "Two were held in the lower parts of Virginia. . . . Similar meetings were held in Georgia, South and North Carolina, and in Maryland, at all of which there were remarkable displays of the awakening and converting power of God," Bangs wrote.[10] Methodism virtually exploded in the Chesapeake Bay area as well.[11]

Jesse Lee, writing in 1810, reports that by 1805 both blacks and whites were present in large numbers, and thousands were converted.[12] Charles Johnson's exhaustive study on camp meetings also comments on the presence of blacks at early camp meetings, primarily in Maryland, Delaware, and Virginia, since these states held high percentages of blacks.[13]

While all histories of American Methodism include the camp meeting as part of the Methodist story, some early historians such as Bangs and Abel Stevens tended to interpret camp meetings as a phenomenon that, while wildly successful for a time, soon faded into obscurity as the Methodist church moved on to matters such as education, involvement in social and political issues, and maturity as a religious institution.[14] Even Matthew Simpson—first president of Indiana Asbury College (which became DePauw University), who was himself converted at a camp meeting—spends less than one page out of one thousand on camp meetings in his massive *Encyclopedia of Methodism* (1878). Perhaps the standard assessment is given by Sweet, who wrote extensively on Methodism, and especially Methodism in Indiana. He noted:

> In its earlier phases revivalism grew largely out of frontier conditions, and performed its best work in the newer sections of the country, and here also it often produced unfortunate excesses. But whatever may be said in criticism of frontier revivalism, this must be said in its behalf: it was perhaps the only method by which the frontier could receive any of the benefits of Christianity, warped though it often was, almost beyond recognition. The camp-meeting, one of the by-products of frontier revivalism, served a very large social and religious need and has developed into the present-day community Chautauqua and summer assemblies. This peculiar phase of American Christianity has been gradually passing, just in proportion as frontier conditions have been disappearing, while the more adequate academic training of the ministry has lessened the emotional appeal in modern preaching.[15]

Sweet seems to suggest that revivalism and camp meetings were effective for rough, uneducated, and not-yet-fully-civilized persons, but with progress and education camp meetings and revivals faded into obscurity. Sweet mentions the Chautauqua movement as a development in the evolution of camp meetings. According to Annie Wardle, writing on the Sunday School Movement of the Methodist Episcopal Church in 2004, "It would be more accurate to say that the Chautauqua movement was a part of the effort to use the camp meeting's popular outdoor setting to redirect the church's interest from revivalism to Christian education."[16] The primary criticism of camp meetings was that they were barbarous, ill-mannered, and did not present a positive image of Methodism or of Christian faith. This study will examine to what extent these criticisms were justified.

Another theme in Farmer's story is the importance of revivalism in general, and the camp meeting in particular, in changing the religious landscape in America. The study will seek to answer many related questions: What effect did revivalism have on the prevailing Calvinist belief that dominated early American Protestantism? How did the introduction of such practices as "the altar" change the nature of Protestant worship and add to sectarianism? What is the relationship of the camp meeting spiritual to Protestant musical styles and later changes in the nature of Protestant worship? How did camp meetings and revivals change the nature of Protestant preaching? How did camp meetings contribute to the development of a religion of the underclass that seems unique to American religion? And most important, how did revivalism lead to the emergence of an American evangelicalism in which experience replaced sacraments and creeds as the defining marks of a theology?

A third theme in Farmer's story is the relationship of revivalism and sectarianism in Indiana. There is perhaps no place more illustrative in the study of religious sectarianism than Indiana in the nineteenth century, particularly in the 1830s and 1840s. Farmer was at the center of sectarian turmoil in the state both as an observer and as a participant.

A fourth theme is the relationship between the Western Revival and populism. The growth of sectarianism in America brought with it a corresponding shift in the American Protestant understanding of the doctrine of the church. During the Western Revival in Indiana and the other states of the Old Northwest, sectarian doctrines of the church, which had only existed before on the fringes of Protestant belief, came, if not to dominate, at least to strongly influence the mainstream American expression of Christianity. Growth in the influence of sectarian thought was accompanied by a form of Christianity that was developing from the religious experience of ordinary people, and not one directed by the intellectuals and the elite.

One observation might help put this study into a broader perspective: The influence of the Methodist camp meetings extended far beyond the passing of the physical gathering on the Indiana frontier known as the camp meeting. A further study of camp meetings and camp meeting revivalism would trace early camp meeting ethos and influence across the United States as American pioneers moved west, through the "Holiness Movement" of the latter part of the nineteenth century, and into Pentecostalism in the twentieth century. There are more Pentecostals today in the world than any other Protestant group. It can be argued that there is very little difference between what happens every Sunday in a Pentecostal church in Brazil from what was happening in early frontier Methodist camp meetings in Indiana.[17]

Farmer's autobiography is not meant to be a history, an interpretation of religion on the frontier, an exposition of doctrine, a critique of Methodism, or a defense of Farmer's Christian Union Church. The autobiography is his story, or a group of his stories. The stories are interesting enough that the book has merit for no other reason than for these stories. Nevertheless, in the process of telling the stories, Farmer gives insight into Protestant religion in general, Methodism in particular, and Methodism's place in early Indiana religious history. Farmer's stories also add to our understanding of America's Second Great Awakening or Western Revival, and so Farmer's stories are placed in this historical context.

In this study the word "Methodist" will refer to the Methodist Episcopal Church, by far the dominant group in Indiana. In some cases, where noted, it will include other Methodist bodies—the Methodist Protestant Church, the Evangelical Association, and the United Brethren Church—that today make up the United Methodist Church.

In addition to addressing some of the differences between Farmer's account and the account of some historians of frontier religion in Indiana, the book will address some other general subjects that are specific to Methodism. It will explain the Methodist connectional system—with bishops, conferences, presiding elders, lay preachers, exhorters, and classes—and how these contributed to the growth of Methodism in Indiana and how the system was ideally structured for the problems of the frontier. This part of the discussion will also include such Methodist features as the practice of short-term appointments, the circuit system, the quarterly conference tradition, the freedom given preachers to improvise and initiate, and the unique doctrines of Methodism. The book will also provide an analysis of Methodism's spectacular growth in the first half of the nineteenth century in Indiana and throughout the nation.

Farmer's original manuscript contains 286 handwritten pages. The material was transcribed by the author and has been abridged here. While there has been no serious attempt to apply literary criticism to the manuscript, it is possible to speculate that, although he sat down to write his autobiography late in life, some of the material may have been written earlier.

1

Eli Farmer's Family and Childhood, 1788 to 1813

Any study of religious and social development in America after the Revolutionary War must take into consideration the Methodists. Methodism was, in many ways, a new religion for a new nation. Methodism was spawned in England under the leadership of John and Charles Wesley, after John Wesley had his "heart-warming" experience at a place in London known as Aldersgate. In England Methodism was not, at least through the eighteenth century, considered a separate denomination, but a movement within the Church of England. It was more specifically a revival movement. In an age of deism, the "rational religion" of the Enlightenment era that understood God as a creator who did not interact with the creation, and growing skepticism, the Methodists offered a different message in a different way for a different kind of people. The Methodist message was based on religious experience, on supernaturalism, which included visions and religious enthusiasm, or emotionalism, and on John Wesley's vision of personal and social holiness.[1] The message was communicated by field preaching—preaching in the open air and in small groups led by lay persons and often by women. Its main appeal was to the lower classes, especially miners. Meeting houses built by the Methodists were never churches but "chapels." Wesley's preachers were not clergy but laity.

Some of those early Methodist converts in England migrated to America, but because they were from England, and because the Wesleys were known as Tories who were loyal to the King, Methodism did not thrive during the period before and during the Revolutionary War. Wesley had sent eight missionaries to America in the 1770s, but these missionaries encountered such resistance that seven of them returned to England. The one who stayed, Francis Asbury, ministered with a low profile.

When the war ended, Wesley realized he could no longer oversee his movement from England and made arrangements for the Methodists in America to organize themselves into a church. He sent them instructions that included doctrine, discipline, and a Sunday service. In December 1784 thirty-two lay preachers gathered in Baltimore, Maryland, and elected a leader, Francis Asbury, who, in Church of England style, understood himself to be a bishop. The lay preachers were ordained and sent forth with the instructions: "You have nothing to do but to save souls."

With that Methodism in America was born. It was ready-made for America, and, as will be seen, especially for the western frontier. Its doctrine was settled, as were its rules for living, its structure, and its constitution. These were contained in a book titled *Doctrines and Discipline of the Methodist Episcopal Church*. The *Discipline*, as it came to be known, could only be changed by the Conference, at this time, the annual gathering of all traveling preachers, and served as Methodism's rulebook from that day forward. While the *Discipline* set important parameters, the American Methodists felt free to develop their religious life independently from Wesley, the Anglicans, and the English.

They needed to. The new church arrived at a time in the new nation when there was not a lot of promise for religion. The American Revolution had not been kind to the Christian faith, especially the evangelical Christian faith. The presumed faith of the founding fathers has been overstated. George Washington probably did not pray in the snow at Valley Forge. Benjamin Franklin's respect for evangelist George Whitefield did not result in an evangelical-type conversion. References to deity in early American documents were not necessarily references to the God of orthodox Christianity. As one nineteenth-century historian observed:

> With rare exceptions the condition of the churches all over the country was that extensive revivals had ceased. From 1750 to 1800 was a long period of turmoil and distractions. The French and Indian wars; the agitations preceding the Revolution; the evils of the post-bellum period; the French infidelity and English Deism; the gross wickedness; the political controversies, sharp, violent and vindictive ... with the adoption of the Federal Constitution; the evil influences of the French Revolution, with which so many Americans sympathized,—are some of the elements which worked unfavorably to the cause of religion.[2]

It is true that Christian faith permeated the life of earliest colonial America. The Puritans spoke of their settlement as the New Israel. William Penn made treaties with the Indians and wrote of a peaceable kingdom. New England experienced a religious stirring in the 1730s under Jonathan Edwards and Whitefield that later came to be known as the First Great Awakening. Gilbert Tennent and his brothers led a religious awakening in New Jersey and the mid-Atlantic coast. American ideals of liberty and republican democracy were fueled by Calvinist convictions about the equality of the sinful nature of all persons before God, the necessity of restraints on power because of that sinful nature, and the dignity of God's elected individuals.

But religious revivals die out, and ideals in themselves do not necessarily bring about religious fervor. By the 1760s Edwards had been relieved of his pulpit in Southampton, Massachusetts; the Tennent revival had faded; Congregationalism was being influenced more and more by Unitarians, who did not believe in a Trinity of "God, the father; Jesus, the son; and the Holy Spirit"; and deism and enlightenment philosophy were infiltrating the aristocratic thinking of the founding fathers.

The rebellion against the King of England had been in part a rebellion against the established church and the established clergy, and, in many ways, against the supernatural God represented by that clergy. The Anglican Church in America, with its links to England, had so suffered from the radical zeal of the American patriots that some observers felt it was in danger of dying out in America within a generation. The sectarian peace churches—Quakers, Mennonites, Brethren, and Moravians—were less than enthusiastic about the revolution, and actually faced persecution from other colonists. With or without persecution, these churches did not thrive during America's war with England. Only the Baptists and the Presbyterians—the two groups that would compete with Methodists on the frontier—escaped the war relatively unscathed, and neither was known in post-Revolutionary days for religious zeal.

At the close of the Revolutionary War, only 10 percent of the citizens of the new United States of America were church members, and of that number only 2.5 percent identified as Methodist. In 1750 there was an organized church for every 706 Americans. By 1800 it took 1,122 Americans to form a church. In the West, Methodism, despite the fact that it had come early to Kentucky, actually declined from 1792 to 1800. During those years, while the population of Kentucky grew from 73,000 to 264,000, Methodist membership decreased from 1,808 members to 1,704.[3]

But Methodism was not deterred. Taking its cue from the country's burst of energy that had accompanied independence, Methodism was characterized by unbounded optimism. Other religious groups may have been discouraged by efforts that seemed to produce little fruit, but Methodists could speak only of the new opportunities that God would bring about in this new nation. Asbury was consumed by the vision. He wrote in a letter to a friend in England after the Revolutionary War: "'O America, America, God will make it the glory of the world for religion.'"[4]

The Methodist passion was for nothing less than to save that world. The Puritans spoke about America as a city set on a hill. That suggested a Christian civilization. The Methodists spoke in grander terms. They were post-millennialists.[5] They did not think in terms of a Christian civilization but in terms of a converted world that would hasten the day for Jesus Christ's return to earth. Even as the Americans had been successful in a political revolution, the Methodists were convinced that what the nation needed was a spiritual revolution, and they set themselves to be a part of it. At their inaugural meeting in Baltimore, Maryland, they declared as a grand purpose for their church, "to reform the continent and spread Scriptural holiness over the land."[6]

The new nation did not know exactly what to do with these Methodists, who soon were invading their communities to spread this vision of scriptural holiness. When Jesse Lee, the first preacher appointed to New England, arrived in Boston in 1790, he began his career by standing on a gambling table on the Boston Common and singing Methodist hymns.[7] His efforts were scorned by Congregationalists and Unitarians, but Lee and his comrades were persistent, preaching anywhere they could find an audience, and they soon established a Methodist foothold in New England.

The western frontier presented a different kind of challenge. Religion was almost nonexistent in the scattered settlements west of the Appalachian Mountains. In her study of early Kentucky, Ellen Eslinger described churches before 1800 as suffering from stagnation, slumber, competition, and lack of leadership. Settlers were seen as lawless and immoral, unrestrained by the culture and polite society of the East.[8]

In 1818 Isaac Reed, a Presbyterian missionary, came to Indiana and wrote a report to the Presbyterian Societies of New England on the status of religion in the fledgling state. In it he reported:

> We came into Madison, and put up with Mr. D. M'Clure. In my travels in Kentucky, which have included about 700 miles, I have learned much of [Indiana's] religious state. This is truly low, though it is thought better than a few years since. There are many which wear the Baptist's name, but they have neither the knowledge, order, nor the apparent piety of the Baptists in the northern states. The Methodists are not very numerous and the Presbyterian cause and interest is low. There are some precious people, whom I highly respect: they are walking in the ordinances of God, and sighing over the abominations of the land, in which their lot is cast. And there are some faithful ministers, who are zealous for the cause of the Redeemer. But they are so few,—they are so very few,—more than 30 counties, containing an immense population, are without a single Presbyterian minister. Several of these counties have in them little churches, but they have no pastors. Poor souls, how I pity them. Since I came into the state, most of my time has been spent with such. I hope some good has arisen, and will arise from it.[9]

Eli Farmer was born into this western frontier world. Since his autobiography is basically his personal story, he does not comment on whether the western frontier as he remembered it was "lawless" or in a state of spiritual "slumber." But the account of his early life fits the image of the West as a wild frontier, with Indian wars, hardship, alcohol, violence, and very little evidence of religion—that is, until camp meetings. Farmer begins his story with his birth:

Native Americans were very much present during Eli Farmer's early years in Kentucky and Indiana. Forts, such as this one built in southern Indiana, ca. 1805, helped pioneer settlers defend themselves against raids. Violence was perpetrated by both sides during the territorial period.

I was born according to the history furnished by my parents on the 15th day of February A.D. 1794 in Franklin County, Kentucky; about five miles northwest of Frankfurt at Dr. Ennis Station. My father's name was Joel Farmer; my mother's maiden name was Sarah Rice; both of whom were of revolutionary stock; my father being of Dutch and Welsh decent, and my mother of Irish and English extraction. In the spring of 1788, he accompanied General Wayne to the West to assist in fighting the Indians.[10]

Farmer starts his autobiography by telling some stories passed down to him by his father. One of those stories has to do with adventures in General Anthony Wayne's army:

A severe battle came off with the Indians. Many were slain of both armies. . . . During this engagement, Wayne made a decisive charge upon the enemy, causing a general stampede among the Indians, and following up the advantage thus gained, his army slaughtered a great [many] Indian "braves". After pursuing the red man about two miles he caused his bugles to sound a halt and desired the army to stop; but as the boys had never learned their "stop"—they being Kentuckians and Virginians—he found it impossible to halt his forces; which trifling insubordination somewhat annoyed the old "Chieftain." While his anger was kindled against his troops he arose in his saddle and cried out quite lustily "Go to halt them." This was the last battle I remember hearing my father talk about.

The Farmer family moved several times from Virginia to Kentucky and back, as Farmer relates:

Upon the expiration of my father's term of service, he with two other young men began to look back with longing hearts to the home of their birth and as soon as an opportunity offered itself they concluded to return of way of the Ohio River. They stole their way along so as to avoid discovery by the Indians who infested the region of country they traversed, some five or six hundred miles through wilderness, and in the fall of 1789 they arrived in London County, Virginia, the land of their nativity.

My father remained with his relation and among his friends, until the following spring. At that time he became acquainted with my mother, whose name was then Sarah Rice. He courted and married her, when she was the age of fourteen years, contrary to the wish of her friends and family, thereby creating a serious disturbance in the relation of the two families. This young girl had given her destiny into my father's keeping in the early period of her life, when she knew that she would most likely be taken far away into the distant frontier of the settlement of Kentucky. Once there she would have no opportunity of seeing her friends, which fact, no doubt was the inception of the difficulties.

This affair aroused the revolutionary fire in both families, and my father determined to return to Kentucky.

Back in Kentucky, there were encounters with lawless men, wild animals, and Indians as Farmer describes:

The first attack was made upon two men who with their wives were shearing sheep in their dooryard, both of whom were shot and killed, one of the men dying instantly, while the other one crawled into the house, where he helped the woman to bar the doors, and then laid down to rise up no more. The women, determined to save themselves if possible, dropped a little colored girl and some children under the floor, "out of the way." Expecting to be rescued soon, they fought with great determination. When an Indian came to the door and tried to break it down with his tomahock one of the women fired at him through the door and killed him. During this tragic scene the other woman was up in the "loft," trying to keep the Indians from setting the roof on fire, and from breaking in. Fearing they would be captured, they gathered up the dead body and fled, shortly after the Indian was killed.

Farmer explains how the stories were passed down:

The facts which I have thus narrated, I received from conversations in our family, and from conversations with old settlers, who used often to meet at our house, where they would "fight over," time after time, the conflicts of the past. Many of the stories would call forth forbidden tears, while each of the company would partake now and then of the whiskey-tady, whose very soul seemed then to unite the company in bands of closer union, all of which was so repeated, that these stirring events although became printed on my young mind, and now, after the lapse of the long years which have intervened, seem very much like events in which I myself was an active participant.

Not all went well with the Farmer family. The work was hard and families were isolated. Farmer states:

During one of these hours of depression and gloom, a certain man proposed to my father to "buy him out," offering him a good price for the property. The offer was accepted, and the property passed over to the new purchaser, my father waiting in accordance with the terms of the contract, a few weeks for the purchase money. After the fellow succeeded in getting possession of the property, he sold the same and then absconded, and thus my father lost all his property, never getting anything subsequently from either party.

Having been twice broken up by the Indians, and once by a white man, my father became greatly discouraged and conceived there was some strange fatuity attending him, from which disaster he never recovered. Finding himself without means, and with an increasing family, he was compelled to work for others as a day laborer, and began attending to certain kettles, used in the manufacture of salt.

The little village where he lived was settled by the rougher cast of soldiers and hunters and their manners were quite as rough as the clothes in which they were clad. Yet, they were frank, liberal, tender-hearted, sociable, and fond of sport.

Despite these problems, Farmer had good memories about his childhood:

In those days many of the frontiersmen, were under neither law or gospel, every man seemed to consider himself, "a law unto himself" and yet, a man's word was as good as his bond, and they were so friendly and sociable, that they owned almost everything in common. Their jokes were sometimes costly, and yet the subjects thereof usually bore their inflictions with great good humor. A certain man came to the furnace one day to buy some salt, and as pack saddles were pretty generally used at that time, he had a good one. He "hitched up" his horse at a point near the furnace, one of the men who was working at the furnace, and who had a pack saddle which he wished to sell, witnessed the proceedings; watching his opportunity, the vender of the packsaddles carried off the saddle of the stranger, and carried it to be burned up in the furnace, and then at the proper time, proposed to sell one to the man to supply the one which had been mysteriously misplaced; but the fellow rightly suspecting the fate of his property, refused to purchase, and went away apparently, little annoyed by his lose. Shortly afterward, he returned to the furnace with another pack-saddle, the pads of which saddle, he had previously provided with about a pound of powder, and again secured his horse, at about the same point as before, and went off about his business. In his absence, the old trick was repeated, but with different results, for the powder exploded, and blew up the whole concern.

At this time while we were attending some sort of gathering in the neighborhood, our home caught fire and everything we had was consumed. Col. Thomas Martin a prominent citizen in the community, took an active part in seeing that the family was provided for. While we were under a cloud which this misfortune had caused to gather over us, Richard Rice, one of my mother's brothers paid us a visit, by whose liberal aid, as well as the assistance of the neighbors, we were nearly restored to our old home again.

I now began to feel the need of an education, and I managed to attend school for a little while until I got a start in reading and writing. I was now in my eighteenth year, and I began to feel my young manhood vigor. The school closed in the summer of 1812 and thereupon I turned my attention to other business.

There is no mention of religion in Farmer's account of his early years. But then, at the age of eighteen, he introduces it:

In the fall of 1812, at a camp meeting in the vicinity of a certain meeting house called "Gillbad", I was deeply convicted of sin, under the preaching of a gentleman by the name of Lord: I had a "godly sorrow that worketh repentance not to be repented of". I attended the meeting every opportunity, living "in the use of my means" that I could think of in order to obtain salvation. I worked on until exhausting my strength, I came to a point where I could say "Oh wretched man that I am, who shal deliver me from the body of this death!" While struggling one day laboring with these feelings and while on my knees, I felt that God quenched me by his Spirit, my load of guilt fell off, The Savior on the cross appeared <u>before me! Before me! Just before me!</u> My light having Thus come like lightning, and I arose from my knees, rejoicing in the love of God. All nature most beautiful unto me and most glorious. I rejoiced I had a God to serve.

I proposed to my parents, although both [of] them were not professors of religion, to conduct family pray[e]rs, deeply impressed with the idea that I had something of a public nature to perform, in connection with the duties of my new position. They refused to grant my request, which refusal somewhat cooled my religious fervor. But still firmly fixed in my purposes, I availed myself, of all means which I could command. One night we had a prayr-meeting at a neighbors house, and as the night was very dark, we could not get home very easily, so a number of us concluded to tarry all night. Bedcloths were spread upon the floor of the same room, and when we had all lain down, there was very little space of the floor left unoccupied. My position was next to the door, and while lying there upon that floor, I heard a voice, at about the hour of midnight, calling my name as plainly as I ever heard anything in my life. apparently just outside the door close by me; which voice loudly declared, "you have not made good use of your Talents."—This occurrence made a deep impression upon my mind, and occasioned me a heavy load for a long period of Time.

In the Spring of 1813 I made an arrangement with one Mr. Jeffs, to collect and drive some cattle of what was called the "green glades" which were on The Yohegany river, some fifty or sixty miles from Harpers Ferry. I herded the cattle there during The summer, counting, herding and walking them twice a week. My custom was to enter The "glades", scatter the salt at various places, then climb a tree and blow a horn, when they would come running and bellowing to the "salting place". Should any of them be missing, I would search about for them, and after finding them, drive them to the herd. I employed my leisure hours in fishing, usualy catching a beautiful fish called "Trout".

When I got tired of this sport, I would cross the river at the bridge, and go in among the tall pine trees, most of which waved their green foliage more, than one hundred feet above my head, while The[i]r stately tops, seemed to pierce the sky far beyond. It was a delightful place for reflections, and more than once, was my soul filled with awe as I communed with nature and natures God. The summer went by quickly, and I found The cattle placed under my care improving finely. Shortly afterward Mr. Jeffs and I drove them to a town called Mooresville, on the south branch of the Potomac, to market and after selling the same, we returned home.

Hearing of a campmeeting after our return home, at a place in Pennsylvania, called Beasontown I thought I would attend it. While attending this meeting I worked almost constantly at the altar. Many convictions were made at the meeting. Feeling that it was my duty to do so, I continued to pray at the altar. A young man who had been for some Time struggling at the altar, sprung up judasidly and cried out loudly, "Lord, take me, take me!" and Then he began pulling off his cloth[es]s, first his coat, Then his vest, and then he began pulling of his pants, when I caught hold of him and persuaded him from continuing. The charge was so powerful this man thought he was going right up to heaven. We continued to struggle for a time, and then he became calmer, when I asked him why he desired to divest himself of his clothes: his answer was that he had read in the Scriptures that when a man goes to heaven he had to "leave all behind."

In these times of excitement, some would be crying, some shouting, while others would be singing and rejoicing. At one of the meetings, one of the preachers came into the altar to labor

Methodist camp meeting, early 1800s

with the mourners, and while doing so, there came into the meeting an exceedingly intelligent and handsome young lady, who took a position near the preacher, and whom seemed to be in deep reflections. As the preacher raised from a kneeling posture, he saw the young lady standing by him with a quantity of ribbons upon her person when he cried out "ribbons, ribbons, ribbons, what will be the end of them?" She replied "I will wear them out, sir, that will be the end of them," and he found he had encountered an uncommonly shrewd lady, and he wisely concluded to let her severely alone. The meeting closed after a number were added to the church. I remained in Beason-town about a week after the meeting closed, when one of my grandmothers brothers who was a wealthy Methodist, and who had crossed the mountains with what were called the "whisky boys" and whose home was childless, desired some one of his relatives, to go to his house and live with him, and at his death heir his estate. My father wished me to perform this service, and take care of the old folks, but after praying over the matter, I finally refused to be confined thus for money, and I returned home much strengthened in my spiritual concerns.

In this introduction to his life, Farmer mentions ideas that were of importance to the Western Revival and to early Methodism, foremost among them "the altar." The altar was a place down in front of the preachers where people wrestled with their souls and sought God and often experienced God's presence. The altar and other camp meeting and Methodist ideas will be discussed more thoroughly in subsequent chapters.

2

The Formative Years, 1814 to 1818

A major portion of Eli Farmer's autobiography describes his formative young adult years between the ages of eighteen and twenty-five (1813–20).[1] Farmer had a number of adventures during these years and traveled between Kentucky and points east. He served in the army during the War of 1812 but saw no action. He met a number of people, including Sam Houston, and held a number of jobs. Farmer's autobiography devotes more space to this period than any other period in his life. Chapters 2 and 3 give an abridged account of these years. During this time, religion played very little part of his life. These are his "backslidden" years. The significance of this will be discussed later in the chapter.

Farmer's story picks up here as he becomes a soldier:

On the third day of March 1814 the President issued a call for soldiers, and the citizens of Monongahold [possibly Monongahela, Pennsylvania] held a public meeting and made up a company, to go to Norfolk, Va fixing the third day of May as the day of starting.

My health having greatly improved [from a bout of measles] I determined to go with this company, and I met them at the appointed time and place. When I arrived there I saw a man standing off to one side weeping, whom I asked to tell me the cause of his grief; and he replied that he was compelled to enter the army when his wife was then lying at home in a critical and probably dying condition. I then asked him how much he would give me to take his place. His reply was, "I am a poor man but I will give you that black horse and all my equipage now, and $400 upon your return." I told him I would agree to that arrangement if the officers would take me in his stead. We stated the case to the officers and they received me accordingly. I took his note for the amount specified, and then put on his equipage, and then sent the note and the horse back to my home. I was now only entering my twenty-first year and weighing 96 pounds. And I thus entered the army for six months.

I soon became acquainted with our 1st Lieutenant Michael Shively, whose uncle partly raised me in Kentucky. I found him a very clever man, and I soon expressed a warm feeling of friendship for him, which was by fully reciprocated, and he treated me with great kindness, and favored me whenever he could, as I was then very small. He could not have shown his own son more marked or tender attentions. Traveling on for a while our boys became very mischievous, and pretending that he had deserted, they tied him and took to a house, where the fellow told a mournfull story about his misfortunes, how [he] had been dragged from his family when in fact he was an unmarried man, and in this manner the feelings of the woman were terribly wrought upon, and in order to manifest their sympathy provided the party with plenty of eatables. The day following was a wet rainy one. The rain falling incessantly, and coming up to the residence of a wealthy farmer, we stopped for shelter.

The officers entered the house, took their swords off, and threw them over on the bed, which act insulted the landlady, and she threw their swords out of doors, and then the officers in their turn became insulted, and refused to control their men, which fact caused the men to become reckless. The landlord was also much insulting in his demeanor, which caused the company to pay their attention to him. They compelled him to unlock his distillery, after which they drank all the whiskey they desired, [and] drove him out before them while the band played the "Dead Man's March."

Our captain returned home and died during our service here, whereupon the command of the company, devolved upon Lieutenant Shively, who proved to be a good officer. Our company were all stout, healthy, active mountaineers, between whom and the "Townlanders" as well as the regulars, feud existed. Our higher officers, were regulars, which feud grew more bitter during our stay. On a certain occasion, three or four of our boys, were engaged in a game of "ball," throwing the ball against one end of the fort, when the colonel's waiter, a black boy, came running along and caught the ball and threw it over into the fort. One of the men caught the lad and cuffed him, who went immediately and complained to the colonel of the treatment he had received. The colonel was very severe upon us, and he came out and called for the man. One of the modes of punishment was called "cobbing" which consisted of pulling down one's pants and stretching ones self over the top of a barrel, when some comrade would take up a board, the end of which was filled with little holes, with which the culprit was whipped. Every stroke almost would raise numerous blood blisters. We soon ascertained this was to be the punishment which the colonel intended to mete out to our comrade, and after counciling together, we went to the colonel and informed him if he whipped the man, he should whip all of us, for it was illegal to whip a person who had not been first tried and found guilty, and we then called the man up. The colonel became very angry and threateningly said that he would get the "regulars" after us. We carried the prisoner away with us, and the colonel turned into the tent swearing violently. The next day we understood that the colonel remarked that we were "d—d good soldiers, but the hardest men to manage [he] had ever seen."

A few days subsequently one of the fellows we called "Sand lappers" (a low lander) passed by me, who remarked as he went by, that he would bet five dollars that their company could furnish a man, that could outrun any man in our company. Which barter I was ambitious enough to accept. When my comrades heard of it each one desired to hazard something on the result, and so many of them took shares in the affair, that after beating my competition I received only fifty cents. Which was the only time I ever made a bet, or ever received anything from one. The man ran one hundred yards, across the fort in the presence of a large and excited crowd. After our man beat, the defeated party cried out to the steak holder, who was a low-lander, "not to give up the stakes" which aroused the angry feelings of our "drum-major" who was sick and an inmate of the hospital, and he struck the fellow, which act led to a great disturbance and the officers were compelled to draw their swords before their commands were heeded by either party.

* * *

Some time after this we were ordered to make preparations for celebrating the "Fourth of July." The colors were to commence firing the cannon at Gran[n]y Island [Virginia] and fire 18 rounds with 18 pounders. Then at Fort Norfolk [Virginia] 18 rounds with 18 pounders, would be fired. Then the "Consolation" which was half a mile above the fort, would fire the same. Then Fort Nelson, yet above the Consolation: and the "Cross Roads" above Norfolk each the same except the latter where six pound guns were used. Fort Poorbury, Port Orchard, Lombard's Point out on the bay, were assigned the same duty, with light and heavy artillery. After this the order was for the infantry and horsemen each to fire off 15 rounds. This program was carried out on the brightest day I ever saw, the rays of the sun which furnished our arms glisteningly. Most of the windows of the houses were broken.

About this time the sickly season came on. Just above us was one general hospital to which all who were thought to be beyond recovery were conveyed. There two experienced surgeons were placed. Near this hospital were some houses that were used as shops where coffins were manufactured, from which wagons were kept going to and from through out the day.

The deaths were numerous. About every four weeks I cleansed my stomach and bowels, fearing that I next might fall and be carried to the vast charnal house for the dead.

Some time after this, the "British" appeared in the Chesapeake Bay, threateningly, and we exercised great vigilance, lest we might be surprised. We had to secure passports before we could either leave or enter camp, and if any one in passing failed to come in this way, such person was fired on. About midnight on one occasion, we saw a vessel passing which we hailed, our officers speaking loudly through a speaking trumpet, but no attention was shown our call, and in a few minutes she had passed beyond our range. The following night, another vessel was also passing, when we also hailed her, to which she paid no attention, and two guns were fired at her. Our officer told us to fire the whole body in case she now refused to "come to." But she "came to" and we found she was a market-man. We were thus kept in suspense for more than a month, expecting a fight every hour. The enemy suddenly disappeared and when we next heard from them they were menacing the "Federal City."

About this time our term of service expired and our captain called for volunteers to go to the capital to help defend the beleaguered city. All but seven of the entire company reentered the service, whom he mostly besought to volunteer, and gave them another day during which to decide, but when the morrow came, he ascertained they needed fourteen men to make up the company and he then handed over our discharges.

* * *

In the fall of 1816, I concluded to return to Kentucky: this was a little while before the Holidays; I determined to go through by what was then called the "nigh way" to Kansiwawa salt works on the Kansiwawa River.[2] I passed through Clarksburg and journeyed on, taking a "by way" which led me along the side of an extensive range of mountains. I was not aware of the fact that this road would lead me through a dense wilderness, until I had traveled a day's journey on the road. The gentleman with whome I tarried the following night, asked me if I had made preparations, for a lengthy trip through a howling wilderness. I told him I had not done so, from the fact that I knew nothing concerning the road. He then told me it was through a wilderness of several hundred miles. I told him then, to prepare some provisions for me, as I didn't wish to turn back. I had a knife, so I got a good flint with which to start up a fire of a night. When I was about ready to depart he charged me to be very watchful, telling me among others things that his reason for this putting me on my guard was, that some two or three days journey farther on was a region which was infested with robbers, comprised of three men and their wives and one old man with his wife and their two sons and their wives. These folks lived out there, ostensiously by hunting but many circumstances favored very strongly a very different occupation.

Seven men had undertaken at various times previously, to pass through that region, but had never been heard of more, after making the attempt and it was generally believed by all who were conversant with the facts in the case, that they had been foully dealt with by these bad men.

On the second day after leaving the house where I had been warned of danger, I reached the place where the robbers lived. In the meantime my food for my horse had given out and I stopped and tried to replenish my stock. As I rode up the women were at a little branch, almost in a state of nudity: and they fled to the house. Riding up to the door of the little cabin, I inquired for the man of the house, and was told the men were out hunting. Observing a crib of corn close by I asked the old woman if I could get a mess of corn for my horse, adding by way of giving my request greater emphasis, that my horse was very hungry, and was getting to be very feeble, and was almost starving. She said "no." My horse was at that time licking the inside of a homing-block most piteously. I again urged her to comply with my request, but she mercilessly said "No. I will give you none." I urged her vehemently, to sell some grain for the horse assuring her I would give any price she might name, to which she replied "you cannot get it sir." I then unthinkingly inquired,—"don't you think you are a hog?"

Communing with myself a moment I concluded to befriend my faithful horse and I deliberately went to the crib with the view of getting some corn and leaving the full price of it with the woman but upon more mature reflection, I abandoned the impulse owing in a great measure to the desperate character of the family.

After leaving the house, well aware of the harsh failings my conduct had provoked and being unarmed, I rode on as rapidly as possible.

When I left the house the sun was almost two hours high. Darkness came on after a while and then the stars came trooping and in the sky beautifully. My over-tasked horse had kept up a continuous lope, from the time of leaving his mortal enemies till a late hour in the night, when leaving the path some distance to one side, I dismounted and found a suitable place for my camp, where my fire could not be observed from the path I had left. I now found myself in a low, flat brook bottom, the soil of which was covered with a dense growth of green "Fern." Using my knife and flint I soon had a fire cracking and blazing near by, and I then took my saddle off my horse and turned him loose. He seemed very much jaded and feeble, and I gave him a portion of my biscuit, which morsel he seemed to relish with great gusto, after which he began eating the "Fern" at my feet, and ate as he moved about our fire. As soon as he had eaten as much of the "Fern" as he wanted, he came up to me and laid down close by my side.

Daylight had almost dawned before I went to sleep, as I was studying about my situation, for there I lay in a wilderness, more than a hundred miles from any one I knew to be my friend. Besides as I have already remarked, I had no weapons with which to defend myself, and in addition thereto, my provisions were exhausted, while I [had] more than a hundred miles before me.

While resting myself at this place, I made a sort of general understanding with Eli [P.] Farmer that in the future, I would see to it that I would be better prepared under such circumstances if I could possibly do so, and not be thus situated again. Morning came, and at an early hour I resumed my journey, returning to the road I had left the night before, which I found without any trouble.

* * *

I was troubled very little in the afternoon with apprehensions of danger, and as my horse possessed a very strong constitution, I traveled on until a late hour at a pretty lively pace, when I came to a high hill on the head waters of the Kansmanawa, at which place I supposed there was somebody in my vicinity. I traveled on about four miles, when I came up to a cabin in the bottoms just at the river, in which cabin the occupants thereof had not yet retired. Hailing the folks within, the landlord came to the door of whom I asked a feed of corn for my horse and refreshments for myself. There was a big kettle near the fence in which he fed his own horse, into which he threw ten ears of corn, and after I had taken the saddle and bridle off my horse, I led him to his meal.

After entering the house, the only bed I saw was one comprised of a little straw and a few seedy looking bed quilts, which were lying on some rough board that were secured to some wooden forks and poles, all of which were connected with the wall of one side of the cabin. The ground answered for the floor of the house. Looking about the room, I espied a round powerful looking back-woodsman clad in "buck-skin" cloths near the fire place who was resting his head on a chunk one end of which was a part of the blazing fire. He was stretched out and at full length, and was unctuously greasy all over. I sat my saddle and saddle-bags down by my side, and mine host gave me a three legged stool on which to seat myself. I confess I felt very suspicious of my oily friend who was reclining at my feet. I asked the landlord whether he could furnish me with supper, and was told he could not do so, assigning as a reason therefore that he had no bread. I had some venison with me, and when I had learned that he had some bear meat I succeeded in getting him to join larder with me and cook the same out of which in connection with a few biscuits I still had we managed to furnish ourselves with a tempting and satisfactory feast, both of us dining together.

Farmer traveled through back country from Virginia to Kentucky after the War of 1812. Settlers along the way were tough and sometimes dangerous. He may have met people similar to the Appalachian family pictured here in 1910.

After we had dined the fellow on the floor shuffled around to one side and I spread out my saddle blanket on the ground and put my saddle and saddle-bags down for a pillow where I laid down to rest, pulling my overcoat over me as a covering. Becoming restless, I laid there for a long time, my thoughts busily engaged in running over my situation. The landlord and his wife were occupying the little bed which I have heretofore described, while my greasy terror maintained his position on the floor. I felt myself in great danger, being naked of weapons.

Towards daylight I dozed off into a little unrefreshing slumber, from which I suddenly awoke finding this huge greasy fellow sitting on a stool almost immediately over me, and gazing steadfastly and fiercely upon me. I was afraid every time he made a movement that it would be a movement to take hold of my saddle-bags and run off with them, and so kept slyly watching his actions. I slipped my hand into my pocket from which I took my pocket knife, after which I opened the same, and kept up my watching, in the meantime arranging what I would do to defend myself and property in case the matter came up for a prompt decision. After lying there some time I rose up quickly with my knife firmly grasped in my hand, and he moved around to one side, and taking possession of another stool I sat down to await the dawn of day. Neither of us felt communication, and so, without exchanging a word, we both sat there watching each other in sullen silence.

About daylight my horse came up to the kettle from which he had eaten his supper, and began eating the remainder of his meal as he could not eat much the previous night. I now asked the landlord to get up. I then took my saddle and saddle-bags out to where my horse was, and while he was eating I got ready to resume my journey. About this time the landlord came out who charged me about a dollar and seventy-five cents for my entertainment. I told him the amount was too much, but he said he must have that amount, I am not quite sure that was the exact price, but I do know that whatever it was, the sum was five or six prices for lodging. For prudential reasons, I told him I was scarce of money and that I was on my way to Kentucky; but he insisted on having the amount demanded.

While I was talking with him, a man from up the creek came to his house for fire, who stated that his fire had "gone out." About this time I also noticed a large number of coon skins hanging up around the house and I inquired what they were worth and when I was answered I remarked that as I returned I would have money and would probably buy them, but made no definite arrangement until after I dickered with them so as to get him to reduce the price. I was making these pretenses in order to leave the impression behind that I had no money which was comparatively speaking the truth, for I was afraid they might think otherwise and attempt to rob me further along on my journey, and I was now resorting to these strategies for my own personal safety. He said he had about two hundred skins, and after we arranged what I was to pay for them, he fell a little on the price of the nights lodging.

To advance my deception I also remarked when I saw the neighbor there yet, perhaps he may have some to sell, if so, "just let him have them ready at your home here . . . and as I return I shall purchase them also at the same figure all things considered." I then continued my journey. But I have never called at that house for those coon skins: for it is [not] at all likely now, that I ever shall.

I journeyed on with some expectations of reaching my destination that night. Traveling on all day I reached about night the head waters of "Big Lick" river, where I crossed into the settlements, and was now surrounded by plenty and peaceable friends.

Pursuing my journey on the next day, I crossed the little Elk River, and arrived [at] the "Big Kannwa" about twenty or twenty five miles from the mouth of the river, where I stopped with a design of going into some kind of business, failing in which design, I went up the river fifteen or twenty miles in a "keel" boat, after wood for certain salt works. We shoved the "Keel" boat up the *river to the choppings and while doing so the weather being very rough I met with an accident which resulted in giving me a good ducking. This occurred at what were called the "Shoals." We had succeeded in pushing our boat up to the upper part of the shoals, when it began to float down stream. When I saw this I sprang forward and threw my shoulder and strength against a certain pole, with which in part we propelled the boat, to which pole at one end was fashioned a piece of iron: and while I was pushing hard against the pole, the end to which the iron was attached slipped in the bottom of the stream, and I fell head long into the river. I did not come to the surface until both the board and myself had drifted down to the lower end of the shoals so rapid was the currant. In going to a house about half a mile distant to dry my clothing, my clothes became frozen so as to make them rattle as I walked along. We were near the chopping when this accident happened, so we were not long in regaining our position and in reaching our destination.*

We were engaged two days in loading the boat. My comrades at this time were pretty bad fellows, some of whom were very rough men, and one of whome at one time talked of whipping me, and I talked back "quite saucily" for I was not afraid of my tormentor. We exercised a great deal, and I soon found I could manage any of them. But the fellow never understood the job. We returned with our wood to the salt works without any other accident. Near the works was the first place I saw what we then called "burning springs." We call them now "coal oil." Finding myself again out of employment, I decided to go over into Kentucky, and again crossed over the Kanwawa, and set my feet toward that old commonwealth, crossing the "Big Gayandott," and another pretty large stream called the "Twelve Pole" on my route.

Going down the Ohio River along the road usually traveled in those days, I spent the night at a very good place where myself and horse were well cared for, at which place there were several fine looking young ladies, who were the children of my steady religious and memorable host. In reply to their inquiries I informed them I was going to Kentucky; and as I had a fine horse with me and tolerably presented as to appearance, the young ladies were very attentive to me showing me distinguished favors. I suppose they were of the opinion that I was a very wealthy man. My recollection is now that they believed they [might] take some money for having lodged me. I had quite a lengthy talk with the old gentleman concerning religious matters, and he seemed to take a great interest in my case, so much so, that he walked some distance with me next morning as I came away, engaged in a pleasant conversation, all of which made a favorable impression on my mind in favor of the old gentleman. I was then in a backslidden condition, and he gave me some wholesome advice.

After his initial conversion at a camp meeting at a place called Gillbad in 1812 and a follow-up camp meeting at Beason-town, Pennsylvania, in 1813, Farmer's religious ardor ebbed. There are almost no references to religion in the account of these years except when Farmer mentions he is in a "backslidden condition." It is not difficult to understand why. Away from the spiritual high brought about by the camp meeting and without encouragement from home or a church or religious group, it was difficult to maintain a religious life. Farmer evidently was working and living in places not yet influenced by revival fervor. Whatever the religious influences in his life, in the period from 1813 to 1820 the word "backslidden" identifies Farmer's orientation as Methodist. The word "backslidden" is a Methodist code word meaning to slip away or reject that which has been attained. Because Methodists believed in free will, they believed that a person could backslide by spiritual neglect or willful disobedience. In the parlance of the time, they were susceptible to "Satan's snares."

Calvinists—whether Congregationalists, Baptists, or Presbyterians—could not "backslide" because they either were or were not part of the elect. They were either in or out and could not slide from one state to the other. Either the religious conversion was not genuine to begin with, or God's grace covered them in spite of their disobedience. For Methodists, however, one could and did often move from being in relationship with God to being out of relationship with God.

After Farmer's pleasant stay along the Ohio River, his story resumes:

That day traveled through a pleasant country passing through Lexington, and Herodsburg Kentucky, and in due time I arrived in Shelby county, where I found numerous acquaintants and friends. I had left this place in year 1811, and I returned now after a lapse of nearly seven years. I enjoyed the remainder of the winter in visitation among them.

* * *

In the spring I undertook to put up a number of buildings and employed a number of hands to help me which business I pushed along with success all summer. We hewed the timber out of which we used logs: otherwise we would cut out the lumber and erect houses a little more pretentious than those made of logs. We used "High savers" in getting out the lumber. We made the shingles ourselves in fact; we built the houses ourselves from the beginning till the time it was completed.

A man by the name of Shelman worked for me. We became so successful that our heads were turned somewhat out we thought ourselves to be important personages. One day "Bob" and I were racing to see who would make the greatest number of shingles by night fall. . . . [After the day's work] he had riven and shaved out seven hundred shingles during the day while I had riven and shaved eleven hundred shingles in the same interval thus beating him by four hundred shingles during the day.

I labored in this vicinity in this business about a year, during which time I realized considerable money, a part of which I now concluded to pay out in giving my self some schooling, and I attended school the great portion of the following year. This was in 1818. During my attendance upon school I didn't take exercise enough, and as I had been accustomed to moving about a great deal, this confinement and want of exercise began to effect my health. To give myself exercise, I would frequently engage in jumping, running, scuffling etc. and in various ways testing my manhood with that of the larger and stronger scholars, many of whom were very strong.

* * *

My military spirit was now so strongly upon me, that I prepared to organize a company, to go to what was then called "New Spain," the country now known as Texas. Spere Spencer, who fell at Reasan River in the war 1812, and who was well known in our vicinity, had a son who had gone to "New Spain" to participate in the strife then in progress in that region, from whome we would get word from time to time, and many of us became anxious to go down there. I formed the company surreptitiously, for we were all afraid to let the older people of the community know of it, for fear they might be adverse to our project. Our secret became known to the public, however, and the parents of the young men of my [company] came to me, and besought me personally to abandon the enterprise, feeling assured that if they could cause me to give it up, the affair would go no further. After a lengthy hesitancy on my part, I very reluctantly consented to comply with their request.

I now concluded to study medicine, entering the office of Mr. [Rin sory?] for that purpose. This man was a very skillfull physican. Soon after entering his office, he one day informed me, that in the early part of his life, he had agreed to marry a beautiful and accomplished southern young lady; and for the purpose of arranging his affairs, so as to consummate the marriage, he had immediately come out to Kentucky, and began to make preparation, during which time he wrote numerous letters to his betroth, but failed to get any answer to his tender missives. This failure was caused by a zealous rival, who up to that period, had been less successful in his wooing, who managed by some fraud to intercept her letters and destroy them. Both the affianced husband and wife, were of course, ignorant of this interference. The rival taking advantage of the various complications, which he there caused to be produced, courted the young lady successfully, and at length led her to the marriage altar, and the twain was made one in the law. Before she gave her consent to this union, she had exhausted all her means of communication with her lover, all her hopes like "dead sea fruits," had turned to ashes on her lips." Supposing that all was yet right, the doctor at length got ready [to] return to the lady, whome he expected to find "adorned for her husband." At the appointed time he called to claim his bride, but was informed, to his and her astonishment, that she was that day to be married to his rival. Stupified and bewildered by this cruel blow, he went to the place where the nuptuals were to be celebrated, and just before the ceremony was performed, asked, to have permission, to have a brief interview with the young lady. Leave was accorded him, and the young couple retired to an adjoining apartment, where an affecting interview was had, at which, the lady assured the doctor, that she had given up all hopes of ever seeing him, from the fact that she could not hear from him. Both became fully satisfied as to the perficicious [perfidious] conduct of the doctors unscruptuous rival, and they exchanged their opinions, unreservedly: the lady strenously declaring that as she was now convinced, that the man had deceived her, she would not live with him.

Upon the conclusion of this interview, the doctor sought out the bride-groom, whome he struck a severe blow, after which he fled and came back to Kentucky: where he subsequently married, and partly raised a family.

After a few years had gone by, he heard that his former sweet-heart, having refused to take upon herself the marriage vow, at the time heretofore mentioned, was living in a state of celibacy, and he went back to the place in the fall of 1818, while I was in his office in order to see the object of his first love. He ascertained that the report was true, on his return, and when he again saw her, how old love came upon him so strongly, that he determined to live with her. He then came back to Kentucky. I had now been in the office four months. Arranging his affairs as rapidly as possible, he left his wife and family, and returned to the south to live with this woman; since which time we never heard of him more.

This mournful affair thus terminated my medical studies, and I determined to return to Virginia. I ought to have stated heretofore, that the family with whome I was boarding at this time charged me nothing for my board. I had been living [with] the family for about eighteen months. They desired my society greatly, and therefore they had me living with them during all these months, for the sake of my society. They had one son who was very closely on the years of his majority with whome I was intimate, and it was more especially for his benefit that they furnished me a home.

Just before I started to Virginia, some-where about Christmas, Samual Houston, who was subsequently governor of, and a United States senator from the state of Texas, paid our house a visit, stopping with us for dinner. We had considerable cider in the cellar, at that time, which was in a barrel, and which was frozen pretty deeply in, from the side of the barrel. By inserting a hot rod into the "bung hole" and thereby melting open a channel through to the center, we found plenty of good cider, of which we all partook freely, and as it was quite strong, some of our company, were not a little stimulated by its use. Sam became considerably intoxicated, and wanted to scuffle with some one. He and I had a number of scuffles with each other on this occasion. He staid all night with us, and while we were bathing our hands and faces at the usual stand therefore, he came out to where I was standing, and threw up his hands as though he wanted to engage in boxing, and I accommodated the young man. Becoming tired of this sport, we quit it, and I commenced washing my hands and face, and while stopping over the basin from which I was performing my morning oblation, and having my hands upon my face, Sam came up to me, and suddenly struck me a severe blow under the right arm, upon my ribs, striking with sufficient force to fracture two of my ribs. I paid him back in the same "fractional" currency, but I did not recover from the effects of the blow for about one month. This was the last time I saw Sam Houston.

About the time I had nearly recovered, captain Scott, whome I have already mentioned in this work, desired to accompany me to Virginia, with a view of returning with a board [boat] loaded with mill-stones and grind-stones. We departed from Kentucky on horseback, and went through the settlement of Ohio, crossing the Ohio river at Marietta. We reached that town at a time when the country contagious [contiguous] thereto, was keenly excited by the fact that their patriotic feelings had been singularly abused. The disturbance was occasioned by a certain lawyer from New Orleans who was then in town, on his way from New York to Louisiana, with a number of Dutch emigrants, who were so impicueneous, that they were compelled to sell their liberty for a season to the captain of the vessel in which they had embarked in the old country, in order to secure a passage over the sea. This was frequently done in those days by poor emigrants, the captains usually indemnifying themselves by selling their interest to such as needed their labor.

This lawyer had bought a number of such claims and was now on his way home with the persons whose liberty he had purchased, in order to have the benefit of their work for awhile, while all parties should be made whole.

This species of human slavery aroused the fierce indignation of the citizens of Ohio in the vicinity of Marietta, while just across the river, there were hundreds of Virginians, who sympathized with their southern friend, the lawyer, and who clamorously contended that he was justly entitled to the labor of the men whom he had ransomed. Some person had informed the emigrants, that as soon as they arrived in the free state of Ohio, they became free, and no man could deprive them of their liberty: and it was this information which had occasioned the disturbance, for when they arrived opposite Cincinnati, these men caught hold of the oars and pulled for the free shore of Ohio, and lawyer had now brought suit for to recover possession of them. The sympathies of most of the community were in favor of the emigrants. A portion of the squad were in Ohio, and the remainder of it in Virginia, at the time we were there.

Leaving Marietta we went to Clarksburg, at the head waters of the Menongahala River, from which point we traveled on to near the town of Morgantown, where my friends were yet residing. Captain Scott being unaccustomed to a mountainous country, became [---] therewith, and returned in a short time to Kentucky.

I remained and opened a three months school. While thus engaged, a fellow pedagogue who was teaching school several miles "up the country" proposed that we have the two schools meet together occasionally, for the purpose of having a "spelling and reading school." So we could have a good time generally. We also made arrangements to give our pupils instructions in politeness of manners. We brought our schools together according to previous arrangement, and held such a school as I had described. My fellow-teacher had been taught under a very old absolute system of pronounciation, whereby he would try to teach our pupils to pronounce such words as "would, could," and "should" very broad – as "wold," cold" and shold." In those days we called that the "old *fashioned way and the scholars were opposed to adopting such a system. I taught the old gentleman differently, and he received my instructions gladly, altho he was a better scholar than I. We usually closed each nights exercise with our "polite school." I had trained myself with great care, and took great delight in imparting instruction in this department, showing time after time, the scholars how to give and how to receive an introduction and giving them hints as to politeness relating to almost every position in life. The effects of my training were such, that I became a very popular teacher all through the settlements, and although every one was well aware the other teacher was greatly my superior in scholastic attainments, yet my mode of imparting instruction, attracted many of his patrons from his school to mine, thereby damaging his business to a considerable extent, but helping mine correspondingly.*

In the formative years of his young adult life, it appears Farmer was too restless to stick with anything very long, and too busy exploring the world to settle down. In those years Farmer served in the army, traveled several times between Pennsylvania, Virginia, and Kentucky, tried to organize a group of his friends to go as soldiers to "New Spain" (Texas), started a business building houses, hauled commodities and families on "keel boats," studied medicine, fought several men, including Sam Houston, attended school briefly, and opened a school.

It is the school that is of interest. Farmer's time in formal schooling can be numbered in months, but he evidently believed he was qualified to run a school. He involved himself in the issue of frontier dialect and pronunciation. His specialty, however, was manners. His was a "polite school." This seems out of character for Farmer early in his life.

It also raises a question that is related to the interest of this study in camp meetings and frontier religion. Who really were the people who inhabited the Western frontier in the early 1800s? The common perception is that people in the early frontier were uncivilized, uneducated, rough, and lawless. There are numerous accounts that characterize the "West" in this manner. For example, one Englishman, William Faux, gives this account of traveling in Indiana in 1828:

> Saving two comfortable plantations, with neat log-houses and flourishing orchards, just planted . . . I saw nothing between Vincennes and Princeton [Indiana], a ride of forty miles, but miserable log holes, and a mean ville of eight or ten huts or cabins, and neglected farms, and indolent, dirty, sickly, wild-looking inhabitants. Soap is no where seen or found in any of the taverns, east or west. Hence dirty hands, heads, and faces every where. Here is nothing clean but wild beasts and birds, nothing industrious generally, except pigs, which are so of necessity. Work or starve is the order of the day with them. Nothing happy but squirrels; their life seems all play, and that of the hogs all work.[3]

Given the assumption of the primitive, uneducated, and lawless nature of the frontier, a number of historians, and especially church historians, have posited the idea that camp meetings, revivalism, and even the Second Great Awakening itself were given to excesses because of the nature of the people who were part of them, that is, the first white people of the Western frontier lived by passion, not by reason. Thus, the religion that worked in those early days was known for emotional extremism. However, following this script, eventually the more genteel and civilized influences of the East would make their way across the Appalachian Mountains and religion would become more respectable. Accordingly, while the camp meeting originally made an impact on religion in America, the impact was momentary. It was a chapter in the development of the West but without a lot of impact on what followed.

A good example of this interpretation is Elizabeth K. Nottingham's *Methodism and the Frontier Indiana Proving Ground*. Revivalism, according to Nottingham, "usually appeals to persons who have little learning or critical training. Their emotions are apt to pass swiftly and impulsively into action. Such impulsive action may take the form of a political revolution, a lynching, or a "red-hot" revival." She further comments:

> It is at least interesting that those parts of Kentucky such as Logan County, for instance, which in the nineteenth century were most famous for their revival meetings, were also most notorious for the number and violence of their lynching mobs. These pioneers had been living in an environment which not only isolated them from the culture of the eastern seaboard but put a premium on the development of bodily, at the expense of mental characteristics. The professional classes, who would normally have acted as centers of self-control, were comparatively few in those pioneer communities in the eastern states by mountain bar; their condition was somewhat analogous to that of those miners of Kingswood and Chowden [England] who felt themselves to be cut off from the bulk of their fellow countrymen by reason of their despised occupation.[4] Poverty, dangerous living, and absence of educational opportunity they also had

Illustration of America's frontier wilderness in Indiana, along the Wabash River, ca. 1830s, by Karl Bodmer

in common. Moreover, the lack of the most ordinary socializing institutions, of the restraints of conventionality and law alike, had bred in both the English and American communities under discussion a spirit of recklessness that not infrequently degenerated into brutality.[5]

Farmer does not fit easily into Nottingham's caricature of the early pioneer. Uneducated, yes. Prone to fighting, yes. Poverty stricken, somewhat. But, given the chance, Farmer seeks out education and then teaches school. He favors teaching manners and politeness to his students. And, as we shall soon see, Farmer was highly moral and moralistic—even in his "backslidden" condition.

3

Spiritual Searching and Conviction, 1817 to 1820

Eli Farmer continues the story of his early life:

About the time I closed my school, a dancing school was opened in my neighborhood.[1] Being still in a backslidden condition, I joined this school. After dancing until I became a little worried on that first evening, I stood by and looked on for a while. It seemed to appear so foolish now to me, and becoming greatly disgusted, I could not refrain from crying out in the midst of the wild revelry, that I would not do so again, and left the room. I was a very unhappy man, though no one else knew that such was my condition and I have no doubt but this had a great deal to do with my feelings of disgust.

After leaving the dance, I went to my schoolroom, where I built a fire, and then sat down to read, remaining thus employed for a long time. This was the only time in my life I ever tried to dance.

* * *

In the summer of 1817 my brother and I prepared a boatload of millstones and grindstones for the Kentucky market. We built two boats, one for the stones and the other for coal. About the times of the holidays, we had our work pretty well advanced, and had plenty of time for amusements. At such times, dances were very numerous, and my brother, who was younger than myself, made arrangements for one, at a tolerable respectable place and asked me to attend, but I declined doing so, for I was then deeply convicted [convinced] of my sins.

While the dance was progressing three or four very large, stout men came into the room, who belonged to another neighborhood, and who attempted to take the girls away from the boys, all of whome were very young, my brother who was the eldest of them perhaps, being only about eighteen or nineteen years old. The boys had some liquor, with which they designed to make some taddy for their girls, a very common occurrence in that day, which liquor these intruders turned over, when they became angered by the refusal of the girls to dance with them. When my brother informed me of what had occurred, which he did the next day, I said, "William, if an opportunity should offer itself in my presence, just say what you please, and as I understand the leader of the band has already threatened to whip me frequently to others, in order to manufacture for himself a wonderful reputation for personal bravery, and to cause people to believe I was not as good a man as I had the credit of being."

We kept on with our work upon our boats, near to which a family lived in a small hut, who were waiting to accompany us down the river to Kentucky.

Some weeks after the dance last referred to, my brother and I went into this little cabin one day, where we found one of the aggressive party, in fact, the fellow who had threatened me, with an ill-mannered looking comrade. The name of the bullie who had threatened me was John Shafer. As we entered the house Shafer said, addressing my brother William, "Mr. Farmer, what do you think of Christmas night?" The answer of brother William was, "Why I think you acted the rascal sir!" This led on to harsh words, and various epithets were bandied back and forth, when I interfered by saying that I desire each of them to be silent, for I was a better man than both of them. I knew this remark would greatly incense Shafer, and I uttered it with a significant demeanor, which was of its self very exasperating. I was sitting upon the side of one of the beds, by the side of one of the young ladies of the house.

After I made the foregoing remark, Shafer came to the bed and sat down on the same, on the other side of the young lady. Meanwhile William and the other man had become involved in a quarrel, and were rapidly tending toward a fight. I now told Shafer I understood he had intended to whip me in order to show people I was not as good a man physically as I was generally thought to be, by my neighbors; about which time my brother was called a liar by his antagonist, which caused William to knock his antagonist down.

When the fight began, of course it was the duty of the young lady to faint, and she promptly did so, falling back on the bed. I sprang to my feet, and called to William to punish the fellow soundly, when Shafer sprang up as though he was going to shove me. Shafer and I agreed to

Eli Farmer's Journeys, 1814 to ca. 1820

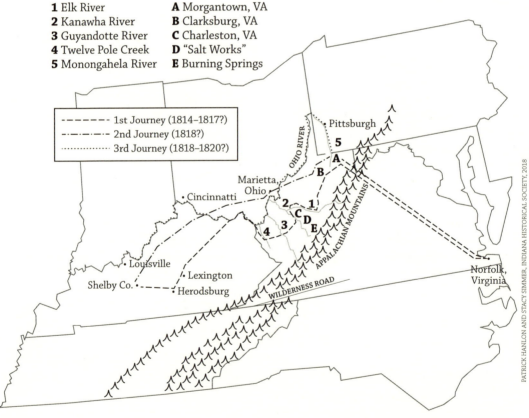

Between 1813 and 1820, Eli Farmer traveled back and forth between Virginia, Pennsylvania, and Kentucky. This map depicts three of his trips, showing the routes he took and the towns and settlements he visited or went by. Much of this region was mountainous, forested, and occupied by rough settlements and Indian villages at this time.

wait till this fight was ended, and then we would fight fairly. After knocking the fellow down, my brother picked him up, and ran with him in his arms toward the fire, as though he were going to throw him behind the fire, the fire being a big one, and one well suited to such a bitter cold day. The man of the house seeing the action on the part of my brother, kicked his foot backward throwing both belligerents out into the middle of the room. As they raised up, they again "clinched"—about which time I carried the young lady to the end of the bed on the opposite side of the house and laid her down. My brother then put his antagonist on the bed which we had just left, and near a barrel of queens ware which was ready for shipment to Kentucky, when the ladies of the house began screaming, crying out that the men would bloody the bed clothes, for the other man was bleeding profusely, and I cried out, "William, take him off of the bed"! and he did so. He jerked him down again, and beat him so badly within one minute that the poor fellow vomited blood. Shafer pushed me at about this stage of the fight, when I told him not to repeat the proceeding again, and after both of us called to our friends again to encourage them, we arranged that we would fight, when the present affair was ended. The battle over I prepared to fight him, but he declined, saying he intended to fight me but not just at that time; I tauntingly replied, "whenever you get ready, by all means let me know it, to which he rejoined by stating that when he did so undertake it he would attend to me.

He put himself in training, for five or six weeks, as though he was making preparation to run a foot race, filling himself for the fight so that by the time he was in readiness, he weighed two hundred and fourteen pounds, he was without a pound of surplus flesh.

All this time we were diligently engaged getting ready for our trip. On a certain Friday night, a furious rain came up, which gave indications to us, that there would shortly be a rise in the river, and we began preparations to get our boats down to our place of loading, which work we labored at until Sunday morning, when we adjusted the steering oar behind the boat, expecting to begin the journey and go down the river that afternoon some fifteen miles. I had worked very hard during the greater part of the forenoon of that Sabbath day, working till eleven o'clock, without having eaten my breakfast. About eleven o'clock, a lad came running down to our board and informed us that Shafer was coming to whip me whereupon I quit my work and concluded to have a brief rest.

Shafer, accompanied by three or four comrades came up soon, to whom I immediately addressed myself, saying that I had understood he had come to bid me a farewell, to which he returned an affirmative answer.

"The sooner then we test the matter" said I, "the better it will be for both of us." We then walked off some distance until we came to a suitable place for the fight, the ground being covered with snow and sleet, and therefore in a bad condition for such business. As we walked along, both of us were engaged in a friendly and even an amusing conversation, so that one of the party was prompted to declare that we were in too good a humor to fight.

When we had reached a proper place, I said, addressing my adversary, "John, I reckon you think you will whip me very easily." "I will give you the damndest whipping you ever got"—was his rejoinder: to which I replied, "I am an unbeliever, John, and now we will soon test it." Meantime I had gotten myself in readiness, and was awaiting him. We pulled off our overcoats, and then took off his close bodied coat, but in compliance with my request, "kept his shirt on." After he felt himself prepared, his friends gave him a dram of "liquor," whereupon he cried out, "Are you ready." "I am waiting you": I said calmly. He rushed towards me with the view no doubt of running right over me, but I jumped forward, putting the heels of my boots firmly in the ground, so as to brace myself firmly, and as he came I parried off his blow, and struck him a severe blow, turning him quickly around, when I caught him and threw him down. I now raised my foot to stamp him in the mouth, but he kicked at me, and I caught his foot in my arms which caused me to fall, my feet now being at his head, and his feet so situated with reference to my head.

Pretty soon we both rose up together, and as we did so, I caught him and succeeded in throwing him on his knees and hands, as though he were ready to receive a pack-saddle.

My antagonist now began trying to hit me in the face, which to avoid, I caught his thumb in my mouth which I bit nearly off. This pain caused him to pull his hand away violently, and in pulling his thumb out of my mouth, the bone of his thumb was left about naked, the flesh having been torn off by my teeth. When he succeeded in freeing this thumb I caught him by a finger, which I also barked off in a similar manner, holding on to it until I beat him down, and he fell heavily and helpless at my feet. After he sank down, he turned over on his back and I fell on him, catching hold of his breast fiercely with my teeth, and at the first venture took out a great mouthful of flesh. It seemed to me I could bite out a mouthful at every attempt. Thinking he could exhaust my strength, and endure more than I, he held out nearly half an hour, toward the latter part of which I skinned his back from the waist-band up, which I did by taking advantage of a slight declination of the battleground. I now ascertained he was about ready to surrender for he was now lying helpless upon his back with his hands thrown over his face to keep me from punishing his eyes and mouth. Pulling his hands away from his face, I began coming at his face with my head, holding his arms in the meantime, and I thus damaged his countenance wretchedly. His friends now interfering and begging for him, he himself being far beyond the power of entreaty, I quit my hold and ceased my efforts, and the war was ended.

His friends sat him up against a stump, and gave him something to stimulate him, when I said to my fellow foe, "Now John, what do you think of it?" His opinion was expressed in the remark uttered in reply to my inquiry—"You are a d—m sight better man than I thought you were!"

I have since been informed that this fellow was confined to a sick bed for six weeks under care of a good physician. After an absence of thirty five years I returned to this locality, and he was so anxious to see me, that hearing I had come back, he came nine miles to see me, which friendly attention he thrice repeated during my sojourn there, until finally upon the last occasion, we happened to have the pleasure of a long interview, at which he informed me that he had never been able to do any good for himself after the whipping he received at my hands, and he was kind enough and honest enough to assure me that he attached no blame to me whatever.

About the same time a cousin of mine with whom I had had a terrible fight long years before, came forty miles to see me, and he also told me he did not blame me for the whipping I had given him, since he, as well as John, had been the aggressor.

At the interview with Shafer he said to me, "Sir I don't expect you drink liquor at all, but you must drink some for old acquaintance sake." The poor man was then showing the effects of the whipping, for one of his shoulders hung down considerably.

On the afternoon of the day on which the fight occurred with Shafer, we descended the river almost fifteen miles to the place of loading, where in due time we succeeded in loading our boats.

It was shortly after this fight when I lost my father. He was coming down the river with me, his family accompanying him, and we stopped to load. While we were loading, my father having some business demanding his attention at Morgantown, went to that place to manage the same; intending to go there in a canoe, he took a by path afoot to go down to the river. Some distance to the point where the canoe had been left. Four days passed, and we heard nothing from him, but supposed he was attending to his affairs at Morgantown. A neighbor passing down that way on the fifth day, found the dead body of my father about three-fourths of a mile only, from the boats. These bad tidings were brought to us immediately, and we brought him to the board, where we prepared for his burial. We buried him close by, his body being the first burial in the first cemetery established in that settlement whereat Indians and white men were buried side by side.

Near this, to me, sacred precinct, and about the same time, the following incident occurred. The children of a certain Mr. Morgan were in the fields planting corn, their father being very sick at the time at the house, and while the children were at work, the father became very uneasy and restless, and although he was very feeble, he took up his gun and started towards the fields where he supposed his children could be found. As he walked slowly along, he met a neighbor girl, who was running and screaming for her life, closely pursued by two Indians. Sending the girl to the house with the children whom he expected to be slaughtered before they could reach the homestead, but quite as fearful they would slay him too, but he proposed to engage these enemies, and thereby favor the flight of the terror-stricken children. The Indians turned their attention to the man and began pursuing him, when he shot and killed one of them. The survivor then furiously attacked the invalid whom he succeeded in crushing to the earth, placing his knees upon the breast of the whiteman, and then attempted to take hold of his bowie-knife with which to kill him. Morgan by a desparate effort, succeeded in getting his hand away from under the Indians knee, and wrenched the instrument of death out of his adversary's hand, and sent it quickly into the quivering flesh of the Indian, inflicting a ghastly wound which caused the savage to cry out, "You murderer" as he made a precipitant flight, the deadly weapon still fastened in the body of the doomed adversary.

Morgan fled to the house, where the neighbors soon collected together, and a large number of infuriated white men went out in pursuit of the foe whom they found after a brief search. He had pulled the knife out of his body and had crawled into a hollow log. He was taken out and at once killed, after which both bodies were skinned, out of which they manufactured numerous saddle-bags, leggings, and straps for razors.

* * *

We came down the Manogasha, accompanied by the family at whose house my brother had the fight, a description of which I have given in the last chapter. We had a boat load of coal, and a boat loaded with grindstones and mill stones. We came down to Pittsburg, where we stopped for a time. After I had no acquaintance with the navigation of the river below this point, I had no fears to alarm me, for I had a pretty good knowledge of the drift of the water. I was however, well acquainted with the channel above Pittsburg. While lying at this point, we were visited one day by some young ladies, who assumed to be very elegant and innocent, one of whom on seeing a frog, cried out with nervous intonation in her voice, "Oh! See! Annie, here is a great 'bull toad.'" Another of the party asked very [artstrey?], apparently, what we called "this"—indicating by her finger that she referred to a pump. This was too much for the simplicity of the simple-minded ladies of our craft, and one of them explained that it was a "pump with which to pump folley out of fools," whereupon our visitors hurriedly decamped.

Traveling on from Pittsburg day and night, we arrived without any accident to befall us, at a point near Limestone, Kentucky, my brother managing the boats half of the time, and I attending to them the remainder of the time; and thus by the aid furnished by the hands on the boat we kept going all the time.

* * *

We went on then until we got within less than half days journey of Limestone, Kentucky, when a furious storm arose, during the early part of which my brother tried to govern the boats, but *failed. I was asleep at the time, and was feeling stupid from the effects of a severe cold I had contracted previously, but I got up out of my bed, and told my brother to quit rowing until I could find out which way we were drifting. Finding the direction in which we were drifting, and giving orders to my mother, whose family was aboard, to prepare herself with an ax and when she saw either of the boats about to sink, to cut the ropes which bound them together, and then remain with the one which was not so situated. The water by this time was pouring over both sides in great quantities, during which time she stood in readiness to do as I had bid her. All this time I was exerting all my energies to avoid running afore of a vast number of floating limbs, and trees, and timbers thronging the shore, trying to drift into the bank without injuring either of the boats. We succeeded in getting ashore safely, but were exhausted by the time our object were accomplished.*

After the storm we started out again and began floating rapidly toward Louisville, where we landed on Saturday night. This was in the year 1820, and this city was then very small. I was then under a pretty deep conviction, and desiring to attend church on the next day, I went up into the city and bought some material out of which to manufacture a pair of "trousers," to supersede the seedy ones I then wore.

On Sunday morning I hurriedly stitched up a pair of new pantaloons and had them ready to wear to the ten o'clock services, all of which work I did myself. I wore them to the Methodist meeting, at which place of worship I heard the noted preacher Henry B. Bascom deliver a sermon. He was considered one of the most powerful men of his day, and I had often heard his eloquence admired. He stepped into the pulpit dressed in the most fashionable of apparel, at which I became disappointed, and insulted. I had formed such [a] widely different opinion of him previously that this was violation of what I then esteemed the properties and decencies of religious life and my disgust and regretful feelings rendered me so miserable, that I derived neither pleasure nor profit from his discourse. I could have wished most heartily that he had been a different sort of a man.

Primitive Methodism

Henry Bascom was one of the best known men of early nineteenth-century Methodism. Matthew Simpson, in the *Encyclopedia of Methodism*, indicates that at one point Bascom was perhaps the most popular pulpit orator in the United States. At the age of twenty-seven Bascom was made chaplain of the U.S. Congress. He became president of two colleges, served as president of the American Colonization Society, worked as editor of the *Southern Review*, identified with the Methodist Episcopal Church South in 1844, wrote a book on the defense of slavery, and was elected bishop.

In 1820 Bascom pastored one of the most prestigious Methodist Episcopal churches in the West, located in Louisville, although he was only twenty-four years old. Later, Farmer formed a different opinion of Bascom, but in 1820, in a "backslidden" condition, Farmer reacted to Bascom with "disgust." This was not because of anything Bascom said but because of his "fashionable" apparel, which Farmer believed was in violation of the proprieties and decencies of religious life.

Farmer appears to be an enigma. On the one hand, he nearly killed a man in a fight. On the other hand, he was highly moralistic, even in his "backslidden" condition. Farmer understood he was out of a relationship with God, yet he had strong views about what religion should be. For him, it meant simplicity and separation from the world, including fashionable clothing; ribbons, ruffles, and all pretence was to be avoided. Thus, he comments on two ladies who saw themselves as "elegant and innocent." Dancing was a sin, and he could not tolerate it when he attended a dance. He states elsewhere in his autobiography that even in his backslidden condition, he did not swear or use alcohol.

American Methodism inherited its understanding of strictness in religion from John Wesley, who inveighed against fashion and extravagant living. Methodist believers were to put distance between themselves and the formal, wealthy, but spiritually dead Anglicans of Wesley's day. The Methodist General Rules, which are arguably mandatory for Methodists even today, include prohibitions against "laying up treasure on earth," "the putting on of gold and costly apparel," "the taking of such diversions as cannot be used in the name of the Lord Jesus," and "buying or selling spirituous liquors, or drinking them."[2]

Early American Methodists out-Wesleyed Wesley himself when it came to strictness. The first American Methodist *Discipline* explained that Methodists were to be a holy people, set apart from the world to live for God. It expanded on fashion in instructions as to who can receive tickets for the love feasts, or fellowship meals:

> Question. Shall we hold to the rules concerning dress?
> *Ans*. By all means. This is not time to give encouragement to superfluity of apparel. Therefore give no tickets to any, till they have left off superfluous ornaments. In order to this, 1. Let every one who has the charge of a circuit, read the thoughts upon dress, at least once a year in every large society. 2. In the dress be very mild, but very strict,

On a flatboat like this one Eli Farmer and his brother hauled coal, grindstones, and millstones from Pittsburgh, Pennsylvania, to Louisville, Kentucky.

3. Allow no exempt case: Better one suffer than many. 4. Give no tickets to any that wear high heads, enormous bonnets, ruffles, or rings.[3]

This primitive Christianity implied a radical lifestyle distinct from the general culture. One of the first Methodist preachers to enter Indiana was Peter Cartwright. His Kentucky circuit of 1804 stretched across the Ohio River and included Clark's Grant in southeastern Indiana. In his autobiography, written in 1856, he fondly recalls the primitive Methodism of 1804:

> We had a little Book concern then in its infancy, struggling hard for existence. We had no Missionary Society; no Sunday-school Society; no Church papers; no Bible or Tract Societies; no colleges, seminaries, academies, or universities.... We had no pewed churches, no choirs, no organs; in a word, we had no instrumental music in our churches anywhere. The Methodists in that early day dressed plain; attended their meetings faithfully, especially preaching, prayer and class meetings; they wore no jewelry, no ruffles; they would frequently walk three or four miles to class-meetings and home again, on Sunday; they would go thirty or forty miles to their quarterly meetings, and think it a glorious privilege to meet their presiding elder, and the rest of the preachers.[4]

As Methodism grew and came to dominate early American church life, it more and more reflected the Henry Bascoms rather than the Peter Cartwrights. In 1820 Methodism was still very much a lower class, frontier, revivalist, and anti-establishment sect. In that form, without pretense, its egalitarian nature is what attracted Farmer. And, as will be seen, this conflict between despised sect and growing respectability would be an issue for Farmer until he finally broke with Methodism.

If early Methodists railed against ostentatious fashion, they also railed against showiness in church buildings. An editorial in the July 18, 1834, *Western Christian Advocate* expressed this concern:

> [If] "Methodism would one day give itself to 'fashionable appearance' and 'popular address' and suffer sinners and delinquent Methodists to pass unreproved, that it would be followed and caressed by the wealthy and fashionable and popular crowd, and when it shall have declined thus far, another part of the plan would be to erect houses of worship more for show than usefulness. Instead of multiplying plain, cheap, and convenient chapels, with increased numbers as they are needed, and as the means accumulate, efforts will be made to rear a few stately edifices with bells, steeples, vestibules, cushioned pews, velveted pulpit, etc.

Convinced that he was a sinner, and because of Bascomb's ostentatiousness, Farmer was at least momentarily repelled by the Methodists. But Methodism was not his only option. The Baptists and the Christian Church (to which eventually he gravitated) also offered a strict understanding of Christianity, as Farmer relates:

I stayed at Louisville until I sold all of my millstones, selling them with the boat on which they had been shipped, and helped to get all safely over the "falls." I had previously left the grindstones above the "falls" on the shore where I had sold the coal. Subsequently we conveyed the grind-stones up into Shelby County where we dispersed of them at a good profit, in fact both of us were pretty well paid for our summers work.

I had also brought with me down the river, a fine stable horse, called Abraham Leopard, I afterward brought this steed into Indiana, in the spring of 1822, I believe, where he became during the first season the sire of eleven stallions. He is the common sire of most of the spotted horses now to be found in central Indiana. I kept him for several years, and took a great deal of pride in him, and made considerable money with him.

But money was no object with me, for I felt so miserable on account of my spiritual condition. After the summer season was over of the year 1820, I concluded to see whether there was any relief to be found for my sorrowful feelings, and in order to get light and helpful aid, I talked with a "Baptist" preacher upon the subject of religion. I told him I was greatly troubled with infidelity, and I followed him from place to place from one of his preaching points to another for some time. I also told him I was troubled with "Calvinistic" views, and was an unhappy man, and that it seemed I could find no resting place, while I experienced such an "aching void."

He told me one day, that he was about to start out on a preaching tour of some eight or ten days duration. He asked me to accompany him, and I consented to do so. I traveled with him for some ten days, during a portion of which time, I was in search of a wife, and part of the time praying to the Lord to convince me in some way that there was such a thing as Christian religion. As we traveled on the preachers became very numerous, all of whom went on with us. At one appointment the preacher with whom I was traveling told the congregation of my spiritual condition, some of whom encouraged me, telling me to seek on. I replied to them by saying "but if I am of the elect I shall be saved; and if I am not I shall be damned in spite of every thing." I knew they were Calvinists, and I thought I would apply their own doctrine. I attended their meetings and examined and questioned the preachers and also many of those who heard their sermons, all the while seeking light, watching anxiously to see whether there were any indications of supernatural power among them.

Calvinism and the Frontier

If Farmer had a problem with what he felt was Methodism compromising with plainness, he also had a theological problem with the Baptists—Calvinism. For three hundred years Calvinism had offered to a significant percentage of Protestantism an ideology that not only outlined the relationship between God and humanity, but also served as a basis for the idea of a Christian civilization. Calvinism, the theological system of choice for Congregationalists, Baptists, and Presbyterians, dominated religion in colonial America, especially in New England. The Calvinistic Puritans brought with them a grand vision for the Christianizing of America, and then the world. It was the Calvinists who first postulated the idea of American exceptionalism, of America as a "city set on a hill." Post-millennialists, such as Jonathan Edwards, further believed in the progress of civilization until the entire world would be Christianized. Calvinism was flexible enough to reconcile its belief in election with the revivalism of the First Great Awakening.[5] But it did not handle Methodist revivalism well. In New England it sought to combat the Methodists by scoffing, but that did not work on the western frontier.

In simplest terms, Medthodist revivalism was based on the assumption of free choice. However, free choice was difficult to reconcile with the doctrine of election with its understanding that God decrees who is saved. This has nothing to do with free will, which is exactly the point Farmer made after spending ten days with the Baptist preacher.

The Methodist challenge to Calvinism did not originate on the western frontier. Wesley in England based his theology on Anglicanism, but added features to his Anglican theology that were in large part reactions to Calvinism.[6] He derived many of his ideas from the Dutch theologian Jacob Arminius, who was himself reformed, but with modifications. Sometimes Methodist theology was called Arminianism, and sometimes Wesleyanism. Chief among Wesley's beliefs was the affirmation of "unlimited atonement," the understanding that Christ's death was for all persons, not just for the elect.[7] If Christ died for all, then everyone could be saved based on their personal response to an invitation. People had free will. It is not without significance that Wesley first spread this message in open-air or field preaching to miners, the poor, and others on the fringes of society. All were chosen. All were loved. All were special. Out of this message came the Methodist revival in England.

There were other distinctive differences between Wesleyanism and Calvinism. Most Christian religious music transcended denominational differences, but there were exceptions. Methodists introduced "invitation" hymns, songs that urged those who were sinners and those who were lost and wayward to repent.

Calvinists were scandalized that religious music would be addressed to sinners instead of to God, or to God's people. If some were elected to be saved and some not, then human beings were usurping God's prerogatives by suggesting that anyone could respond to the gospel. When Calvinists used the word "come" in a hymn it was almost always addressed to the people of God, for example: "Come, ye that love the Lord." For Methodists, however, invitation hymns expressed perfectly what the doctrine of unlimited atonement was about. Along with a new understanding of "altar" (see Chapter 4), it was an integral part of the camp-meeting ethos.

There were some other elements of the Wesleyan–Calvinist controversy that had an effect on American life. The Methodists in America took Wesley's practices, such as field preaching, and ideas, such as unlimited atonement, and applied it to their new setting.[8] The message fit well with American ideas of freedom, liberty, and democracy. The idea of freedom in post-revolutionary America would expand in a number of areas. In the minds of the fathers of the country, freedom meant freedom from political despots and from stifling tradition. In frontier preaching it also referred to freedom from evil supernatural forces, from sin, from spiritual bondage, and from all hindrances that kept the world from its utopian destiny. In spite of the dire preaching about judgment, death, and hell that many people associated with revival preaching, the frontier revival conveyed a tremendous optimism. After successful camp meetings preachers often spoke of millennial glory and the coming of God's kingdom. In biblical terms, the world would be set free from its bondage to decay and obtain the glorious liberty of the children of God (Romans 8:21). It is not by accident that a favorite camp meeting hymn was Wesley's famous "Blow Ye the Trumpet Blow." As sung in camp meetings, the hymn was based on Leviticus 25:8–17, the first mention of liberty in the Bible and the passage from which came the inscription on the Liberty Bell: "Proclaim liberty throughout the land."

While not within the parameters of this study, the optimism and view of the reordering of society has an important component in social reform. Instead of being a conservative force politically and socially, the revivalists were among the most progressive segments of society, at least until the Civil War.[9] The revivalist, populist Methodists who led the split with the Methodist Episcopal Church to form the Wesleyan Methodist Church in 1841–42 were antislavery, pro-temperance, antiwar, pro-gender equality, and post-millennial. The Civil War song, "Battle Hymn of the Republic," with its words, "Mine eyes have seen the coming of the glory of the Lord," used an old camp-meeting tune with words that many Americans associated with millennialism.[10]

This revivalism that challenged Calvinism was not limited to Methodist revivalism. Presbyterians and Baptists were also experiencing and advancing their own forms of revivalism, and with these forms their own challenges to strict Calvinism. Presbyterians were involved in the famous camp meeting at Cane Ridge, Kentucky, in August 1801, and many of the reports from there spoke glowingly of the cooperation between Presbyterians and Methodists. But from the Presbyterian side, Cane Ridge was a divisive event. Barton Stone, who was the main instigator of the revival, had given up on his Presbyterian Calvinism before the meeting and was eventually tried for heresy. Stone left Presbyterianism and with Alexander Campbell helped start the Christian (Campbellite) Church, which had as its features primitivism, restorationism (a return to the original practices of early Christians), and millennialism.[11] Two other Presbyterian ministers involved in Cane Ridge, Richard McNemar and John Thompson, were soon charged by the Washington Presbytery for preaching like Methodists and for holding "dangerous" Arminian doctrines. The ensuing controversy eventually led to the formation of the Christian Church, also known as the Disciples of Christ and the New Light Church. In his autobiography Farmer referred to this group as New Lights.[12] Meanwhile, Presbyterians divided into Old School and New School and into Cumberland Presbyterians.

But it was the Baptists who were the champions in the areas of theological controversy and church splintering. Baptist polity lent itself to splintering. With no centralized authority, and with their strong insistence on local church autonomy, Baptists associated and disassociated with such regularity that one despaired of keeping the groups straight. Baptists often split for little reason: differences between strong individuals, or even arguments among family members. But the Calvinism controversy and revivalism were the reasons for the major theological differences. The more Calvinistic Baptists were the Primitive Baptists, the Anti-Mission Baptists, and the Regular Bapists. The less Calvinistic Baptists were Missionary Baptists, Separate Baptists, and Free Will Baptists. None of the Baptists, however, were prepared to admit to "backsliding." Backsliding became a Methodist term.

According to historian L. C. Rudolph, the compromise of Calvinism was not all positive. Rudolph, author of the monumental study of religion in Indiana, *Hoosier Faiths*, and also of the Presbyterian history in Indiana, *Marching to Zion*, offers this assessment:

> The slow spread of Presbyterianism was not a result of automatic Arminianism in the forest. To argue this, one must hold that the success of the Baptists on the

frontier depended on their keeping their Calvinism secret. The awesome aspect of the forest, the helplessness of man before the weather and disease, the ever-present suffering and death would argue as well for a natural Calvinist theology as a natural Arminianism. When the frontiersmen were Arminian, it was because the most effective of the folk churches, the Methodist, sprang from the Anglican Church when the body was Arminian. It was reinforced on the frontier by revivalism, which, when long continued in an extreme form, undercuts theological maturity as well as church doctrine and practice. "Revivalism thus tends to lean theologically in an Arminian or even Pelagian direction with the implicit suggestion that man saves himself through choice."[13]

While Farmer had little formal education, and not a lot of church experience, and while still in his "backslidden" condition, he nevertheless worked through Calvinist issues of theology and some issues of strictness in religion by meeting for ten days with a Baptist preacher. After that, he knew what he had to do and he knew where he had to go to do it. Farmer reveals this knowledge as his story continues:

At the expiration of the ten days, I compared my condition at that time with my situation at the beginning, that I should be assuming to be in search of religion, and now find myself engaged in laughing. I found my brethren gone from me, and I raised to my feet, saying "I believe the Lord is about to bless me." Opening my mouth to tell what had been done for me, a mighty power came fully upon me then: and I felt that I knew my duty now. O, yes, I saw it all as plainly as any path . . . to ascertain whether I had gained any spiritual strength at all in the interval. I then concluded to leave, and attend a Methodist campmeeting then in session above Louisville several miles.

Before I reached that point, I gave my heart a close scrutiny. I felt ashamed of my overpowering proneness to sin, especially to engage in fighting, and felt satisfied that I could and would do much better.

4

Reclaimed, 1820 to 1822

After evaluating his time with the Baptist pastor, Eli Farmer seeks help in another Methodist camp meeting:

Just before I reached the campmeeting, I met a party of young men and young ladies, coming away from the campgrounds.[1] As I passed them I accosted them civily and politely, saying "how do you do gentlemen and ladies?" One young man raised in his saddle and shouted back, "Why did you not say ladies and gentlemen?" and before I was aware of what I was doing, I had stopped my horse and was about ready to stop and chastise him, but thinking myself of my former resolutions, I rode on to the meeting. The first person I met on entering the camp-ground, was Hanah Buskirk, with whom I had been personally acquainted all my life. I knew her to be a good Christian woman. She was aunt of the now distinguished jurist, the Hon. Samuel H. Buskirk, of the present bench of the supreme court of Indiana, and also an aunt of Judge George A. Buskirk, a prominent lawyer, financier, and banker of the city of Bloomington, in that state.

I had informed this estimable woman of my back-slidden condition so she, one day, introduced me to a young lady by the name of Polly Parker, by saying, "Miss Parker, I introduce to you, Captain Farmer, a back-slider!" I was decked out in a great deal of "finery" at the time, having, I remember, my shirt frilled with ruffles.

"Now," said Hanah, "do you go right into this work, go right along to the altar and be prayed for!" and she forthwith began exhorting me to seek religion again. These ladies then went away, and I went forward to the altar where I leaned forward upon the same, resting my self on the rails thereof and behold what I then thought to be the most motly throng I had ever seen. To me the scene was a very strange one, but by and by I slipped down under the railing and got down on my knees and began to pray. I felt singularly enough, and finding I could do nothing there, I again took up my position at the railing where I continued my prayers for the Lord to convince me, promising if he would do so, that my life should be wholly devoted to his service.

Standing there praying earnestly, I soon felt a softening touch of sovereign grace which melted my heart, and ere I knew what I was doing I was weeping. While thus weeping, I asked myself, "Is this sympathy, or is it some supernatural power?" and began to closely examine myself, to account for my present state: and I finally became satisfied that it was some supernatural power, that was dissolving my heart so tenderly. I had not experienced such feelings for more than five years previous to the time of which I speak. I then promised my God, that if I should not feel any stronger witness than this one, I would regard that as an answer, and would be determined to live for him the best I could.

The Camp Meeting and the American Evangelical Ethos: The Altar

It is the contention of this book that the American frontier camp meeting introduced practices and ideas that eventually resulted in a new American religious culture that would be identified today as evangelicalism. A quote from Ernst Troeltsch, historian of the social ethics of churches, will serve to preface this discussion:

> The really creative, church-forming, religious movements are the work of the lower strata. Here only can one find that union of unimpaired imagination, simplicity in emotional life, unreflective character of thought, spontaneity of energy and vehement force of need, out of which an unconditional faith in a divine revelation, the naiveté of complete surrender and the intransigence of certitude can rise. Need upon the one hand and the absence of an all-relativizing culture of reflection on the other hand are at home only in these strata. All great community-building revelations have come forth again and again out of such circles and the significance and power for further development in such religious movements have always been dependent upon the force of the original impetus given in such naïve revelations as well as on the energy of the conviction which made this impetus absolute and divine.[2]

In his very first camp meeting in Virginia in 1813, and in almost every one he attended thereafter, Farmer referred to "the altar." With the introduction of a new understanding of "altar," the revivalists changed the nature of worship and Christian ministry, the Protestant doctrine of the church, and eventually church architecture.

The altar in the camp meetings during Farmer's time referred to an area set aside for persons to "get religion," or, to put it in Christian terms, to "get saved," be "filled with the Spirit," or to receive some special anointing of God. How big the altar area was, or what items were within that area, or what people ministered within the area, or even what the area was called, depended on the circumstances. Sometimes the altar was not an area, but just a rail, a bench, or a place to kneel. For the scoffers it was sometimes referred to as "the pen." It was also known as a "mourner's bench" or an "anxious bench," especially when the altar area included a pew or a bench. In a rapidly changing religious culture, language had not been standardized, and the implications of words and language would evolve.

It is possible to posit an approximate date for this new understanding. There is no precedent for anything like the revivalist's altar at any time or at any place or for any other group within Christendom before the first decade of the 1800s. The American camp meeting introduced the use of the altar; it was not used by the Wesleyans in England or during the First Great Awakening in the North Atlantic states.[3] It was, in fact, not used even at Cane Ridge, nor in any of the camp meetings described before about 1807 to 1810.

The new understanding of altar reflects Troeltsch's suggestion of "unimpaired imagination." The altar was an improvisation introduced as a practical way to deal with seekers or "mourners" in a mass meeting. And it entered into camp-meeting culture so unobtrusively that no one documented its history. As in Farmer's mention of the altar in 1813, and again in 1816, the use of the altar appeared in camp-meeting accounts as if it had always been there. Henry Boehm, an early Methodist who helped organize the

Evangelical Association, reflected on some of the claims as to when and where the idea of inviting mourners to the altar for prayers first took place in his book of reminiscences. He places the introduction variously between 1802 and 1807.[4]

The camp meeting use of altar changed the understanding of what was the nature of sacrifice in religious worship. For Roman Catholics and all groups influenced by Catholicism, the sacrifice offered on the church altar is Christ. This sacrifice is patterned after the Hebrew altar in the temple. In each mass Christ is offered anew on the altar and in his offering the bread and wine become the body and blood of Christ. There are variations and some compromises of this view in Protestant churches but the concept is the same. Groups such as Presbyterians, Puritans, Baptists, and Anabaptists, in reaction to Catholics, sometimes dropped the word altar in favor of a "communion table," and often simply deleted any understanding of altar from their gatherings, but none ever reinterpreted the meaning of the word.

What was different in camp-meeting revivalism was the idea that it is the individual religious seeker who is offered to God. The revivalists did not in any way seek to diminish the importance of the cross as the central Christian symbol, but they understood that Christ's sacrifice was made once and for all and did not need to be reenacted in the worship service. What the revivalists did want to emphasize was the sacrifice of the individual, to be laid on the altar and made a living sacrifice.[5] Thus, the emphasis is on the decision. If fire consumed the sacrifice in Old Testament symbolism, in this new understanding fire stood for the Holy Spirit, or the ecstatic experience as the sign of God's receiving the offering. There was a reason for the shouts and emotional intensity. In modern evangelical religious culture this is related to the understanding of the "new birth" and is at the heart of evangelicalism. This understanding shifts the focus of worship from offering praise to God for God's sake, whether any human feelings are involved or not, to the seeking of the religious experience as a confirmation that worship has taken place.

When Farmer encounters the women exhorters on the way to the camp meeting "above Louisville" around 1820–22, he is urged to "go to the altar." Within a very few short years the new interpretation of the altar had worked its way into evangelical religious life.

The camp meeting understanding of altar undermined the high role of the priest, or ordained minister. In Catholicism the priest must be present at the altar to effect the transubstantiation of the communion elements. The priest is the mediator between God and the people. Martin Luther could speak of the "priesthood of all believers" but still insisted that what was accomplished at the altar was the responsibility of the ordained clergy. For camp-meeting revivalists, the sacrifice on the altar did not require the presence of any clergy. This was taking the Lutheran and Protestant doctrine of the priesthood of all believers to its logical conclusion. In Farmer's case, godly exhorter women served in a priest's role.

This development affected even the terminology used about clergy. In Catholic-type churches the clergy are treated with respect and are addressed as "father," "pastor," or "reverend." In the camp meeting, and in later evangelical culture, the leader is referred to almost always as "preacher," and often simply as "brother." Thus, in camp-meeting culture persons needed no special standing or training to minister at the altar, other than the anointing of the Holy Spirit. It is significant that in his second camp meeting in Beasontown, Pennsylvania, Farmer "worked" the altar. A Catholic priest spends years before he is qualified to officiate at the altar; Farmer needed only two camp meetings. This was perhaps the most egalitarian religious development in American church history.

The new understanding of altar led to the popularizing of the testimony or recounting of personal experience. In the camp-meeting revival, or in any revival for that matter, a divine encounter or transaction is validated by a public witness. The new understanding of altar also changed the understanding of the word "holy," which means "separate." In Catholicism the altar area is so holy that only the priest or those designated by him can enter the area. This is based on the Hebrew understanding of degrees of holiness in the temple: from the Holy of Holies (where only the high priest ministers), to the altar area (where only priests minister), to the worshipping congregational area (where only men participate), to the area where both Jewish men and women can gather, to the Court of the Gentile (where non-Jews can gather). In the Catholic pattern the altar area is reserved for the priest and his appointees (except for special occasions).

In American camp meetings "holy" referred to all things given totally to God (such as the Bible), but especially to persons made pure by God's action. The separation came when believers separated themselves from thoughts, actions, and attitudes that were not pure; in the outside world believers separated from things considered worldly, such as fashion, dancing, alcohol, and gambling.

The altar area at a camp meeting, ca. 1829, which was in front of the preacher

The new understanding of altar would also soon influence church architecture. In traditional church architecture, almost always derived in some way from the Catholic understanding, the central focus of worship is on the center altar, associated with the cross and the sacraments. Early Presbyterian and Congregational churches used the pulpit and the "communion table," usually in front of the pulpit, as the focus of worship. But revivalist Methodist and Baptist churches focused worship on the pulpit, which usually held a Bible, with or without a communion table, along with an altar railing that could double as a communion railing. In revival culture then, the altar was no longer a table but the kneeling rail, the place where persons would pray, make religious commitments, or receive communion.

Methodism did not sustain this understanding of altar and worship in later years. As revival culture waned and many Methodist churches became more catholic and less sectarian in their understanding of the church, and especially into the twentieth century, Methodists exchanged their center pulpits for the "divided chancel" that allowed for a central altar as the focus of worship. In Baptist and other sectarian-type churches, the altar is still the kneeling place of prayer and commitment.

In early years no one was theologizing about this new understanding of altar. These developments were growing out of the revival experience and taking place apparently without comment. They were able to be incorporated into revivalist church life because of the absence of the moderating influences of traditional church teaching.

The person who did develop a "theology of the altar" was a prominent Methodist laywoman in New York, Phoebe Palmer. During the 1830s Palmer conducted Tuesday prayer meetings in her sister's New York home. Her altar theology grew out of these meetings. In 1840 her book, *Guide to Holiness*, posited the view that entire sanctification or Christian perfection was possible instantaneously by "sacrificing all on the altar." This book, along with her teaching and other articles, did more than any other influence to launch what was known as the Holiness Movement.

While it is beyond the purview of this study, the point should be made that camp-meeting revivalism based on an altar experience developed into Palmer's sanctification altar theology, which developed into the Holiness Movement in the latter part of the nineteenth century.[6] The Holiness Movement developed into Pentecostalism, which now claims sixty million adherents worldwide. Except for the phenomenon of speaking in tongues, the Pentecostal services today carry the same features as the early Methodist camp meetings, including being "slain in the spirit" (fainting), dancing, shouting, and the use of the altar.[7]

Farmer's story picks up just after his experience of grace at the altar at the Methodist camp meeting near Louisville, Kentucky:

I returned home with Hanah Buskirk and Polly Parker, both of whom were young ladies at the time, and we stopped on the way, at the residence of squire David Huffs to take dinner. That worthy gentleman is now a resident of Green County, Ind. Previous to dining, I was walking the floor of the room, earnestly engaged in prayer for a happy and speedy deliverance. Just before dinner, I felt a sudden flash, which I can compare to nothing so suitable as electricity, and with it I felt a gleam of hope and light spring up in my inmost heart. At one time I thought of saying to my lady companions, that I was of the opinion the Lord was about to bless me, but I did not express the thought. I regretted many times afterward my neglecting to do so.

This feeling wore off, by and by, and we ate dinner and went on home, where I made an engagement with the ladies to meet them at Jones' campmeeting, nearby Shelbyville, Kentucky, in a few weeks thereafter. I became more and more despondent, and more and more miserable as the days and nights succeeded each other.

These accounts from Farmer challenge the various theories that seek to explain the success of frontier camp meetings by economic, sociological, and psychological analysis. One of the best studies on camp meeting origins, Ellen Eslinger's *Citizens of Zion: The Social Origin of Camp Meeting Revivalism* relates theories of camp meetings that emphasize "cultural conflict, loneliness, poverty, [and] the broader development of southern culture." According to these theories, camp-meeting revivalism was an escape from a harsh life, or perhaps a reorientation that attempted to "reintegrate a society rent by economic hardship, political partisanship, and cultural conflict."[8]

Basing much of her study on Kentucky, Eslinger concludes that conditions in that state were not quite as harsh as often portrayed. Even before Cane Ridge, Kentucky was experiencing the rapid development of economic and ambitious enterprises of every variety. Population was multiplying as settlers flowed into the new land. She believes Kentucky was developing a political culture that was much more than just an extension of Virginia. Among other observations she rejects the idea of some historians that "little if anything that happened in [camp meeting revivalism] was new."[9] Eslinger posits a spiritual explanation for camp meetings.

If Farmer thought any about the origin and extent and the social context of camp meetings and revivalism, he certainly did not make his thoughts known. Nor did he express anything about loneliness, poverty, or the need to reorient values or establish a new religious culture. He does not even explain how or why he attended his first camp meeting at Gillbad. But the early camp meetings he describes would set the tone for his life and ministry for years to come. To Eli Farmer and his contemporaries the explanation for the popularity of camp meetings was much simpler: they were seeking a supernatural intervention, a blessing bestowed by God. Farmer speaks to this point in the next passages of his autobiography:

At the appointed time we met at the before-mentioned campmeeting in accordance with our agreement. I spoke with a Methodist preacher, to whom I made known my condition, who in turn exhorted me fervently and often. I told him that I wished to serve God, but my heart was so hardened I could not do so—declaring also, that I <u>repented because I could not repent</u>. I was greatly burdened, and my heart seemed to swell up ready to burst within me. I felt that I was defenselessly occupying an open field of destruction, having no way or power of escape, and that God was just in damning me, because I had not been a better man. I here saw the great deformity of my own nature, and I jumped from the altar and ran far out into the forest alone. I fully hated myself. I sat down on a log, and all at once my heart was melted, tears again flowed freely, when I felt considerably better.

About this time some men rode by, one of whom inquired to know what troubled me, and I replied, "I want to serve God, but am so great a sinner I cannot!" "Go back to camp!" was their rejoinder. I returned to the meeting, thinking I would saddle my horse and return home, for I feared I was becoming worse, and making myself by my attendance here, more unhappy and miserable. Looking up I saw the sun but a little way above the treetops upon the west side, being then only about two hours above the horizon, whereupon I concluded I would not have sufficient time in which to reach home before night-fall.

I remained. I said I shall remain and see what the Lord will do for me. Again I began praying among the mourners, but could feel no relief. I now returned to the tent, my heart, causing me to fear, absolutely swelling within my body. While thus engaged, a young lady came up from the altar and began telling me her experience, how miserable she had been, for she was also a backslider, telling a terrible story, but it chance to be but a repetition of my own desperate case, so I thought in case I went to hell, I should go trying to seek religion and go praying.

About this thrilling moment the thought occurred to me, that if God would only save me, I would, should He so will it, go to hell and preach to sinners. As this thought flitted across my brain, it seemed to me, I instantaneously received a power by which I was enabled to loose any hold upon every thing, and I found myself, ere I was aware of it, laughing. I thought then, that this was a strange proceeding never trod before or since that blissful hour. Praising God with all my strength, I began telling them anew what he had done for me, and as I touched them, each one seemed to receive some kind of a shock: in fact it seemed like there was such a power upon me then, that my very touch would help others who were stricken on account of sin, for such as I touched soon came to light and liberty. I was so happy all through the following night, that I did not sleep at all, but unweariedly kept watch through its blessed hours, holding sweet communion with my appeased God.

On the next morning "volunteers" were called for, and I arose and gave my hand to the preacher, and jumped upon a bench and began exhorting people to come forward and enlist in the army of the Lord. A great many joined the church at that time, and the meeting was kept up several days beyond the Sabbath. I took a very active part at the altar in laboring with the mourners. A bevy of young ladies, with all of whom I was acquainted, came walking around the altar on one occasion, one of whom remarked to her companions, "Darned if I am afraid to go in there." She came right in but was immediately stricken with conviction and started to run away, but I touched her lightly upon the shoulder, saying to her, as I did so "Don't run, Debby, don't run from the Lord" whereupon she fell. I felt it my duty to preach, and I have singled this woman out as an object of my especial prayers.

Previous to the occurrence which I have just narrated, praying that she might become a Christian, I did the same for the gentleman whom she afterward married, and with the same success. He went from the altar after the services there had been concluded, and I went out in search of him, to see whether he could be brought to Christ. I found him down on one side of the campground, where a great many people were praying over him. The name of the young man was James Dabney. I had named these persons especially in my prayers because they were about as wicked, as any persons within my acquaintance at the time, and I told the Lord, that if He would convert these people, I would take such conversions as an indication that it was my duty to preach the gospel. I now promised the Lord, I would endeavor to give myself to him, and live for Him, laboring for Him, as provident might open up the way for me.

The meeting was continued over Sabbath. During preaching Sabbath morning, a rumor ran through the camp that Henry Bascomb was upon the campground. A consultation among the old ministers was held at once, to decide whether an invitation should be extended to him to preach. The deliberations of the consultation were conducted privately, owing to the fact that no little prejudice existed in the minds of many good Christians against Mr. Bascomb on account of his persistence in wearing fashionable clothing. He was exceeding neat and careful in his wearing apparel, and it was feared by many, that this was a sin which might not be overlooked. The council decided to request him to preach at 2 o'clock, and sent a messenger to him with their request. The messenger found the object of his search far back in the congregation, occupying a seat among the sinners. The messenger also requested him to come forward, and it was duly announced that he would preach at 2 o'clock in the afternoon. I was very glad of an opportunity to hear him again, and when he entered the stand, at the appointed time to preach, I found myself within the altar close by in a much better frame of mind for receiving his sermon, than I had found myself at the time of hearing him at Louisville.

I closely observed every action on his part upon the occasion, and from the beginning, I was charmed by his winsome and impressive manner, every look and every action, and tone of voice, seemed to shed additional light upon every thing he did. His devotional manner of reading hymns, and his touching prayers affected me powerfully. His expressions in every respect during the delivery of the powerful sermon which followed, seemed to be ladened and freighted with a double weight of power, and the old men who had formally been so prejudiced against him, soon began to weep, and shout, and thank God for such efforts, and every thing seemed to melt away before him. His countenance seemed to be lighted up as though a lamp were shining through every lineament of his face, and his eloquence as a mighty power, before which nothing stood unmoved.

On Monday the camp was broken up, and I returned home.

On my way home, I stopped at the residence of the wife of my brother. She had at one time been a Methodist; but was now in a backslidden condition and I began exhorting her. The spirit of the Lord seemed to be upon me, and she encouraged me greatly to go on, telling me she had once enjoyed the light. I went on then to my mother's house. My mother was a widow woman now. She never made a profession. On the contrary, I was the first one out of a wicked family to make a profession. I told her what the Lord had done for me, the recital of which seemed to effect her sensibly. About the usual hour for retiring for the night, I asked permission to pray in the family, and she granted me that liberty. My brother Thomas who was then ab[o]ut fifteen years old, seemed to be somewhat effected but slipped off in time of prayers and went to bed, which discourteous act greatly troubled me, for I feared he did not have confidence in me. Such fears so troubled me that I had thoughts of abandoning prayers in the family, but it seemed to me that I could hear the cry ringing in my ears continually, "Keep up family prayer," and I continued it.

I now asked the Lord to give me my mother as a witness, that, He, had called me to preach, and in a very short time, she became very much concerned and soon professed religion, coming out very brightly on the Lord's side.

Feeling greatly encouraged, I began talking to the neighbors. The settlement was one in which the Baptists held the ascendancy, and many of their oldest members thought I was entirely too enthusiastic. There was a young man among them by the name of Lantz Johnson, who had professed religion a short time before, and who was the only company I could find whose society was agreeable to me. I found him warm-hearted and zealous in religion.

One day I asked him to accompany me to [a] Methodist meeting and he did so. He had previously entertained strong prejudice against the Methodists, thinking there was nothing good among them. During the meeting he became warmed up considerably and he concluded to remain longer and attend class-meeting. He became so happy during the class-meeting that he jumped to his feet and began shouting, crying out loudly: "The Lord is here! The Lord is here!" We returned home, and this young man became a warm friend of the Methodists, so much so, that his brethren became alarmed lest he should leave their church and join the Methodists. To frustrate such action on the part of the young brother they began to work against me, among other things, industriously circulating the report that I was deranged. He afterward came to be a resident of Indiana, and we had no more trouble because of him.

My mother being an earnest Christian, began telling her experience to the neighbors, and a Baptist minister came to see her, who after a satisfactory interview, pronounced her a true disciple in whom there was no guile.

The Baptists labored assiduously to cause her to unite with their church, but I persuaded her to wait until she should hear a Methodist preacher, and then choose for herself. I got a Methodist minister to come into the settlement and preach in order to assist my mother in her selection of a spiritual home. On the night of his arrival the Baptists had a prayer meeting, and he attended, and upon invitation, sang and prayed. At a proper time he arose and gave a brief exhortation, and "opened the doors of the church" to receive members. Mother came up to him and gave her hand. This action on the part of the Methodist minister created considerable prejudice and ill feeling, so that some of the Baptist members left the church. Subsequently I took my mother to Methodist meetings some distance off, as frequently as my arrangements would allow.

I continued in that country for some time, trying to be religious, examining the moral and religious standing of the youth of my vicinity, and holding meetings occasionally. I would go out from among my own people into settlements where I was less acquainted and less known, and where I felt a greater liberty. I still felt it to be my duty to preach, and finely [finally] concluded I could not be successful where I was so well known, among people with whome I was so familliar. So I concluded to settle up my business affairs, and leave the country. My mother being a poor woman, I did all I could towards helping her on in the world, and bought her another horse, and also a cow, and paid for the schooling of her children, and started them to school.

5

"God Has Given Me This Place," 1822 to 1826

In the next passage of Eli Farmer's autobiography, he travels to Indiana to begin preaching there:

In the spring of 1822 I came over into the state of Indiana, with the view of preaching to the Indians.[1] I left my widowed mother, and my brothers and sisters, and started out upon this adventure, at about the time I was entering my 29th year. Believing I would have no use for such a thing I came off with out a church letter. I was firm in the belief that the Lord would direct my steps rightly, and I would not fail to go to the best place for me. I crossed the Ohio river at New Albany, and traveled northwestward until I came to the town of Bloomington, at which place I found an old acquaintance in the person of Abraham Buskirk. I was riding my spotted stallion at the time, and was plainly clad in a round breasted coat, common janes clothing, and my money was nearly exhausted. I tarried with Mr. Buskirk. He was a professor of religion then, as was also his wife, a most estimable lady and a noble christian. They soon ascertained that I was a professor, and both of them besought me to join the church at that place. At length I gave my name to them as a member, not expecting however to remain long among them. Meantime a sister of Mr. Buskirk, living in the vicinity of my friends in Kentucky, hearing that I had come off without getting a letter and ascertaining my whereabouts caused a letter to be issued to me, and sent it to me in a letter. This lady was the person whom I have heretofore mentioned as introducing me to a lady as being a back-slider.

I remained here until fall, during which time I was struggling for what the Methodists call "sanctification or full redemption." I would fast, and pray almost constantly, and I felt so wretched, that I could scarsely rest day or night. My convictions became so deep and solemn that I fairly loathed my own nature.

The Methodists and Sanctification

Any study of Methodism in the nineteenth century must deal with the Methodist doctrine of sanctification, or, as it is known by its various names, holiness, full redemption, full salvation, perfect love, or second blessing.[2] The doctrine can be traced to John Wesley in England and grew out of Wesley's differences with Calvinism and his optimistic view of grace. For Wesley, it was not enough that one could be *forgiven* for sin; the Bible suggested that the believer could be *cleansed* from sin. The difference is significant. Calvinists taught the doctrine of "imputed righteousness," which asserted that while God looked upon the believer as righteous because of the work of Jesus Christ, the believer was still a sinner. The believer was a forgiven sinner, but a sinner just the same.

Wesley taught what was called "imparted" righteousness, which meant that God looked upon the believer as righteous because the believer had been made righteous and was righteous. The goal of Christian life was more than just forgiveness; it was rather to have a pure heart or to be perfected in love. This purification took place not by works or good deeds but by grace through faith.

During the Second Great Awakening, or the Western Revival, sanctification began to be identified more and more with Methodist revivals and camp meetings. Sanctification could happen gradually or instantaneously. When it happened instantaneously it was preached as another (or second) blessing following the salvation experience. The importance of this historically is that in the evolution of camp meetings, and mostly after 1865, preaching on holiness soon became the major theme of these gatherings. One of the first actions of the National Association for the Promotion of Holiness, which dates from 1865, was to announce plans for national camp meetings. At the very time when camp meetings had fallen into disfavor among Methodists, they took on new life among that portion of Methodists committed to the kind of populist religion characterized by frontier Methodism. The rallying cry for these populist Methodists was holiness, and by the 1880s the Holiness Movement had developed into its own church culture complete with its own hymns, preaching themes, literature, and traveling evangelists. In 1888 there were four publishing houses devoted exclusively to publishing holiness literature; in 1891 the National Holiness Association listed 304 "holiness" evangelists in America; in 1892 there were forty-one holiness periodicals being published throughout the country.

The Holiness Movement was at first supported by Methodist church leaders (many of whom were products of the preaching) until the movement became more and more critical of the coldness and formalism of establishment Methodism. At the same time it was moving toward emotional and behavioral extremes—shouting, dancing, being "slain in the spirit," and other activities not unlike those that characterized early camp meetings. The pejorative term "holy rollers" was the label used by cynics. At that point Methodist leaders withdrew their support. The result was a mass exodus in the 1880s and 1890s and the beginning of the Church of the Nazarene, the Assemblies of God, and any religious group with "Church of God" in its title. This was taking place among several different ethnic groups and also in missionary situations.

When the phenomena of "prophecy" and "speaking in tongues" was superimposed on the Holiness Movement, the Pentecostal Movement was launched in the early 1900s. This represents the fastest growing segment of Protestantism worldwide in the twenty-first century. Persons who believe that what happened in early Methodist camp meetings was only a passing phenomenon have only to go to a Pentecostal service in the present day to experience the same worship characteristics.

Back toward the beginning of this movement, on the Indiana frontier, Farmer left his sick bed to go to another camp meeting because he was seeking sanctification:

About this time a camp meeting came on above Spencer a few miles, and I was somewhat ill at the time. I was very anxious to attend this meeting, but was afraid to do so for a while lest I might endanger my health. My desires became so strong and overpowering that I concluded to go, having an understanding with my self that if I should find myself growing more feeble, I would seek shelter at some farm house where there would be less exposure, and where I could receive the full benefits of the medicines I had prepared for the occasion.

On my way to the meeting I fell in with a young man who was of the opinion that his mission in life was to preach the gospel, and I pretty soon discovered he was in pretty much the same condition in which I found myself. Arriving at the camp ground, we found the meeting well under way, everything getting on satisfactorily under the leadership of Samuel Hamilton, the presiding elder. Under the preaching of this zealous and old servant of God upon this occasion there came upon me such a divine shock of divine power that I was made sound in soul and body. Just by the touch of the power, of the Holy Spirit and I was made as sound as I ever was in my life. The young man who had accompanied me a portion of the way to this meeting, to whom I just referred retired with me to the woods, long after night fall, to pray. The object of our united prayers was to be, that the Lord would lead us safely into his vineyard to be useful workers therein. While on my knees struggling for light and full sanctification, a beautiful light appeared before me, like a flash of lightning. Heaven appeared to be seen in the most attractive form that I had ever thought of even in rapturous visions of nights, and it seemed to me in that hour of dazzling splendor, and enrapturing joy that I could see the celestial city, with all her beauty, Her partly lifted gates of precious stones, her streets of gold, her angelic choirs, her stately trees, whose boughs are for the healing of the nations, and her flowers of perennial fragrance and blooms margining the eternal river, whose waters are flowing for the nations: and the scene seemed wedded to my very soul, so that I was loath to turn away from it. Some time afterward it disappeared and we returned to camp. We continued to work in this meeting until it broke up, after which I went down to Spencer. . . . Spencer was then a little village of a few small log cabins.

* * *

While at Spencer, I boarded with a very excellent man by the name of David Johnson. . . . About this time I told Mr. Johnson we ought to have a prayer meeting and gave out an appointment for one accordingly whereat, I organized a regular prayer meeting. I was aided by brother Johnson and an old widow lady by the name of Johnson, and who was the mother of Findley Johnson, a respected citizen of that locality at this time.

We three persons constituted the class, and we agreed to hold a prayer meeting regularly each week, in a little hut in the village. We took up our cross, and went forward with our christian duties, and I suppose these were the first meetings ever held in the town of Spencer.

In one of these meetings the old lady got so happy, that she ran out into the street, and shouted aloud, which aroused the people, and they gathered in from the various little huts and a great deal of excitement was thus created. A day or two afterward I retired to a dense thicket near the village and held secret prayer. I got down on my knees, and standing myself by a pawpaw bush, began praying most earnestly, and suddenly, while thus engaged, the beautiful city again flashed before my enraptured vision, and it seemed to be drawing nearer and nearer, evolving itself into an awful attractive scene as it approached me. My soul seemed to be quitting my body, so strong were my heart's longing to be made a partaker of its celestial light. I remained upon my knees, and gazed with awe-stricken wonder upon the blessed picture I feared would fade away. While thus engaged, it seemed to me, that I saw the Savior coming out of the city, and he was a beautiful, though plain man. He seemed to be approaching me, and I felt that I should fall were he to touch me. He came up to me, and placing his hand upon my head, I was thrilled through by a flood of light, which seemed to permeate my mind, and heart, and body. I *cannot now state whether I fell or not, for the first thing I remember to have occurred afterward, was joyously shouting and praising God. I felt I was purified and cleansed and as I understood it, sanctified.*

I was then in public business, and examining myself, I found out that I had got rid of my former selfishness, and was far less sinister. In fact, "I loved my neighbors as I loved myself." I ascertained that I was quite as much disposed to look after the interests of my neighbors in business affairs, as I was to look after my own affairs. I knew no difference. I found in my renewed person a fulfillment of the passage of Scripture in the first Psalm, "I delighted in the law of the Lord, and meditated therein day and night." Whether asleep or in my waking hours, I was happy. And I could feel that my "peace flowed as a river," and "righteousness as the waves of the sea" encompassed me round about. I enjoyed this blissful state for many years.

Marriage and the Frontier Circuit Riders

For a short period of time in early American Methodism, marriage was forbidden, or at least greatly discouraged, for the traveling elders who were circuit riders. One person who spoke strongly about this was Bishop Francis Asbury, who believed that if the task of the circuit rider was to save souls, marriage could only be a distraction. Furthermore, many circuit riders had no permanent home and their income was too small to support a wife and family. There was an option for Methodist preachers who married and that was to be a local pastor. Local in this case referred to the fact that some pastors helped with the circuit but had homes and did not accept a yearly appointment. They were also, for all practical purposes, second-class citizens in the Methodist hierarchy. Only the traveling elders were members of the annual conference.

Farmer and other preachers were quite aware there was a reason for the rule. Circuit riding was not conducive to nurturing a stable home life. Nevertheless, the prohibition against marriage soon broke down. In Farmer's case, it seems quite certain that he was not about to be constrained by a rule advocated by authorities. However, marriage and settling down delayed Farmer entering into "the work," as he relates:

Soon after this I became acquainted with my first wife Matilda Allison. I found by association with her, that she was a very pious, holy woman. Failing to sell my house in order to get means with which to go out among the red men on a missionary tour, I concluded I would do better to marry her, and establish myself in business and await the indications of Providence. I bought a tract of land, from a gentleman by the name of Sweeny. I had few means with which to pay for it, and it was quite difficult, to meet my engagements with reference to its purchase by me. The land referred to, is situated some three miles west of Bloomington, and is a portion of the farm on which I now reside.

* * *

Late in the fall a camp meeting was held at Stephen Grimes: and I attended it. The Quarterly conference was held at the same time and place.[3] I was licensed to exhort. The first intimation I had of any such intention on the part of the said conference was the presentation to me by their committee of my credentials already made out.[4] Taking the paper in my hand I examined them in an abstracted manner, and was for awhile, undecided as to the course I ought to pursue. I at length I returned them, and begged to be excused from taking them. By this course I at once lost

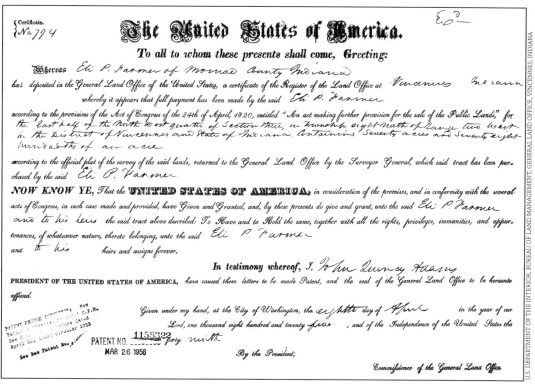

Original land deed for Eli Farmer in Monroe County, Indiana, dated April 8, 1825

considerable spiritual strength. My intention was to open up my farm and prepare it for cultivation, after which I hoped to be ready for the ministry, and would then give myself wholly up to the work. But I soon discovered I was retrograding in spiritual matters. Some times while at work in the forest, chopping or grubbing, the Spirit of the Lord would come upon me, and I would drop everything and run out in the neighborhood in search of some one, to whom I might talk. I kept promising my conscience, that just as soon as I could do so, I would give my self up to the work, and thereby paying her hush money, that her rebelling voice might be stilled. In this manner, I came near losing my spiritual life entirely, notwithstanding I prayed almost constantly. My wife rightly interpreting my feelings, urged me, to go into the work of the ministry. I told her she was too feeble to take upon her self the hardships, incident to the life of the wife of a Methodist preacher: when she silenced me, by saying that in order to aid me in the work of the Lord, she would attend me to the uttermost ends of the earth, and I became so troubled, I could rest neither day nor night. My fears so alarmed me, when I thought of my neglect, that I was absolutely afraid to go into the woods to work, lest I might be killed or maimed, by a falling limb or tree. I was sorely distressed, and I concluded I must preach or be damned forever, and my heart kept echoing back the warnings of my soul—"Woe, woe is me if I preach not the gospel."[5] I was so distrustful of myself, that I asked the Lord, if consistent with His will, to remove me from the earth, if I could be counted worthy of a triumphant and happy death. Death would indeed, have been a good and welcome release to me.

Meantime there was a man by the name of John Raper, who was working for me, in order to pay a debt due [to] me from him, and who annoyed me not a little, just at this period. He had frequently commented to others, upon my physical manhood, as he had known me in Kentucky. On public occasion, he would pretend to be very anxious to test my manhood, and he would frequently assume to be very angry with me, and talk violently about whipping me.

He did this in order to manufacture a representation for himself, as a brave and powerful man. He not infrequently carried his vexatious conduct so far, as to abuse me personally in the presence of others, and threaten to whip me, all of which I meekly and patiently bore. We had been prompted to this course I had no doubt, by a foolish remark he had heard me utter to the effect, that I would not strike a man, and he was disposed to presume a great deal upon that declaration. A re-examination of my quakerish proclivities and principles, caused me to see that my views on that subject were incorrect. God's people, I saw, by this examination, had always been prepared to properly defend themselves, and they had always been accorded the victory in unsought battles. The result was, I concluded it would be less criminal, to whip him, and thereby, learn him his place, than to longer bear his torments and insults, provided I could do so in the proper spirit. In addition to my own investigations and studies upon this question, I consulted with my father-in-law, Mr. John Allison, who was a class leader, addressing him thus;—"Father Allison, what am I do to with this case," and I referred him to the whole matter, withholding nothing from him. His advice was like this:—"Sir, the next time he does so, do you pull your coat off and go out and whip him," and I found this council was very acceptable to me.

A few days after I was traveling along a county road when I met John Raper, and I commanded him to get down, telling him I had made up my mind to whip him. He refused to comply with my demand, and I again ordered him to dismount, when he promised to never molest me again. I told him he was such a liar I could not believe him, and that he must get down, as I did not intend he would go away unwhipped. I soon saw, however, that he was already whipped, and relenting, I agreed to let him go, by putting him on his good behavior in the future. It afforded me a great satisfaction to be able to state that he was ever afterwards my steadfast friend under all circumstances, and he used often to declare in my hearing and else where, that I had taught him a good lesson.

My trials were destined to afflict still further, as will be seen as my story progresses. In the following spring Mr. Abram Buskirk, required my services to assist him with his corn crop; the only help he then had, consisting of his son John B. Buskirk, who is now a resident of Bloomington, but who was then only a lad, probably about nine years of age: and I went to his house to help plant corn. I had arranged with my wife, that she was to come to Buskirks in the afternoon, and return home with me after supper. As she came down to be in pursuance of our arrangement, accompanied by my little dog, she received a grave insult, from a family by the name of Allsup, who resided just across the road, or nearly so, from Mr. Buskirk's house. This family had a couple of vicious dogs, one of which was an uncommonly large one, and he had either bitten or had attempted to bite nearly every person in the settlement. At one time, the children of Leroy Mayfield, were going to school, when they were attacked by these dogs. They had become so savage, by the encouragement they had received, that they had come out into the road, and were fiercely assailing the little fellows, when I chanced to pass along. The children ran screamingly to me, closely pursued by the dogs. I stepped in between the children and their pursuers, and knocked one of the dogs down with a club, and when he had recovered from the first effect of the blow, he ran off howling. I never intended to say anything about it, but the little fellows published it abroad, and the people soon come to know all about it, and of course I fell under the displeasure of the family.

Well, as my wife came along as I have stated, this family hissed their dogs upon mine,—I was working in the field adjourning [adjoining] the place where the disturbance began. These vicious dogs had caught mine, and were about to dispose of him summarily, when a couple of my neighbors shouted to me to rescue my dog. One of these men Matthew Boreland jumped the fence, and cried out he would help me, and began encouraging one of the Buskirk's dogs to attack those fighting with mine, and succeeded in getting him to attack the larger one. I ran up and used my hoe upon them, in such a manner as to do them as little damage as possible to effect a separation. The sons, of the family to whom the dogs belonged came rushing up and became very boisterous. Mr. Boreland knew they had urged the dogs to make the onslaught, and he began abusing them with great vehemence, directing his remarks to the elder one, a lad about fifteen years old, whom he at one time threatened to chastise with a whip. After Boreland had got through with them, I told them not to carry away bad stories home, and to tell their father to come and investigate the matter, while the witnesses were ready to testify, in case he thought we had wronged him, or his family, or his property. The owner of the dogs came up to where we were at work, in great haste, pretty soon after the children had departed, and in a very angry manner, began to abuse Mr. Boreland. Mr. B thereupon returned his insulting language, and profainly told him that unless those dogs were better mannered and put under some restraint he would kill them. I had kept silent. The old fellow after a while turned to me and opened the vials of his wrath upon my head, and abused me in a violent and insulting manner; but I kept on at my work. He finally said he would catch me out sometime when he would whip me. As he turned off to go home, he savagely said, addressing me, "Bring home that pint of salt you borrowed of me."

We went down to Mr. Buskirks for supper, where we found old Thomas Buskirk, an uncle of Abram Buskirk, who had long known me. While at supper, we held a council relative to the fuss, at which sister Buskirk said—"do you go now, bro Farmer, as soon as your supper is finished and get a bowl that will hold a pint, and take it into our smokehouse, get a pint of salt for him, for he may sue you right off;" and I did so. My feelings and passions, although highly wrought upon, were still under my control, for I had fully resolved to resent nothing coming from them, unless it was offered me.

As I was going to his house, I met him and he was leading a horse to a branch to water the animal. I informed him I was going to his house for the purpose of returning the salt, and express my regret that we could not get along pleasanter, and added that I hoped he would not abuse one so again, as I had rights and feelings like other men. He jumped forward and caught hold of a club, his horse meanwhile breaking loose from him and running off. As he raised the club to strike me, I dropped the salt, and caught up a club myself to keep him from hitting me. While I was parring off his blows, a flash of anger took possession of me, and I decided to cure him at once. Holding the club with one hand, I struck with my other hand, and he staggered away from his bludgeon, and as the opportunity presented itself, I gave him a severe kick in his stomach. I then struck him on one side of his head with my fist, and knocked him fully twenty feet. I struck him hard enough to break the skin from his ear, leaving nothing but the grissle. He now began hollering "murder," and I was greatly alarmed, fearing I had given him a fatal blow. Mr. Buskirk, and the Allsup family, with the Allsup dogs, came running out to us, but by the time they reached us, my antagonist had got up, and still fearing the effects of his injuries, I walked rapidly away.

I went down to Buskirks, where a general council was held, and we all decided I had not done amiss, but yet I felt badly about it. I was feeling dreadful, when Thomas Buskirk addressed me thus, "now sir, you have done right, and you must not get discouraged, but continue to do right. I am counted an infidel, but I am not of that faith. There was a time, when I might have obtained religion, but that time has gone by unimproved by me, I put if off too long, and it is now too late; so be careful, I beg of you and do not backslide." I returned home in a miserable frame of mind, and with a mashed and swollen hand.

At the earliest opportunity, I went before the church, and asked for a trial.[6] It seemed to me if I were punished a little my feelings would be less tormenting. The church, after an informal inquiry was made, refused to investigate my case, and encouraged me by assuring me, I had done no wrong. I remained in a dreary condition for some time, feeling myself under a cloud which *seemed loath to be lifted, and its shadows were unlifted by a single star of hope.*

After a season I made up my mind that if God would reclaim me and endow me with the Spirit for preaching as I had once possessed it I would enter upon the work, though the attempt should slay me.

About this time I heard of [a] campmeeting which was to be held near Bedford at the farm of Michael Farmer, a distant relative of mine, and I concluded to attend it. My brother Thomas had come out from Kentucky to see me, in pursuance of a proposition I had made to him, to the effect that if he would come out and live with me, I would pay for his schooling; and I urged him to go with me to the camp meeting. We both went down to the meeting. Thomas was converted and made a profession of religion at that meeting, returned to Kentucky where he afterward became a minister, and accomplished a good work. He died in the faith of a Methodist preacher, and I have no doubt to this day, although long years have intervened, "his works do follow him."

I was also benefited at that meeting. I was reclaimed, and the spirit returned to me. I determined to cut loose from the world. I told my wife that I had to go into the work now, but she said, I could not go then, for said she, "I feel that I shall live but a little while now, I am in the way, but will soon be removed."

I thought her words were the language of a delusion, born of her afflictions. Soon after this, she was attacked with a violent fit of bleeding at the lungs, and in a few weeks she died. While she was dying, she thus addressed me, "I am now dying, and I am going strait away to my home in heaven; let our little boy (our boy John) live with father and mother, and you go out and give all we have to the glory of God and we shall live together again." "John," said she, "will die a good man." And sure enough John died shouting.

After burying my wife, my Presiding elder sent me to Piola [Paoli] circuit, where I labored till a man was secured to fill the appointment. I returned home, but soon afterward went down into Greene County, to form a new circuit at a point in the White River valley. Truly I went "weeping, bearing precious seed." And the good book says, such "shall doubltess return with their sheaves in their hand."[7]

Methodist Ideas of Church Growth

Writing his autobiography approximately fifty years after this event, Farmer found nothing unusual in the way he reported going to Greene County to "form a new circuit." But it must be noted that his call to preach and his crusade into Greene County were not according to any established tradition, and would invite comment.

The Methodist system of deploying preachers was an "episcopal" (having authoritative bishops), "connectional," or "sending" system. Preachers were assigned by the bishop at the annual conference or at least by a presiding elder who held the authority between annual conferences. Preachers were credentialed by the annual conference, which was the gathering of all preachers once a year to report on their work, to credential other preachers, to set boundaries for circuits, and to be assigned to new appointments. All of this was under the standard of the *Discipline*, the Methodist constitution and law book that was revised by a general conference of delegates held every four years.

On paper the system suggests accountability and well-defined lines of authority. In practice, however, at least in the early years, it was chaotic. Preachers formed new circuits and abandoned old circuits at will. They got lost in the wilderness or became sick and frequently did not make their circuit appointments. Preachers adapted as necessary; they recruited their own helpers, and they organized camp meetings that were never authorized by annual conferences or bishops.

When his call finally came, Farmer launched his preaching career. But the call and Farmer's authority to preach came not from a licensing committee, nor a bishop, nor a committee, but from God. This was true of all of the religious groups that thrived on the frontier, whether Methodists or Baptists or preachers of the Christian Church. These groups might well be called American indigenous denominations. The idea of credentialing directly by God led to individualism, independence, and sectarianism in religious matters. A Farmer contemporary and Disciples preacher, Abraham Snethen, gave his version of how preachers got started in his autobiography:

> In those days when a man felt himself called of God to preach the gospel, he went straight at it. He conferred not with flesh and blood but straightway preached the gospel. Instead of hunting up a college, or theological seminary, he hunted up a horse, if one could be found, a pair of saddlebags, a hymn book, and a Bible, and without money or change of raiment, he went forth to proclaim the truth as he understood it. His theme was salvation from sin, and his test was "Behold the Lamb of God, that taketh away the sin of the world." Thus equipped, he went forth through hail, snow, storm, wind, and rain; he climbed the hills, crossed the mountains, traversed the valleys, plunged through swamps, swam swollen streams, slept out doors nights: wet, weary, hungry, yet ever triumphant.[8]

Farmer did not enter Greene County to do a survey or to determine if it was of interest for Methodist work or to check if the field was being covered by any other denominations. Farmer had a plan: to start a circuit and do warfare for God:

I went to Bloomfield, which place I found filled up pretty well with infidels.[9] I went in among them and began an aggressive warfare, and the Spirit of the Lord was with me and upon me. I had prayed so earnestly, and fervently, over this place that I seemed to have a sort of witness that it would be given to me in spite of men or devils. The infidel element of society seemed to be insulted, and for some cause treated me coolly. An old gentleman by the name of Vanclives actively and thoroughly canvassed the community near the land of which he himself owned, and did all he could for the cause of Infidelity. He even gave all his landed state to be used as infidel property, for the furtherance of their interests, in order to build up an infidel community.

One of their number, a man by the name of Doctor Pattan came to me one day, and rudely said to me, "Dam you leave this place, or you will frighten our women and children to death." My reply was equally plain, but less profane, for I observed, "I shall let you know in due season, that God has given me this place, despite the opposition of men or devils."

Vanclives came up with his cane and pretended to cane me, but I told him he was mistaken in his man, and that God had given me the place, and that I would have it.

Squire Presmore, a noted infidel, invited me to take dinner with him one day, and I accepted the invitation. We were sitting in the barroom of his hotel, just before dinner, when he accosted me thus, "I dislike and despise these black coated fellows who go about making their living in this way."[10]

I replied about like this, "You need not be frightened on my account at all, sir, for I am abundantly able to pay my way; the gospel shall never go a begging so long as I have a cent." After I had eaten my dinner, I proposed to pay him but he would not have a cent; and I then told him

I should not sup with him any more, for when I came to a public house, I wish to be a free man with an undisputed right, without any restraint, to say what I believe to be right.

I labored on there, and the people came out in great numbers to hear me, and I could see that the Spirit of the Lord was working among the people. After preaching I would frequently go several miles into the country to get my horse and myself provided for. After preaching on a certain occasion, Squire Passmore, who was a cousin of Benjamin Neeld of my own country, came to me and said, "Sir, it seems you have no place to stop here, and the court room is getting to be a cold place, and as I have been thinking over the matter I am of the opinion that I shall try to be a Christian, and I would like for you to go home with me."

I saw he was powerfully convicted, and I said, "Squire, your offer is so fair I must accept it, but I am prepared to pay for my accommodations."

"No," said he, "come and make my house your home."

I then told him, that in about two weeks from that time I would begin a protracted meeting at that place, and that if he would care for the preachers, including myself, with our horses, who might be in attendance, I would pay him for it at the closing of the meeting, telling him I would have quite a number of such at that time.[11] Said he, "Come to my house all of you, and come free of charge."

After leaving Bloomfield on this occasion, I attended another appointment on the opposite side of the river, at a place called Fairplay, and then went on to another appointment.[12] While at this last appointment, in the evening of the day I left Bloomfield, a messenger from squire Passmore came for me, having a message to the effect, that squire Passmore was about dying and wished to [see] me, but I did not get to see the messenger.

When I heard the intelligence I observed, "I hope he is dying to sin," but did not go to him. When I got around to Bloomfield again, I found the Lord had blessed him powerfully, and from that time everything seemed to yield to the good cause. Judge Wynds, Doctor Patton, and other leading infidels, sold out and moved to the Owens settlement at New Harmony, on the Wabash, where they joined the Owens society. Meanwhile our work went forward at Bloomfield successfully, and all who remained joined the church.

The last one who joined the church was Mr. Leonard, a noted fiddler. During the earlier stages of the meeting Leonard had become angry with us because his wife had joined the church, and he frequently tried to interrupt our meetings by swearing loudly and playing on his fiddle in his house close by, and made himself generally as great a nuisance as possible. He did this to drown our noise. The work increased, and became such a power that at last he dropped his fiddle, and coming up to the door where our meeting was in progress thus addressed me, "Sir Farmer, I want you to have meeting at my house tonight." I announced that we would [be] meeting that night at the house of Mr. Leonard, that we would have a prayer meeting there, and I wanted all to come out to it. This gave a new impetus to the work. We met at the time appointed. Leonard arose in the meeting and asked all of the friends to forgive him, and he soon became a happy member of the church.

This was in 1826. During this year I met with good success wheresoever I went. I was blessed with revivals at all my appointments.

During that year, Jane, the daughter of an old Kentucky friend of mine by the name of Milum attended some of my meetings and finally professed religion at a Methodist meeting in a certain neighborhood. The old gentleman was a strong Calvinistic Baptist, and he made light of the matter. I thought I would go over to his house one evening, and see how Jane was getting on. Entering the house I spoke to the family in a friendly way, feeling determined to take no offence at anything their faith might prompt them to say or do.

Illustration of an early Methodist circuit rider

Pretty soon Jane came into the room from the kitchen. When I asked her how she came on, before she could find time to answer, the old gentleman said, "O you Methodists have something which you give the people to make them act as they do."

While we were talking, a New Light sister came in, and asked me very soon after entering the room whether I was not going to hold a meeting for them that night. I replied by saying that the hour was so late that a congregation could not then be had: when she rejoined by saying that if I would consent to preach, she would secure an audience for me. Sister Milum also insisted on having a meeting, and said if I would consent to preach, she would send her boys out to notify the neighbors.[13]

I consented to comply with their wish and active preparations were at once begun for the meeting. The neighborhood was sparsely settled, yet all came out, and we had a pretty good congregation. When they had all gathered in I began the meeting, taking this for my text, "Fear not little flock, it is your Father's good pleasure to give you the kingdom."

By the time I had got pretty well through with my discourse, the power of the Lord came down in a remarkable manner and Jane jumped up and began shouting, and praising God, and pretty soon the old lady did the same. The old lady had never done such a thing previously, and the old gentleman hurriedly left the house. Nearly all of the neighbors professed religion before I left the meeting, and I continued to hold meetings at that place, having an appointment there every time I came around on my circuit. The old man's eldest son, who had been absent from home a great deal, was the last one to join the church. At one of the meetings the old gentleman was standing by when his son William made a profession of being converted, became very happy. Before he was aware of the fact, the old man was thanking God, "Thank God," said he, "These people are doing a great deal of good."

The work began to spread till it ran out into many other communities.

Soon after this, I became acquainted with an old Quaker preacher, who lived near Newberry, down in Green County in the White River valley. Their name was John O'Neal. He came to my meeting one day, and my attention was attracted to him by his peculiar cloth[e]s, his old fashioned round breeched coat, and his broad brimmed hat. I supposed he was an old fashioned Methodist. He was with an acquaintance of mine by the name of Jason Cary who was similarly attired.

We had a good meeting on that occasion, and when it was over, both of them came to me, and the old Quaker, having ascertained my first name, thus addressed me,—"Eli, I want thee to come and see me."

He then went on to instruct me with great particularity about the way to his house, and I promised to visit him on my next round. I informed him that just four weeks from that day I would be back again, and I would manage to find him, and to visit him at his home. He again gave me very full directions as to how I might find him, telling about following certain roads and paths, leading to a certain gate, within sight of his house in order that I might not be trouble[d] in finding the way.

At the appointed time, I went to my meeting, and after it was over, following his directions, I had no difficulty whatever in finding my Quaker friend. The old gentleman was watching for me, at the big gate. He gave me a cordial welcome, and we started towards the house, which was about half a mile distant. When we drew near the house he said, "Now, Eli, go down to the house and I will come down directly. I went down to the house, and was there received by a very good looking woman, an elderly looking old lady who wore a neat clean cap, and whose other clothing was of a plain though neat order. She was at the yard gate, and when I came up to the fence, she saluted me by saying, "Eli, get down, thou art just as welcome at our house, as thou wouldst be, was thou a Quaker preacher."

I dismounted and took her by the hand. "Now," said she, "Eli, come into the house." I followed her into the house. When she had got about midway of the floor, she turned to me and said, "Eli, what wilt thou have for thy supper, wilt thou have coffee, tea, or milk."

I bade her make me some coffee, and by this time her husband the old gentleman came in from the barn. He gave me the privilege of his library, which I found on examination, to be one of rare excellence in that early day. When supper was announced, we all sat down at the table, when the old gentleman said, —"Eli, we will now hold a Quaker meeting," and we maintained strict silence for a few minutes. This was their manner of returning thanks.

"All right, Father ONeal" said I, as soon as he had after their manner returned thanks, and asked a blessing, he said to me,—"Now, Eli, thee is at liberty" —and I asked a blessing with his request.

We now helped ourselves to the bounteous repast. After supper, I enjoyed myself very pleasantly. In fact I always found a pleasant home with this good family upon every occasion a home was there sought for. At the hour of retiring for the night, he again said to me, —"Eli, we will hold our Quaker meeting again."

"All right, Father O'Neal," I replied. As soon as they had finished their devotions after their own manner, he said, "Now, Eli, thee is at liberty." And I said, "Let us pray." We knelt down on our knees, and had prayers after the manner of the Methodists. When I got ready to leave on the next morning, I was assured by both of them that I could make that place my home always should I desire to do so. When the old gentleman could, he attended my meetings, and I would frequently call on him to close the meeting. He would sometimes exhort, and weep, in a very affecting manner, and his family nearly all professed religion under our labors.

"Now," said he, after these professions had been made by them, "they are at liberty to be either Quakers, or Methodist, and I think you had better establish a regular preaching appointment here, and put this place on your list," and I did so.[14] We made up a church at his own house, and I never enjoyed more freedom, and more happiness in my life, than I did at my appointments at this Quaker preacher's house. The last time I ever saw this worthy old couple, was while I was on my way to Davis County, to fill one of my appointments, on which occasion I had the pleasure to tarry with them over night. Next morning, the old man came out to the big gate with me, he was on his way then to attend a Methodist classmeeting nine miles distant at Bloomfield, and he at our parting said, "I want thee to tell me whether I ought to join the Methodists, or remain a Quaker as I am."

"I cannot say, Father O'Neal," I replied, "I do not know that joining the Methodists could make you a better man than you are already."

"Well," said he, "the Methodists know me, and their preachers will come to my house and preach for me any hour, but were I to join them, my brother Quaker preachers maybe might abandon me, and preach no more for me."

This was the last time I ever saw him, though I have since heard from him. I understand he is now dead, if that be true, I have no doubt his soul is now resting in the bosom of his God.

6

Officially Methodist, 1825 to 1826

Although Eli Farmer had been riding a circuit around Greene County, Indiana, for some time, he began his official career as a Methodist preacher at a camp meeting in Bloomington, Indiana, in late 1825, as he relates below:

At our last camp meeting at Bloomington, I was recommended for the traveling connection, and I became a licensed minister, at a time when our numerical strength was very full.[1] This state and the great state of Illinois comprised but a conference. At the time I entered upon my ministerial duties Ohio and Missouri, were cut off from our old conference leaving the above described states as the territory over which our conference was extended. By this new arrangement I found the Rev. Peter Cartwright had been left in our conference.[2]

At the first conference after my becoming a traveling preacher, I was sent to Bloomfield circuit, a circuit which I had formed the year previous, and I went to work with hearty good will, determined to do all I could.

Farmer and the "Traveling Connection"

In September 1825 Farmer officially became a preacher in what was called at that time the Illinois Conference of the Methodist Episcopal Church. Methodism was growing so rapidly, the conference lines were changing almost annually. At the general conference of 1824, Missouri and points west were made a conference, Ohio was made a separate conference, and Illinois and Indiana together became a conference known as the Illinois Conference.

Structurally the Methodist Episcopal Church was organized very much like the U.S. government with legislative, executive, and judicial branches. Legislatively, the general conference was a delegated national body that met every four years and had authority to revise church law. This law was published in a book known simply as the *Discipline*. The general conference also elected bishops and set annual conference boundaries. The annual conference was made up of ministers who were appointed to serve the churches within the conference boundaries. The annual conference set district lines, rearranged circuits, and credentialed ministers. The quarterly conference was the gathering of different classes and churches that made up a circuit. The presiding elder was to be present for these meetings, and the sacraments were to be administered. Often one of the quarterly meetings was scheduled for several days; at these times camp meetings were held.

Thus Methodism had built into its very structure the incentive for camp meetings. All of the churches or classes or preaching points on a circuit were already scheduled to gather for the quarterly meeting. In some instances this could add up to thirty different congregations. Since the distances for these meetings could be up to forty miles, it made sense to make arrangements to camp or stay overnight or for several nights. Camp meetings became a part of the schedule, usually at the quarterly conference held in August or September. These were always unofficial, or at least quasi-official. That is, they were not prescribed by the church *Discipline*. Because of this they were called not by the presiding elder but by the preacher in charge of the circuit.

The executive branch of the Methodist church government included bishops who were overseers for the denomination and the conferences, presiding elders who were overseers for districts within the annual conference, and preachers who were overseers for the classes and churches of the circuit. The bishop, with the assistance of the presiding elder, made the appointments for the preachers. This system of church government was called "episcopal," meaning, as with Catholics and Anglicans, it was based on the authority of bishops. It was also called "connectional" because each church was part of a larger whole, and each pastor was part of a larger fellowship of clergy. From this "connection" preachers felt free to call in fellow preachers to help with services and camp meetings.

In spite of the well-defined hierarchical structure, the system, at least in its early years, allowed for a tremendous amount of freedom, flexibility, and improvising. Farmer

A record of Eli Farmer's first official appointment as a Methodist preacher, reported in the September 9, 1825, Indiana Palladium

COMMUNICATED.

At the Illinois Conference, held at Charlestown, Indiana, the Preachers were appointed for the ensuing year, to the districts, circuits, and stations as follows, viz:

Madison District.—JOHN STRANGE, P. E.
  Madison Station—Samuel Basset.
  Madison Circuit—G. K. Hester.
  Lawrenceburgh—J. L. Thompson.
  White Water—James Havens.
  Connersville—Nehemiah B. Griffith.
  Rushville—Stephen R. Beggs.
  Flat Rock—Thos. S. Hitt, James Jones.
  Indianapolis—Thos Hewson.
Charlestown District—JAS. ARMSTRONG, P. E.
  Charlestown—Allen Wiley, George Randal.
  Corydon—Samuel Low.
  Paoli—John Miller.
  Bloomfield—Eli P. Farmer.
  Eel River—Daniel Anderson.
  Crawfordsville—Hacaliah Vrederburgh.
  Bloomington—Edwin Ray.
  Salem Station—Wm. Shanks.
  Salem Circuit—John Cord.

acted as his own "bishop" within the bounds of his given circuit area. He organized classes and churches, (and sometimes discontinued classes), recruited additional preachers for the circuit, and arranged camp meetings when the spirit moved him.

Farmer's license to preach was based on a recommendation from a quarterly meeting, which, in his case, took place during a camp meeting. He was "licensed," not ordained. In 1826 he was then made deacon and elder and a full member of the conference, which may not have impressed him too much since he does not mention it in his autobiography. Even then Farmer must have considered himself an outsider since he would make disparaging remarks about "the authorities" or the "traveling preachers" (as opposed to the "local preachers"). The more influential traveling preachers and the presiding elders would later be associated in Farmer's mind with "tyrannies."

That he was only licensed in 1825 seemed to make no difference to Farmer, who was called to preach, and not to advance in a career. He had established the Bloomfield circuit on his own initiative the year before. The circuit was received by the conference, and Farmer was appointed as its official Methodist preacher. His story continues:

During the year I held a camp meeting near Fair Play at which we accomplished a good work. This meeting was attended by several persons from Bloomington, and one of their number, Mr. Frank Ottwell, professed religion. We had some of our best preachers there, but the interest began to die out pretty soon, under their preaching, and I forbode any further preaching for a Season.

I called for all the old sisters who could pray to come within the altar and unite in prayer for God to remove the obstacles to success.[3] We got down on our knees and then and there had a quaker prayer meeting. I told the sisters to wait till I called upon them, I desired them to pray.

After a season some of them began to feel happy, and it was very difficult for them to restrain their feelings. The work soon became a success, the good old sisters laboured valiantly; and much good resulted from the meeting.

Soon after the meeting just mentioned, I held another camp meeting, at the place where Newberry now stands, where we had a powerful work among the people. At this meeting, a certain young man experienced a great deal of mental anguish, lingering a long time at the altar, until the meetings were nearly over. I went to him and addressed him after this manner, "Sir, are you not a backslider." "I am, Sir," said he. "I once enjoyed the life of religion." I told him to kneel down, and when he had done so, I called up all the people whom I knew to be powerful in prayer, around him. Encouraging him, I told him to look up and try to take hold of the promises by the proper exercises of faith, and that we would try to do so, and in this way he was delivered of the Lord. A powerful shock of divine power came upon him, which shocked all those in his immediate vicinity. His sister who was near by, caught hold of him, which act in some mysterious manner caused him to temporarily loose his hold upon divine mercy. I told some of the folks to take her away, and we then surrounded him again, and we began praying as before and in a few minutes, a similar shock visited him, and he was made shouting happy.

"Getting Happy": Revivalism, Enthusiasm, Healing, and Visions

It has already been observed that camp meetings played a major part in frontier revivalism, and revivalism played a major part in the development of Indiana Methodism. Religious revivalism may be understood as an intense expression of Christianity that focused on preaching, invitation, and emotional response. Revivalism was not opposed to religious education, liturgical worship, and the sacraments, but these traditional ways of being Christian were deemphasized in revival culture.

In the East, in areas dominated by Episcopalians, reformed Christian groups, Presbyterians, and Congregationalists, revivalism, and for that matter, Methodism itself, tended to be viewed as religion on the fringes. Methodist preachers were looked upon with suspicion as untrained, uncouth, and disruptive to the established religious traditions. George Whitefield, the British Methodist who was a key figure in the First Great Awakening, came under severe condemnation by the religious establishment in the East. In 1744 Harvard College issued a thirteen-page statement titled *The Testimony of the President, Professors, Tutors, and Hebrew Instructor of Harvard College Against George Whitefield*. Among other things the statement said of Whitefield:

> First, as to the Man himself, whom we look upon as an Enthusiast, a censorious, uncharitable Person, and a Deluder of the People. . . . We charge him, with Enthusiasm. Now that we may speak clearly upon this Head, we mean by an Enthusiast, one that acts, either according to Dreams, or some sudden Impulses and Impressions upon his Mind, which he fondly imagines to be from the Spirit of God. . . .
>
> In the next Place, we look upon Mr. W. as an uncharitable, censorious and slanderous Man; which indeed is but a natural Consequence of the heat of Enthusiasm, by which he was so evidently acted; for this Distemper of the Mind always puts a Man in a vain Conceit of his own Worth and Excellency, which all his Pretences to Humility will never hide, as long as he evidently shews, that he would have the World think he hath a greater Familiarity with God than other Men. . . . Hence such a Man naturally assumes an Authority to dictate to others, and a Right to direct their Conduct and Opinions, and hence if any act not according to his Directions, and the Model of Things he had form'd in his own heated Brain, he is presently apt to run into slander, and stigmatize them as Men of no Religion, unconverted, and Opposers of the Spirit of God.[4]

The statement also faulted Whitefield for "extempore manner of preaching" and his "itinerant way of preaching," whereby he preaches anywhere, including places where he had not been invited by the ministers in charge of the area.

The effect of this sort of criticism was to protect the established religious culture from various forms of religious extremism. But in the West, at least in the opening decades of the nineteenth century, there was no established religious culture and, therefore, no established standards to determine what constituted religious extremism. Revivalism did not challenge the prevailing culture since there was nothing to challenge. Revivalism became part of and helped to create the religious culture on the frontier.

Thus, if revivalism stressed religious experience, religious experience became part of the religious culture. If distinctions based on class or wealth or gender or race were blurred in revivalism, so, too, were they blurred in the religious culture. If revivalism emphasized the importance of the individual as opposed to outside authorities and traditions, so developed a religious culture that lent itself to sectarianism, or the creation of numerous Christian denominations, each with specific doctrinal beliefs that separated them from other denominations or sects. If revivalism was scornful of formalism and ritual, so a religious culture developed that was scornful of formalism and ritual.

The most common word used against the Methodist revivalists in England and then in America was the word "enthusiasm" or "enthusiasts." Enthusiasm could be defined as the uninhibited expressions of religious ecstasy that seemed beyond the boundaries of polite behavior. The Harvard paper used the word in its critique of Whitefield. It was used by Eastern travelers who chanced into Methodist camp meetings. In the general society the word always was used pejoratively.

On the Western frontier, enthusiasm was taken to a whole new level of intensity. Farmer would speak of "getting happy" or "being happy." Getting happy might refer to shouting and dancing; it also included fainting ("being slain in the Spirit"), healings, barking, seizure-like jerking, uncontrolled laughter, miracles, visions, and what outsiders called barbarian and uncivilized behavior. This went so far as "snake handling." In his study *Frontier Mission*, Walter Posey sought to put "enthusiasm" into context:

> In truth, the camp meetings' appeal was not just to the spirit of man hungering after righteousness, but to his gregarious nature seeking surcease from the loneliness and hardship of the frontier. Homes were deserted, settlements temporarily abandoned, and fields left unworked, for the whole countryside turned out to the "holy fair." The discomfort of a wagon trip of thirty miles was a small price to pay for the social and spiritual tonic of a "religious holiday."
>
> At first sight these meetings presented a scene of confusion. The crowd talked freely and walked from place to place during the services, and several preachers and recruits from the laity performed simultaneously. Trees, stumps and wagon beds served as pulpits or as rostrums for the song leaders. Each new preacher had a gathering around him, and for his hearers he depicted horrible prospects unless one "got right" with God. At times as many as six hymns were sung at once, with discords punctuated by hysterical shouts so that the melodies were hardly recognizable. With conversion sinners took the stand or were hoisted to the shoulders of comrades, from which vantage point they added their exhorting to the confusion of tongues. Both laity and clergy abandoned themselves completely to excesses of emotion.[5]

Farmer not only is not bothered by this, but he encourages it and is a participant. In the meeting "above Spencer," at a time when Farmer was ill, he received such a "shock of divine power" that he was "made sound in soul and body." He also reported seeing a vision of heaven opening and rapturous visions of lights; it was as if he could see the celestial city, including partly lifted gates of precious stones, streets of gold, angelic choirs, stately trees, and flowers of perennial fragrance.

In his next passage, Farmer describes another delightful experience he had—this one while traveling to a camp meeting:

My labors during this year were crowned with good success. During this year, another camp meeting was held near Bedford, at Michael Farmer's campground. I made arrangements to attend it. I was then some thirty miles distant about the time the meeting began, with a dense and howling wilderness intervening. After eating my supper one afternoon, I started across the country through this wilderness, to attend the meeting; with the view of traveling through during the night. The moon shown out beautifully, when I struck the trail made by hunters, and which ran through what was widely known as "Paddies Garden;" and which also led to the sulphur springs. We then called those springs—"Sulphur's Creek." I never enjoyed such a happy night in my life. Riding along I preached several sermons to the forest trees, as I passed through the wilderness, encompassed around about by innumerable wild beasts, and which was considered a dangerous country. I reached the campground about day light, and found the camp yet quietly sleeping. I remained at the meeting until it was over, and felt greatly benefited by it. Indeed that was a happy year to me.

7

Good in Prayer and Singing, 1826 to 1827

In the next section of Eli Farmer's autobiography, he addresses the second year of his official career as a Methodist itinerant preacher:

Conference came on in the early fall of 1826, and I was appointed to Vermillion Circuit in Illinois.¹ When I reached my appointment, I found my work was widely scattered, and the people had not yet been advised of my coming.² On my journey around my circuit, and while fixing my appointments, I met a young man about seventeen years of age who was of Quaker antecedents, and who had professed religion among us. He was very anxious to preach, so much so, that he seemed almost wild with excitement which such thoughts had suggested, and wanted me to aid him in opening up the way before him, by securing a license for him. I told him that he would have to adopt the course provided in our Discipline. But he said the Discipline was too slow for him, and that he would be damned in case he put the matter off, and he must go to preaching at once. His father had already disinherited him, and refused to assist him.

The young man could not rest day nor night, but went about the neighborhood praying and crying, and I regarded him as a very holy boy. He elicited my liveliest sympathies, and I too was greatly troubled on account of his case, and I gave him a field in which to labor, putting him within a convenient distance of me, for my watch care.³ He returned to his home, and his father gave him an old broken legged horse to use in the prosecution of his work. As soon as he secured the horse, he started up the Wabash Valley, and I soon heard from him. He was actively engaged in preaching some where about Attica [Indiana], and near the mouth of Pine creek.⁴ He had found a few families there and began preach to them.

On one occasion, probably on one of the first sermons preached by him, he began preaching about the power possessed by the apostles, whereby they were enabled to lay hold of serpents and drink the most deadly poisons without receiving any injuries. He came out pretty strong upon the doctrines connected with his subject. Returning to his boarding house, upon the conclusion of his sermon, he went out to the stable, to look after his horse, and after a time came back to the house, and proposed to refute the arguments of those who had derided him in a novel manner, for He had a rattle snake on his person, which he had captured at the stable, and he produced the reptile and handled it fearlessly, as proof of his marvelous power over it. This was indeed very forcable, as well as a dangerous illustration of his views. I have been told by reputable citizens who witnessed the wonderful spectacle, that he threw the reptile down in the yard, and it was one of the most vicious and deadly of snakes, and of a very large description. After throwing it down, he went up to it, and inserted a portion of his foot into its mouth, and annoyed it in various other ways. The spectators were afraid to go near it.

Snake, or Serpent Handling

The idea of snake handling is based on several verses in the Bible, such as Luke 10:19: "Behold, I have given you the authority to trample on serpents." Methodists were already known for bizarre and what were deemed irrational practices. Stories such as the one reported by Farmer added to the reputation that Methodists brought not a religion of stability but of religious extremism. Snake handling as a regular religious practice was not known in American Christianity until 1910, when it became part of the Holiness–Pentecostal movement and was practiced primarily in Appalachia.[5] It should be noted that southern Indiana, Ohio, and Illinois, as well as Cane Ridge, northeast of Lexington, Kentucky, are sometimes seen as part of the larger Appalachian area and in many ways share a similar religious culture.[6]

Farmer continues the story of the snake-handling young man:

It was a custom of this boy, to fast and pray often, one night of every week being spent in prayer by him. He never slept a moment during such nights. He was so good and holy a boy I could not find it in my heart to check or restrain him, in fact, I confess I was afraid to do so. I could not decide what I ought to do with him. I so managed him however, that I could generally control him. I finally succeeded in getting a license for him, and he became a good preacher.

Prosecuting my journey still further for the purpose of arranging my appointments, I arrived at another regular stand. At this place I incidentally heard the brother with whom I was stopping, mention the name of Nelson Moore, a neighbor, when I inquired as to what kind of a man this Mr. Moore was, and was informed that he was a large fleshy man. "Where is he from?" I asked. "From Indianapolis," said he. "That gentleman is my brother-in-law," I observed, "and I must get my horse and go to his house tonight." I ascertained that he lived about a mile distant, and saddling my horse I rode over to Mr. Moore's house. As I drew near his residence I heard him chopping wood near his house and I turned off in his direction, and when I got within easy range of his hearing, I addressed him in this manner: "Sir, have you seen any sheep around here today?" I was then in a position where he could not see who I was. He answered that he had seen none. I rode up to him and put my hand on him and said —"I will take you for a sheep, if you have not turned to be a goat!"

I made this remark because I was aware he had once been a good methodist but was now in a backslidden condition. He inspected me very closely and succeeded in recognizing me. I staid all night with him and he urged me to make his house one of my regular preaching places, and I did so, stopping there every round, and preaching to the people. We had many pleasant and profitable meetings at this point.

Going still further on in my journey around my field of labor, I was informed that at a certain grove, there resided a noted universalist, who attacked every preacher that ventured near him, and like the demons of Gennesaret, he was so troublesome that it was "dangerous for a man to go that way."[7] I at once began to prepare for him, for from the intimations I had concerning him, I greatly feared his power for evil. When I arrived in this neighborhood, I found that he and a number of his friends were at a house-raising, near to the place where I had concluded to tarry all night. I went to the house-raising and announced that at a certain time, specifying the hour, I would preach at a certain place in the neighborhood, also specifying the location, and gave all a hearty invitation to attend the meeting. One of the gentlemen present, stepped out towards me and said, "Sir, I want you to preach before you leave this time." I looked around, to see whether I could recognize any one who would meet my surmises as to [how] my adversary ought to look. I was now assured that if I would consent to preach, they would all go home for their families, and all come back again to the meeting, at the usual place for preaching.

I consented, and in about one hours time, we had gathered in a good congregation. Being fully prepared in every way, I had great liberty in preaching. At one place in my discourse, I attempted to strike universalism [the idea that all humans will be saved] a severe blow, and I saw the congregation all look at a certain man in a questioning manner, and I soon came to know who he was. He was powerfully affected, and when near the close of the services, I opened the doors of the church, for persons who might wish to join us; both he and his wife, gave me their hand.[8] As he did so, he said to me, "Sir, I believe the Lord has sent you here, especially for my case, and I am determined to quit my universalistic opinions." Said he, "I have been a universalist for fifteen years, and I shall now abandon such doctrines right off." He was a very intelligent man and said further: "Well, sir, I shall have a great deal of labor to do now, for I must undo what I have been doing for years." I left him and his family firmly planted in the church, and journeyed on.

The territory over which I had supervision was About a hundred miles up the Wabash, and a hundred and fifty miles along the outer edge of a certain prairie, being a district of nearly three hundred miles square. I kept an accurate account of the number of miles traveled by me during this year, according to my account I traveled that year over four thousand miles. This does not include my little rides through the various settlements. I very frequently preached twice a day, and met with great success at every point.

In a certain neighborhood some fifteen miles below Terre Haute [Indiana], on the Illinois side of the river, there was a large body of outlaws, who had been driven from the "Sandy Salt works" in Kentucky on account of their depredations, and had settled here. Some of them were partly of negro blood, and like the others, were large, stout, and desperate men and women. Soon after establishing themselves here, they began to make themselves a terror to all the country round about, by killing indians, robbing, and the like, as well as now and then setting fire to houses. In addition to these crimes against the persons and property of their neighbors, they were guilty of all sorts of petty misdemeanors, such as robbing the bee queens, cutting off the manes and tails of horses and the like. Should any of their number be indicted, and brought to trial for their offences their comrades in crime would swear them out of it, and the unconscionable scoundrels, would escape punishment from justice.

They were called by the name of the "Creek nation." I said to my friends I would go into that region with the gospel. My friends were afraid for me to do so, fearing I should loose my horse if I escaped with my life: but I made up my mind to test them at all personal hazards. I went down to see them, and found an old gentleman among them, who was the owner of a mill on "Big Creek," whome I asked to help me by giving me leave to preach in his house, and he consented. He seemed to be a civil sort of a man, and I was very favorably impressed with him. I made an appointment, and at the proper time went back to fill it, but found a small congregation assembled. They all seemed afraid of preaching, and some of them would come up to the outside of the door and windows and look in upon us. I preached to them as best I could and many of my audience seemed affected by my discourse. After this I had no trouble getting an audience, and they were not near as obdurate and impervious as I had formerly supposed. When the work began among them it seemed like they had little trouble to find the way, and were soon in the enjoyment of the christian faith and happiness. All bore their crosses cheerfully, and the meetings went on in a powerful manner. Some times while I would be preaching several of them would fall down as though they had been shot.

On one occasion a very large young lady fell down while I was preaching, falling heavily and for a while, was apparently dead. Her fall was observed by a big rough-looking young man who was peeping in at the door, and he rushed into the room, and seizing her undertook to carry her away. I in turn seized hold of her also, and told him in an authoritative manner, he must not take her away.

He told me he thought she was dead, but I said "She is not dead; she will get up again in a little while."

He persisted in his attempt to get her out and begone, pulling at her, and I pulled too, so that we straightened her out as though she was being stretched to a considerable extent. Her brother who had already made a profession of religion came to me and helped me, and peremptorily ordered him to desist, declaring that she must not be taken away. Pretty soon the girl arose shouting, and made everything move before her. Being a woman of good sense and talking ability, she began exhorting and succeeded in a remarkable manner in stirring up considerable excitement.

The fellow who had sought to interfere with us now came up and begged to be pardoned, declaring that he had supposed a neighbor's daughter was dead, and of course he was of the opinion she ought to be taken out. We assured him he was freely forgiven by us and he appeared to be ready to do all he could for us.

The people of that community afterward manifested the utmost respect for me. I decided, now that these meetings were closed, to attack an adjoining settlement, and as this point was the strong hold of the bad fellows, I thought then I needed something in the way of a working auxiliary. I sent out for six young ladies whom I had gathered into the church at different points on my circuit. They were all powerful in prayer and all of them were good singers. We all met, in pursuance of my appointment, and went to work. I preached with great acceptance and power, and was very successful. Upon the conclusion of my sermons, I would call for mourners, and then these girls would sing and pray, after which, when the altar would be visited by seekers of mercy, they would labor at the altar with the sinners surrounding it.

Development of Evangelical Culture: The Gospel Spiritual

This remarkable paragraph in Farmer's autobiography needs comment and interpretation. Farmer is entering a spiritual lion's den. He was advised by his friends not to go to the "Creek Nation" because it was unsafe. He goes anyway to one settlement and has such success that he then proposes to go to the adjoining settlement, which is the stronghold of the "bad fellows." He evidently is not going just to establish preaching points, which is the usual custom of circuit riders, but to hold revivals and win converts. He chooses to go unaccompanied by other preachers or by bodyguards but instead takes six young ladies "powerful in prayer and good singers." He lays out an altar area and the "girls" sing and pray after which seekers visit the altar and are ministered to by the young ladies.

An especially noteworthy part of this story is the reference to singing. The place of music in camp meetings and revivals has been largely under-reported and under-appreciated in the accounts of camp meetings and frontier religion.[9] Worship—if that is what it might be called—in frontier camp meetings and revival services consisted mainly of singing, praying, testifying, preaching, and activity at the altar. The Methodists took a page from John Wesley's outdoor services in England and improvised to adapt to the American frontier. The important part of every service, next to the preaching itself, was the singing. But what to sing? Those attending the earliest Methodist services were content to sing the highly poetical hymns of Isaac Watts and Charles Wesley. But there were problems. Persons with no religious background were unacquainted with this music. At camp meetings and often in places where preachers met their congregations, there were no hymn books. How these challenges were met is described by an early Methodist preacher, B. St. James Fry:

> At the commencement of the revival those familiar hymns [Wesley's], known in all our orthodox congregations, were used, but it was soon felt that they gave but imperfect expression to the ardent feelings of the worshipers. The deficiency was principally supplied by the preachers. Hymns, or, "spiritual song," as they were more frequently called, to the cultured ear rude and bold in expression, rugged in meter, and imperfect in rhyme, often improvised in the preaching stand, were at once accepted as more suited to their wants. These were quickly committed to memory, and to a considerable extent usurped the place of the old and more worthy hymns.[10]

Another early Methodist explains what happened after revival songs started to flourish:

> It was not only at the meetings they (the spiritual songs) were sung, but making so deep an impression upon the minds of the people of the period, they were soon learned by the thousands; who made the shops, the fields, the woods, the hills and the vales echo with the melody of their voices. . . . When one was started at their meetings, hundreds would unite, and being divided into many companies when singing would be going on, the sound of their voices "was heard afar off." It was truly solemn and awful, yet melodious! Under the singing the greatest power appeared generally to be displayed. Its charms disarmed and then melted into tenderness the hard hearts of sinners. Even the persecuting and heaven-daring

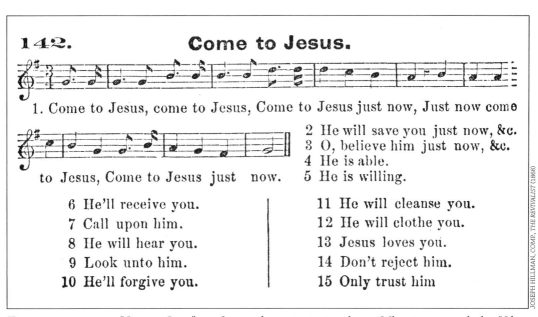

The camp meeting song "Come to Jesus" was first used as an invitation chorus. When it was parodied as "Oh My Darling Clementine," it could no longer be used in camp meetings.

sinner, would sometimes have his attention caught by it, and be suddenly melted into tears; and at other times, seized with a sudden trembling, they would fall to the ground.[11]

More traditional Methodists, especially the Methodists from the East, were appalled when faced with the popularity of the new music. Even Bishop Francis Asbury, though he encouraged camp meetings and was himself a camp meeting preacher, wrote the following warning: "We must therefore earnestly entreat you, if you have any respect for the authority of the Conference, or of us, or any regard for the propriety of the Connection, to purchase no Hymn-books, but what are signed with the names of your Bishops."[12]

In 1848 the Methodist Episcopal Church published its first official hymnal. There were hymnals before, but this one was authorized by the general conference and signed, meaning approved, by the bishops. It was an excellent hymnal, orthodox in theology and consisting mainly of Charles Wesley's hymns. But it was not an American book. Of more than eleven hundred hymns, only two had American roots, with the others being of British or European origin. Meanwhile, the revivalists were publishing their own songbooks by the dozens. Ellen Jane Lorenz has identified at least forty-two of these, issued between 1811 and 1875.[13] One of the best known was *The Revivalist: A Collection of Choice Revival Hymns and Tunes* (1868). The compiler, Joseph Hillman, gathered old-time Methodist tunes and spiritual songs, many of which had never been written down. The list of credits is a "Who's Who" of Methodist evangelists, song leaders, and camp-meeting enthusiasts. It claimed to be not a substitute for the official hymnal, but a supplement. *The Revivalist* sold 150,000 copies during its first four years of publication and went through eleven editions.

Music in *The Revivalist* was exuberant, creative, crude, outlandish, and quite different from anything that had been previously associated with religious music. Much of it was folk music of unknown origin, passed on by word of mouth. Many of its hymns had no credits. Others were simply identified as "old tune" or "western melody." One example is "Come to Jesus," perhaps the most popular of the frontier invitation choruses. *The Revivalist* also contains several texts for "Say Brothers," the original tune now better known as "The Battle Hymn of the Republic."

With the frontier revivals and camp meetings, singing took on a new role. It was not just an expression of praise to God but rather a new version of religious folk music designed to appeal to the emotions and often addressed to sinners or sometimes to "travelers," "wayfarers," or "pilgrims"—labels that reflected the frontier experience. The singing was often part of the gospel presentation, designed to bring sinners to repentance, and was almost always being used when mourners were seeking spiritual peace at the altar. The excesses of camp meeting enthusiasm would begin to moderate throughout the nineteenth century, but the camp meeting music would evolve and take new forms that led to African American spirituals, Sunday school songs, gospel music (whether black gospel or southern gospel), and worship choruses.[14]

The two weapons in Farmer's spiritual arsenal as he invaded the settlement of the Creek Nation's bad fellows were his preaching and the singing and praying of six young ladies. As he stated, Farmer preached, the ladies sang, and the altar was filled with mourners:

173. Say, Brothers.

Not too fast.

1. Say, brothers, will you meet us? Say, brothers, will you meet us?
   Say, sisters, will you meet us? Say, sis-ters, will you meet us?

Say, brothers, will you meet us On Canaan's hap-py shore?
Say, sis-ters, will you meet us On Canaan's hap-py shore?

2 By the grace of God we'll meet you,
  Where parting is no more;
That will be a happy meeting
  On Canaan's happy shore.

3 Jesus lives and reigns forever
  On Canaan's happy shore.
Glory! glory! hallelujah!
  Forever, evermore!

174. Ye Soldiers of the Cross, Arise!

1 Ye soldiers of the cross, arise,
  And put your armor on;
March to the city
  Of the New Jerusalem;
Jesus gives the order
  And leads his people on
Till victory is won.

CHORUS.

Glory, glory, hallelujah!
Glory, glory, hallelujah!
Glory, glory, hallelujah!
  We are marching on.

2 The watchmen they are crying:
  Attend the trumpet's sound;
Take the gospel banner,
  And the powers of hell surround;
Hearts and arms make ready,
  The battle is at hand;
Go forth at Christ's command.

3 Lay hold upon the Saviour
  By faith's victorious shield,
March on in order
  Till you win the glorious field;
Faint not by the way
  Till you've gain'd the peaceful shore
Where war shall be no more.

4 Ne'er think the victory won,
  Nor lay your armor down;
March on in duty
  Till you gain the starry crown.
When the war is o'er
  And the battle you have won,
Jesus will say "well done."

175. *Tune:* SAY, BROTHERS.

1 Now I know what makes me happy,
Now I know what makes me happy,
Now I know what makes me happy,
  'Tis glory in my soul.

2 Lord, give us gospel measure,
  Pressed down and running o'er.

3 Lord, keep the fire burning
  With glory in my soul.

176. Sunday School Song. *Tune:* A Home Up Yonder, No. 20.

1 There is a place I love to go,
  Sunday—Sunday,
In storm or sunshine, rain or snow,
  That's the Sunday School.

Chorus.—For I love the bells ringing,
  Sunday—Sunday,
I love the cheerful singing
  At the Sunday School.

2 I would not stay at home to play,
I'd rather come and hear them pray.

3 We read that Jesus died and rose
That we might flee from sin's dark woes.

JOSEPH HILLMAN, COMP., *THE REVIVALIST* (1868)

Camp meeting spirituals were often composed and verses added on the spot. Many were never written down and most were not harmonized. The music for "Say, Brothers" was later used for the chorus of "The Battle Hymn of the Republic."

One night while I was watching the work then being conducted by my assistants, for I was resting at the time, I observed a short, stout, stubby fellow, apparently about fifteen years of age, who seemed to be greatly affected. Soon he arose from the altar and commenced shouting in a loud voice. Looking about he saw his uncle standing near him. This uncle was a large, rough, burley fellow. The boy turned to him and addressed him in this way. "I reckon you think a boy cannot have religion;" then throwing his arms around his uncle's neck, he began to exhort him to turn from his sinful position and seek the Lord. The uncle braced himself up stoutly, but at last his knees weakened and both fell to the floor, the boy meanwhile praying for his relative with great fervency. This scene created considerable excitement.

In the midst of this excitement his wife came up to the door, and observing her husband thus engaged with the boy, rushed to his rescue, bearing in her arms a young child about a year old. She caught her husband by his coat collar and commenced pulling him away. The boy was still praying in a loud and vehement manner, which [while] the uncle was screaming wildly, and frantically striving to release himself.

The woman dragged him along, running over a bench, which made a great clatter. I jumped toward them, in an effort to prevent his being taken away, but was too late, and the woman succeeded in getting her husband out of doors. Quickly following them, I succeeded in overtaking them, and urged them to return, but she replied that her father had never taught any such religion as she had just witnessed, she hurriedly conveyed her husband home.

Winter came on, and I found our little cabins generally cold, but I was prompt to fill all of my appointments.

My friends of the "Creek Nation" were fond of attending church. I could frequently tell when I had entered their territory, by the foot-prints leading off in the direction of the place of worship, the prints being made with moccasins. The weather never at any time, became too cold to furnish me such proofs. As soon as they would get to the meeting they would at once commence the work. If I ever loved a people in the world, I loved these good people, for the power of the Lord was with them continually.

Thus putting a general trust in human kind, and relying upon divine assistance, I found a good which blood shed could not have gained, and I boldly pressed onward, hoarding the lessons I had just learned in my heart.

I spent this year very happy traveling about from one appointment to another and laboring incessantly in all kinds of weather. In the fall of this year, at our third quarterly meeting, I told my friends that we must have a camp-meeting and they thought we could hold one provided we could find a suitable place for one. I suggested that it be held among the folks of the "Creek Nation," but they said, "No, that would destroy the whole work," for a great number of my friends, of that section did not yet know of the revivals which had been held down that way, and they thought the "nation" would break up the meeting. I replied by saying that I would go there securely, as I had been among them and knew them very well. They still desisted from my view, but I insisted strenuously upon holding it there, stating that I would hold it there whether the Presiding Elder attended the meeting or did not attend it.

At the proper time I sent out the proclamation to the people, and also a cordial invitation to a number of preachers, asking all to come out to the meeting and help us. At the campground, on the first day of the meeting, I selected men who had professed religion and some who had made no such profession, to act as guards outside of our encampment. These guards were selected from among the folks of the "Creek Nation." Before I stationed them at their posts, I told them to be vigilant and careful for people from other sections would be apt to try to do mischief and would seek to attribute their own evil deeds to the people of the "Creek Nation."

I never attended a meeting in my life where better order was observed. The good work went right on, and there were many conversions made at these meetings. About the time we were ready to close the meeting, I announced that we would engage in what we called a "holy march." My announcement embraced the following exercise: we would march around the encampment on its outer side, three times, singing as we marched along, and that all who desired to go to heaven, were urgently requested to join the procession of singers. Many of the brethren and sisters, became so happy during these closing services that they seemed to be kept upon the earth only by a miracle. I also announced that just before the last march around the camp, I would stop and shake hands with them as they made the last circuit. I did so, and as soon as many of them had taken m[e] by the hand, they would file round me and come up again, and thus hover about me, loath to leave me. Some would be crying while there would be shouting and praising God. It was indeed a difficult matter to get away from them. Finally several preachers were compelled to come to my rescue, by forcing their way through the dense crowd, and carrying me bodily away from the immense assembly. I myself was unwilling to separate from them, feeling that I would be quite ready and willing to die under such circumstances so auspicious and so glorious.

At our last quarterly meeting we had a campmeeting on the Wabash at the mouth of big Vermillion River. Previous to that we had made considerable preparation in order that the people who might attend it should be properly cared for. The Presiding Elder came on at the time appointed and we entered upon the work. Our Presiding Elder at the time was Charles Holiday, a very excellent preacher. We both entered our work with great zeal and hopefulness. I was fond of these out-of-doors meetings. They were very popular with all classes. Altho not so fashionable as churches now are, yet the churches in which we frequently worshiped in that day, were gotten up on the old style, very like the first one ever built, for:

> "The perfect world, by Adam trod
> Was the first temple-built by God-
> His fiat laid the corner stone,
> And heaved its pillars, one by one."

On the opposite side of the Wabash there lived some sixteen or eighteen large, rough, bold men, who were in the habit of breaking up meetings where-ever they could do so. They generally took along with them plenty of whiskey, and as much additional help, as their attractive liquid alley would tempt away into such unprofitable business. The captain of this company dubbed himself, "The Big Black Wolfe." Among their earliest mischief was the turning loose of the horse of the elder and myself. We soon ascertained that the object of their visit was to break up our meeting.

The Presiding Elder and other preachers said we ought to give up the conflict and break up the meeting. "Give me Abraham Smith," said I, "as an assistant, and we will take the whole party." This complimentary declaration stimulated my friend Smith, whom I knew to be an uncommonly powerful and courageous man. He expressed himself as being in readiness to help me. Our enemies were at the time consulting together in a thicket not very far off and I got brother Smith to go down to their immediate neighborhood and ascertain if possible what preparations were being made by which to attempt to break us down.

After a careful reconnaissance, he came back and made his report, and about this time these bad men raised a song, and began singing, "Old Father Grimes, that good old man. . . ." I believe there was also some mention of an old blue coat that this old gentleman Grimes was said to have owned at one period of his life, which coat seemed to have been buttoned in some unusual manner "down before." From the general tone and body of that ballad one was led to the opinion that the apparel of this Grimes was altogether strangely fashioned. Upon the conclusion of this song, some one of their band called out, "Brother Bennett, go to praying," referring to the Quaker by whom I mentioned in the last chapter as being so anxious to preach, and then one of their number prayed in the most irreverent manner. After the mock prayer, they most impiously performed the sacrilege of administering the holy "sacrament," using whiskey as a representative of the symbolical emblem of the blood of Christ.

Searching out a couple of magistrates whom I knew to be upon the campground, I placed them in a certain position, so they would be hidden from view, and yet conveniently near as when we should require their services. After our meeting was over, we permitted the lights to die out excepting those near the preachers' quarters. In a short time every thing in camp was still, and in a few minutes their leader "The Black Wolfe," stepped within our camp and came down toward the fire where several of us were sitting; he was at once recognized by us. Just before he got to the fire, however, I slipped around behind him, and coming up in his rear, suddenly caught hold of him and pushed him up so as the light from out [of the] fire, fell fully upon him, and told him to sit down, and he did so.

"Now behave yourself," said I, continuing my addresses to him, "and we will treat you well; and if you do not do so you will be handled pretty roughly."

"Sir," said he, "do you intend to insult me?"

"No," said I, "but you will now be compelled to behave yourself; of this fact you may be well assured."

He now became violent and swore several terrible oaths and we tried him before the court for profanity. He pled his own cause, and as he was a lawyer, he was mean enough to make a pretty good showing on his own behalf. The fine assessed him was two dollars and fifty cents. Upon refusing to pay it he was placed in custody of an officer. His plea was very ingenious, contending that he did not use the "by God" but the word "be God."

We placed him in a chair, and stationed a guard around him. Pretty soon he asked permission to withdraw a short distance, and for prudential reasons we suffered it, sending however, a guard with him, who soon returned with him. We still kept him in charge of the guard.

After a brief interval, two or three of his companions came up to see what had become of their captain. At the proper time I got behind these men and pushed them up so my brethren could identify them; and so soon as they saw that their captain was captured they started to run away. I followed one of them while my friend Smith closely pursued another one, and we gave them an exciting chase. The fellow pursued by me ran along a devious route among a number of wagons that were arranged in a row to the rear of our camp. Dodging about in a skillful manner he finally succeeded in getting out into the darkness where he could not be seen, and thus escaped me, but I had pressed him so closely that he lost his hat, which I brought into camp as a trophy. My friend Smith was quite as fortunate in affrightening his game as I was, for he succeeded in grabbing hold of the coat of his retreating foe, the tail of which he tore off, and which he brought in as souvenir of his exciting and memorable march after a manner of the army of "Flanders."

Smith did not rest upon the laurels already won, nor seek a surcease of victory by the thought that "to the victor doth the spoils belong." On the contrary, determined to make his pursuit as significant a triumph, he bethought himself of a number nine boot in which his right foot was incased, and he brought that number of his personal property in close and sudden proximity, to the rear of the fleeing fugitive. Brother Smith, who is at this time a practicing physician at Bloomington, to this day declares, that he cannot be mistaken in his assertion, that he kicked the fellow over a large brush pile. He stoutly asserts also that this was about as good a job of that kind as he ever undertook to perform. Even had I any such desire it is no part of my duty, as a faithful historian, to modify his statement. So I leave a generous public to decide for themselves, whether this statement of the Doctor shall be shorn of its distinctive features or whether it shall be counted worthy of a reception in spirit in which it has been i[n]varibly made, of truthful candor.

We succeeded in capturing others of the band, however, whom we also placed under guard. Next morning we made preparations as though we intended to try them, but we were very anxious that they might escape, especially their captain, of whom we were heartily tired, and we managed the affair so as to give him an opportunity to get away. To do this we decided to hold their trials near a certain large sugar tree on the farther side of a field of corn close to our camp. The corn had been planted in a rich black soil, in the river bottom and was very stout and high at this time. While we went through this field we gave the opportunity to escape. I gave Smith a certain sign previously agreed upon between us, and he loitered behind somewhat, and taking advantage of this seeming negligence on the part of Smith, "The Big Black Wolfe," sprang out to one side and ran off as rapidly as he could run. I called out with manifest eagerness to Smith—"Catch him, catch him," and "The Big Black Wolfe" made the corn rattle. All of them, fortunately for all parties concerned, made their escape, and we afterward learned, that they swam the Wabash and the Vermillian Rivers in their frantic endeavor to gain a place of safety. It is perhaps unnecessary to state that we were never Subsequently troubled in any manner by this party.

Some seven miles above the place where this campmeeting was held, there were a number of men living near the town of Perryville who had threatened me with violence. Their threatenings were so direfull, that my friends were seriously alarmed, fearing they would kille me, and insisted upon guarding me from one appointment to another.

At one of my appointments, between the site of the campmeeting grounds and Perryville, I preached a pretty elaborate discourse, and at its close I opened the doors of the church. An exceeding pretty young lady, a healthy, stout-looking woman, came forward and gave me her hand to join the church. Her husband came up and said she should not join, saying, "She is my wife, sir." I urged her to be devoted to God. "She inquired whether she might have the privilege of the church." The man now supposed I had taken her name, and went off and told a brother-in-law about it, and he thereupon threatened me with a whipping. I told the husband I feared no man, and he under the pretense that he was reporting me to his brother-in-law, told that gentleman I had threatened to whip him, and he (the brother-in-law) came in search of me. He was a very stout looking man. He came up to me and said, "Sir, I understand you intend to whip me, or have threatened to whip me." I referred him to the brethren who were witnesses of all that occurred. I told him I feared no man, but I did fear God.

"That is right," said he, and he turned away and left me.

I went to Perryville, where I had been told preparations had been made to whip me but I saw no certain indications that such a fate was in store for me. I preached at this place, and as soon as I got my dinner, I went out into the street where I found a number of men engaged in raising a framed building. Stepping up on top of some timbers on the grounds I thus addressed them, "I understand, gentlemen, that I am to be whipped before I leave this place, now I have this to say, that if you are going to do it, you must do it soon, for I am going away soon."

A great burley, powerful-looking fellow said, "I would whip you if it was not for the law."

My reply was this, "The law was made to straighten crooked men, and if I should become crooked I ought to be straightened, and if you, sir, get crooked, it ought to straighten you. I wish to say further that I have never been whipped yet since my mother whipped me. Now I wish to inquire just here—how do you whip when you go to whip a fellow? Do you pray before doing so?

A large powerful man, standing by and listening to us turning to him, said, "Now, damn you, shut your mouth or I will whip you myself," and in this way he silenced him.

This was about the winding up of that year's labor.

8

Taking on Lafayette, 1827 to 1828

After working in the wilderness settlements near the Wabash River in Indiana and Illinois, Eli Farmer was given a new circuit at the annual conference of 1827. His autobiography tells of this new appointment:

Conference that year was held far down the Wabash, below Vincennes [Indiana], at a town by the name of Mt. Carmel [Illinois], I believe, and I was now sent to Crawfordsville [Indiana] circuit.[1] I went to my appointment and began a work at once. Isaac Elston of that town was at that time making arrangements to lay off lots at the site on where Michigan City now stands [south shore of Lake Michigan in Indiana]. He and his family insisted on my boarding with them while I might be in that neighborhood.

I went around to my appointments and organized my forces. A minister of our conference by the name of Henry Buel had been stationed that year at LaFayette [Indiana], and he soon became involved in trouble with the enemies of the Methodist Church. He had been preaching in the courthouse, a temporary structure in that place, and a number of bad men would hover about his meetings to disturb the exercises. They would fire off guns and yell furiously, just outside, and in various other ways annoy the congregation and the minister, and he finally abandoned the field.

Previous to this time I had married my second wife [Elizabeth McClung], and she was with me on this occasion.[2] I began preaching on the Saturday morning following my arrival at the conclusion of which I announced services for the night of that day. Along side of the little courthouse was a grog shop, the windows of which were open. In fact there was no glass in the windows of either building. The patrons of the doggery [cheap saloon] that night were drinking hard and very soon became boisterous. Some of their number would frequently quit the scene of revelry, and come to the courthouse, and put their heads in at the windows, then they would go back to the saloon, after a time of drinking whiskey, they would come back to the windows. I made up my mind after they had gone back to the doggery after one of their visits, that in case they returned to the windows, I would invite them in.

Pretty soon a fellow inserted his head into the room again, and I stopped preaching and addressed him thus, "Sir, if you please, come inside and take a seat with us."

"Why, damn you," said he, "I have not been in the groggery."

"I have not so accused you," I answered.

"Damn you," continued he, "I will cow-hide you."

I tried to apologize to him, and to convince him he was in error in his view of what I had said, and that I did not wish to insult him.

He grew more and more furious, in my efforts to pacify him. I went on with my sermon, while he surrounded himself by his cowardly comrades, to whom he avowed his intention to cowhide me as he did not propose to be insulted by me. I was fully determined that in case he touched me, to defend myself and whip him.

Before the conclusion of the meetings I told my wife to go back to the house where we were expected to stop over night, as I wished to get her away before any difficulty could come up. She was young and had never seen a fight and I was afraid she might be badly frightened in case we had any trouble. But he did not wait for the people to leave the room. He came up to me and pretended to be very anxious to fight with me, making a terrible fuss as though he were going to tear all my limbs off of me. Calmly addressing him, I said, "Stranger, it was not the design to insult you." I was compelled to repeat this declaration several times before I could make him hear me, and then he came close to me. When he came about as near me as I care to have him come, I clapped my hands together, and they popped like pistol shots. I did this to give him timely warning of what I should do in case he touched me. Believing he was getting into trouble, he wheeled around and walked off, and thus left the room.

On the next day I organized the first church ever formed in LaFayette.

That village has grown to be a great city, and her streets and avenues are thronged with busy men and woman. She has marts of trade, and her schools, her colleges, and churches are almost metropolitan. I believe there are now there more than half a hundred places of worship in that teeming city.

Stations and Circuits

In the Methodist connectional system, a circuit appointment was an appointment to an area or to a group of churches. When a single church was strong enough to support a pastor it was called a "station" appointment. The development of station churches changed the dynamics of Methodism. For one, it marked the beginning of the transition of Methodism as religion of the poor to Methodism as a religion of the middle class. Station appointments were highly sought appointments, as they provided a stable means of support, since on circuits there was no guarantee that proposed salaries would be paid. Initially in Indiana, Presbyterians were more successful in towns, and Methodists more successful in rural areas. Methodists, however, soon became more successful in the larger towns, and when established their churches became associated with prestige. Often the title "First Church" implied that prestige.

The development of station churches also affected camp meetings, which were more successful in circuits when all of the smaller churches and classes and preaching points gathered together for the quarterly conferences. Since the circuits often covered wide areas, people came from great distances and, with or without camp meetings, often planned to stay overnight. When a camp meeting was planned with a quarterly meeting, the presiding elder would be present, the crowd was guaranteed, and neighboring preachers were often invited to help with the preaching. Given this setting it is understandable why camp meetings served to address social as well as religious needs. Station churches could be involved in camp meetings but the incentive was not the same. Station churches might still be "revival" churches but they would tend to schedule "protracted meetings," often simply called revival meetings, which were held indoors.

The development of stations did not come quickly to Indiana. By 1827, when Farmer went to Lafayette, there were only two stations in Indiana: at Madison and Salem. By then Lafayette was growing fast. Yet, there was no Methodist presence there since the work had been abandoned because of opposition. Farmer was the right man at the right time at the right place.

Farmer made no mention of a great revival. It is quite possible that there was a core of people just waiting to be organized. By 1827 the Methodist religion was no longer a novelty. The Lafayette church grew so rapidly that in 1830 it became a "station" church. Farmer, writing from memory, is technically incorrect when he said that Henry Buell (Farmer also misspelled the name) was "stationed" at Lafayette. Buell's 1826 appointment was to Crawfordsville; Lafayette was a preaching point on the Crawfordsville circuit. This was the same appointment Farmer had in 1827. The Lafayette church is today Trinity United Methodist Church. A history of the church confirms Farmer's account of what happened.[3]

In his autobiography Farmer speaks of a trip made to the Chicago area as well as a camp meeting in which he shared the pulpit with the famous Lorenzo Dow:

I traveled successfully through my field of labor during this year also. Toward the close of the conference year, I accompanied my friend Elston to Michigan City. This gentleman was very anxious that I should settle in the vicinity of that city, as he had made arrangements to do so himself, and he offered me the choice of all the lots there in case I should remain one year.

While in that region I visited the site of the city of Chicago also and all the country adjacent thereto while yet the red man roamed over these wild lands. Chicago had not then been born, and the cries of her infancy were not heard for years afterward. It would be difficult, no doubt, for me to realize the changes "time's" busy fingers have wrought since then; were I ever to return now the great city sits there enthroned in regal splendor upon the margins of the beautiful lake, notwithstanding the awful calamities that have recently befallen her.

About the close of this year we held a big campmeeting at Crawfordsville, which was made a memorable one, by the fact that I succeeded in getting the noted Lorenzo Dow to attend the meeting to help me. I had gotten acquainted with him at Louisville a short time previously, and was with him for several days, and heard him preach several times on these occasions.

Having collected a sufficient amount to pay for my land, I went down to Vincennes for the purpose of paying for it. There I met this eccentric though very able evangelist again and we went to Vincennes together. While at Vincennes, I made arrangements with him to help me at our campmeeting at Crawfordsville, and Lorenzo and I came on to that place, and at the appointed time we opened the meeting.

We had a powerful campmeeting. Mr. Dow labored with us with all of his marvelous power and energy. He preached several wonderful sermons for us, and was supported in an able manner by brother Aaron Wood and our Presiding Elder Armstrong, and aided also by my feeble assistance.

Lorenzo Dow

Farmer was entering a period of personal effectiveness. Somehow or other he was able to schedule Lorenzo Dow for a camp meeting. Farmer used the word "eccentric" to describe Dow—a word, it seems, that almost everyone used to refer to Dow. He was also known as "Mad Dow" and "Crazy Dow." Twice refused acceptance as a Methodist preacher because of his unusual ways, he was finally given an opportunity to start a work in Canada. In one year he had recruited a Methodist membership numbering 245. From there Dow went to Ireland, then returned to America. When camp meetings were introduced to the East Coast, Dow was in the middle of them. He published a tract "In Defense of Camp Meetings" in which, among other arguments, he listed times and places and numbers of converts for twenty consecutive camp meetings in which he participated or knew about, starting with Rehobath Chapel, Warren County, Georgia, on October 8, 1802, with 100 converts. In those twenty meetings 1,370 persons were converted.[4]

In 1804 Dow spoke at more than five hundred meetings.[5] Three times in his life he went to England, introducing the American camp meeting there in 1807. Camp meetings became so divisive in England that three English Methodist preachers were expelled and a new denomination, the Primitive Methodist Church, was started.

Dow never accepted Methodist-type discipline and basically traveled as an independent Methodist evangelist. He seldom shaved or bathed or wore new clothes and it was said his hair never saw a comb. He preached wherever he was, with invitation or without. While Methodist histories seldom mention Dow, Nathan Hatch used him as the prime example of the place of populist religion in the development of what Hatch called the *Democratization of American Christianity*. Dow probably preached to more Americans than any other preacher in his time. In addition, between 1800 and 1835 more than seventy different editions of his various writings were published, making him for a time America's best-selling author.[6]

Farmer picks up his dialogue just after the camp meeting in Crawfordsville:

I had helped Edmond Day to hold a campmeeting at this town [Crawfordsville], at the time the first church was organized there. At the meeting attended by Dow, just mentioned, our church was greatly strengthened by a rapid and healthy grace among the membership, and also by many accessions to the church. Soon after this I went up the Wabash to preach a few sermons for the brethren at a point where Delphi [Indiana] now stands, at the mouth of Deer Creek.

Returning therefrom, I overtook a couple of young men who were coming down the river to LaFayette, and who had been up the country among the Indians. They had attended my meeting the night before, and they began to deride me, running on for some time with their trifling and insulting remarks, to all of which I paid no attention. Forbearance at length became exhausted on my part, and I retaliated to some stinging remark pretty sharply, which caused them to resort to even rougher and more indecorous language. This aroused me somewhat and I observed, "Gentlemen, you are mean men, and all mean men are cowards, and I want you to understand that I am fully able to attend to you both, and I am not afraid of you. For no gentleman would in this manner help to attack a lone man in a wilderness!"

We traveled on in comparative silence, till we came to the house of a trader by the name of Longlay who was a Frenchman and who was living with an Indian wife. He had been twice married the first wife being also an Indian woman. He had abandoned the first one and was now living with a younger woman.

After stopping at this place awhile, we journeyed on till we came to LaFayette where my companions disappeared. Four years subsequently, I again visited Kentucky, and about fifteen miles above Louisville, on the Bardstown Pike, on my way to see my brother, I met one of these

The original title of this engraving of Lorenzo Dow by Lossing–Barrett was Lorenzo Dow and the Jerking Exercise. *"Jerking" was another of the unusual physical manifestations associated with early camp meetings.*

young men whom I at once recognized. "You are one of the men I fell in with on a little voyage a few years ago, upon the Wabash," I said mentioning the time with greater particularity. He tried to make me think I was mistaken by saying it was his brother whom I had met, but I insisted that he was the man. He made it convenient to leave immediately, and my brother told me after his departure, that the fellow had told him theretofore of the circumstance.

From LaFayette I returned to my circuit and finished my year's labor. About the close of the conference year, I started out on a visit to the Tippecanoe battle ground, or near there, going by way of the French traders, and through a place commonly called the "Weeaw Prairie." I struck an Indian trail pretty soon after starting out on my journey, which led to the trader's place of business. As soon as I reached the edge of the prairie, I observed a number of wigwams and Indian women and children. Riding up to them I saw a couple of Indian men reclining on some robes.

One of Longlay's sons was in the camp, and as I knew he could converse in my tongue, I inquired of him what so many women and children were doing there. He informed me that the Indian men were over at his father's drinking "whiskey," and we have brought these women," he said, "out here for safety." The young man was an educated half-breed. He then informed me that every year after his crop was laid by, they generally took a hunt with the Indians. He himself had a half-bred wife.

I went on until I reached his father's house some fifteen miles from the camp. I dismounted, and gave myself and horse a rest. Entering the house and getting a drink of water, I saw several Indians in the room, drinking pretty freely. One old fellow ran up to me and seized hold of me. He seemed to be in a friendly mood, and I received his rude greeting good humoredly. He was clad in a check shirt which extended down to his knees almost, and he began scuffling with me. We tramped around considerably, but I didn't enjoy his vulgar familiarity, especially so since he smelled badly, and as soon as I could get rid of him without insulting him I did so and resumed my journey.

Riding along at a pretty rapid rate my ears were soon saluted with loud yelling, and I knew that a lot of Indians were somewhere ahead. They seemed to be down in the bottom of Wild Cat Creek. I soon found the main body of Indians where I had supposed them to be, and I concluded I would ride right in among them and buy a bearskin of someone of their number, as I greatly needed a covering for my saddle and saddle-bags.

I rode up pretty close, and found them in a circular row, facing each other. There were about two hundred men in their body. I was riding a very spirited animal at this time, and I rode up pretty close to them before they observed me. Their attention was directed to me by the snorting of my horse who was somewhat loath to venture close to them. When they saw me so close to them they opened up a way for me so [I] could look into their ring they had formed, and I then saw a couple of big Indians in the center of the circle, one of whom was sitting flat on the ground, with nothing on his person but a britch cloth: while the other one was in a kneeling position, and was seemingly engaged in doctoring his comrades eyes. I supposed the two had been fighting, and having become friends again, the victor was trying to repair the damages he had inflicted on his adversary. Some one in the encircling line now jabbered out something I was unable to understand, when the fellow who was performing the part of the "Good Samaritan," quickly turned his eyes to me, and springing to his feet, he yelled out something which was all wild jargon to me, and ran toward me. His actions frightened my horse, and the horse ran off violently, and if I had not managed her carefully she might have broken her neck and mine too.

I then pursued my journey up the Wabash, and on my return I found the Indians had left. I could hear the reports from their guns away off in various directions. As they would eat anything almost, they would kill almost anything, and the consequence was, they did a great deal of shooting.

During this season I broke down under a severe and protracted attack of dyspepsia, super induced by exposures to which I had subjected myself. My wife traveled with me a great deal and rendered great assistance. She not infrequently exposed herself to many and great dangers. Very often we were compelled to swim our horses across dangerous streams of water in order to reach my appointments.

Returning again to Crawfordsville I began active preparations for a removal to Bloomington, or rather to my home, as my health was in a very feeble condition.

I determined to return home and employ the man then living on my place to finish building my house, so as I might have a home to which I might bring my wife. I gave the man directions as to the completion of the building, and telling him when he might expect my return, I went back to Crawfordsville, taking with me my brother-in-law whom I had gotten to consent to haul our family and household goods for us on the return trip.

As we returned we came through Spencer where we stopped for a while. As quarterly meeting was in progress at this place, I concluded to remain there over Sabbath, having arrived there on Saturday night. My brother-in-law, who was not a professor of religion, and who was an inexperienced young man, was opposed to our staying there all day Sunday. He did not enjoy himself at this place and was anxious to drive on again Sunday morning. He came to the window of the room in which my wife and I were sleeping, early next morning and began cracking his whip loudly to awaken us out of our sleep, and when he had succeeded in doing so, he cried out to us, "We must go on this morning."

I tried to dissuade him from his design, but he was intractable. Contrary to my wish, we were compelled by him to pursue our journey on Sunday. After we had traveled a short distance from Spencer, we met a vexatious situation. His riding horse was secured to the rear end of our four-horse wagon. The halter fastened at one end to the horse's neck, while the other end of the halter was secured to one of the rings of the wagon-bed, which ring also helped to hold the wagon cover in its place, the cover being made of something like sheeting.

By a little careless driving, the wagon ran over a small stump which jolted us a good deal and which caused one end of the sheet to become loosened, and it fluttered in the wind and frightened the horse in the rear of the wagon, and he jerked back with a great force, causing the ring and steeple to come out of their places. The wagon cover was still attached to the ring and steeple, and when the horse wheeled to run away, of course the covering was attached to her halter, and she pulled it along fluttering by toward her. This only increased her fears and gave her an additional cause for alarm, and she ran back toward Spencer. As she ran very rapidly the cover stretched away out behind her like an immense banner. There was a great many people who were going to church who were thronging the road at the time, and they were frightened quite as badly as was the horse, when they saw this apparition rushing down the public highway. I called to some of them to give the road but in their bewilderment they stood looking at this strong and overwhelming spectacle, the sheet rising and falling with the rush of the winds. The affrighted animal rushed down the road to the river and there turned and ran down a new road leading down the river.

I followed on after her as fast as I could. I could tell every place where the sheet had come in contact with the ground by the marks left behind. I followed the trail about two miles and gave up the chase. At one place where I inquired of a family whether they had seen a horse pass by that way, I was informed that they had a short time before seen two horses go by. I supposed them to have been mistaken in the number, and attributed it to the fluttering wagon cover which may have seemed to be a horse in the brief interval occupied in the rapid flight by the horse.

Arriving at the wagon we resumed our journey. We soon met other good people on their way to church, and we asked them to be so kind as to make inquiries for us concerning the strayed animal, describing this minutely and the manner of her escape from us.

We came on until we reached the residence of a good friend of mine where I got a horse and went back in search for the animal, and finally succeeded in affecting a capture. She had made a wide circuit around the adjoining neighborhoods, and had returned to the starting point. By night fall we were ready for traveling again on the morrow.

We came on home next morning. When the man (Wm Dusand) who was occupying my place saw us coming, he hurriedly got a crescent saw and fixed a doorway so as to enable us to enter the cabin. The house was up but was not yet provided with the "openings" and fire place. He soon made arrangements so as to allow us to deposit our goods inside. My brother-in-law went back home, while we remained in that little hut, after fixing it up as best we could.

9

Sickness, Location, and Washington Circuit
1828 to 1830

The winter of 1828–29 was a time of sickness and despair for Eli Farmer and his second wife. Years later, when he wrote his autobiography, he could still remember the pain of that period:

My wife and I were both very sick, and we rented out our little farm.[1] I felt at this time the house was very dark and gloomy. Misery born of my wretched temporal condition hovered about my door, and her hateful whine of woe broke in upon my other sorrows, distracting my jarring senses with her wailing cries, while my joyless minutes tediously flowed by with silent pace and looks demure. Sore pierced by wintery winds, we shrank into our sordid hut of cheerless poverty. Could we have been blessed with good health the clouds of gloom about us would not have seemed so threatening and somber. My experience has been this: that nature hath a rule to which she generally conforms in her dealings with God's humble poor, and that is, that where she withholds the comforts of wealth in worldly goods, she yet, as a compensation for the seeming neglect, assigns to such in their stead, health, freedom, innocence, and peace, her real "goods," and only "mocks the great" and wealthy with empty pageantries. But we in violation of her rule, were denied of all, for amid our penury and want, sleep seemed often times to be our only refuge, "and even collegial pleasures were but few."

Had our poverty been superinduced by laziness or selfish waste, we could have felt our lot richly merited. I have no doubt now, that it was the good providence of God that we should be thus schooled in the miseries of squalid poverty in order that we might be better prepared for the stern duties of our subsequent lives. Indeed the lessons learned there embraced more than those which taught us sour dependence upon the giver of all good and perfect gifts for we also learned to sympathize more actively with God's own poor.

> *"Few save the poor feel for the poor;*
> *The rich know not how hard*
> *It is to be of needful rest*
> *And needful food debased.*
> *They know not of the scanty meal*
> *With small pale faces round*
> *No fire upon the cold damp hearth*
> *When snow is on the ground."*

We were very poor. We had nothing but our cloth[e]s and our horse. Our money was exhausted and ourselves sick and discouraged. I was alarmed to tell my neighbors of our very destitute condition. Destitute!! Yes, we were out of bread, and every thing of which bread is made. The floor of our rude cabin was the ground while a blanket served the purpose of a door. We had no chimney even to our hut, and we suffered greatly from the smoke when not otherways annoyed. The tempter, taking advantage of my lowly condition, whispered many times in my ears, "You have given away your once strong and healthy constitution, given up your life, in fact for the cause, and now you are left to die, scorned by the world, and left without a home."

But I kept trying to claim the promises, and my heart answered back to its challenger, "The Lord will fulfill his word and I shall not suffer." Soon I helped to eat the last morsel of food we had, and it was eaten one morning at breakfast. Confined to my bed I confronted my fate, by watching the openings of Providence with a prayerful heart.

About dinner time of that day, an old lady, the mother of the Rev. Draper Chipman, came in with a basket well laden with just such edibles as sick folks ought to be supplied with, and spread them out before us, and it was just at the right time too. Joy springing up in my heart, I exultantly cried out, "Now, Devil, where are you? See, here is provision made for us!" Feeling encouraged I began to improve.

After this we were always supplied with food in some way, some neighbors always handing in something needed by us, and just at the proper time, too, when we needed it, so that we came to be very trustful.

When I had somewhat recovered from my sickness, I rode down to Bloomfield, and the brethren at this place besought me earnestly to move down there, assuring me that they would see to it that I was provided for. I concluded to comply with their request and they sent a wagon for my wife and our household goods, and moved them to this town.

I stayed at Bloomfield some time. The good people meanwhile supplying all our wants with a lavish hand. My health was almost broken down, and I did not preach a great deal. Visiting Fairplay, where I had many friends, I was persuaded to move to that place, and remained there pretty much all winter. I held meetings every Sabbath in a little school house in the village.

Sickness, Near Death, and Satan's Attacks

At the end of a successful year on the Crawfordsville circuit, Eli and Elizabeth Farmer came face to face with the fragile nature of life as a circuit rider when they both became very sick. The conference records show that Farmer took no preaching appointment for the 1828–29 year. In Methodist terms Farmer was "on location," which meant he still had a relationship with the conference as a Methodist preacher but without appointment. He requested another year of location in 1829–30 but was (interestingly) turned down and given the Washington circuit.

Farmer interpreted his year of sickness in religious terms, as a time of spiritual testing. He was under attack by "the tempter," or "the devil." He was sick, isolated, and had no means of support. But at the last moment, before starvation, God intervened through a kindly visitor who brought food, then through neighbors, and then through friends at Fairplay, who had been a part of his first, self-assigned appointment at Bloomfield. The western frontier was supposedly lawless and unrefined. Perhaps, but individuals, at least in Indiana, were hospitable and generous. Some circuit riders would tell of times when in making their rounds they found it necessary to sleep on the ground. Usually, however, settlers would host preachers in their homes.

It would seem from Farmer's account that he and Elizabeth lived for most of the year 1828–29 on the generosity of others. Two persons who now became a part of Farmer's life were the "infidels," Doctor Patton and Judge Wynds, who had given him trouble in 1824–25. It is worth mentioning that when Farmer was first in Bloomfield, one of the criticisms there of the preachers was that they were after money. Farmer had to convince them that he would receive nothing from them and would pay his own way.

A few years later, the situation had changed. Patton and Wynds were still infidels but friends nonetheless. Farmer commented about how good they were to him, doing more even than the supposed Christians. Naturally, Farmer, as soon as he was able, started to preach again. Nothing is said about the Methodist preacher appointed to the circuit that Farmer had started when he resumes his story:

Doctor Patton and Judge Wynds had returned from New Harmony, and they would come over to my house nearly every night, to quarrel with me about my religion, both of them still persisting in their attempts to be infidels. I would preach to them as best I could and always close the interview with prayer. Doctor Patton would not kneel at prayer, and then when prayer was over, I would get up and score him for his being so ill mannerly as to refuse to submit to the rules of a house which he would visit night after night.

His plea in exculpation was that he would be acting hypocritical. Judge Wynds would kneel.

I am reminded just now of a service which I performed for the Judge about this period of my life. He had married into an eastern family and after living with his wife a few years, the loving

Many early frontier cabins were hastily built. Farmer's cabin had dirt floors and a curtain for a door and may have looked similar to this drafty cabin.

couple was separated by the wife dying. Judge Wynds lived a widower more than eleven years, till finding that the affection and love existing between them was inseparable he at length made up his mind to marry a sister of his former wife. Both had striven hard to prevent the marriage, the judge having hastily gone east, whither he had gone on a visit, and where he remained quite a year, in the vain endeavor to school his heart against his marriage with the surviving sister. He found he could not break away from her, and returned to Fairplay with the view to marry her. I saw him one day in Fairplay soon after his return from the east, and he said, "Brother Farmer, I have a job I want you to attend to for me."

"Well," said I, "be quick about it, I'm in a hurry and it is getting late."

"Well," said he, "I will run for the license."

He did so, and we hurriedly made our way towards the house at which the young lady lived. Before we arrived there, however, he told me to call on his brother, who was a judge and bid him come with me, and we were all to be at the young lady's house in just one hour from that moment, and as soon as he gave me the word I was to perform the ceremony as quickly as possible, for he feared opposition on the part of the old folks. Complying with his request I repeated the invitation to the judge. He manifested great feeling, and was evidently adverse to the union. But we both went to the place where the wedding was to be celebrated, and after waiting a few minutes the groom entered.

The parents of the bride were in the kitchen at the time, getting supper, while her brothers were at work in a corn field close by. A significant wink was given me by the groom and he raised from his chair and advanced to the side of the woman. She was sitting down and busy with her sewing, clad in a common cotton dress which she herself had made. The man took her by the hand and raised her to her feet, when she laid aside her work, and just as I pronounced the ceremony finished, the old lady entered the room. She was greatly opposed to the marriage. No objections were urged against him, however, except the fact that he had previously taken a wife out of the family. Altho he was a noble man, this marriage occasioned a terrible fuss, which was conducted in so harsh and boisterous a manner as to attract the attention of the boys in the field, and they came to the house, and soon became active participants in it. The newly married pair refrained from any attempt to a defense or expostulation, and as soon as he could conveniently do so, the groom withdrew, followed by his brother and my self. The lady made him a good wife, and he became a useful citizen, and an excellent member of the Methodist church. At his death he left her a childless widow, and notwithstanding he was very liberal with his family and his church, he left her also a large fortune. I saw the woman a few years ago, and she begged me earnestly to tarry all night at her house.

Judge Wynds taught school during the winter months at Fairplay, and every Sunday morning he would prepare the school-room for our meeting. He was very accommodating to me, but would yet combat my views with all his powers. He would come to my house at such times as my firewood would be about exhausted, and aid me by hauling up a large additional supply. He was even more liberal in his dealings with me than were any of the professors of religion in the church. I could not refrain one day from saying to him, "Judge, the Lord will bless you some time, for your great liberalities. You practice more than our Christians preach and practice, and yet you profess infidelity."

"Oh well," said he, "it is always right to do good."

During the latter part of the winter, my meetings were visited by a Cumberland Presbyterian lady, a noble, kind-hearted, Christian woman, whose interest in the serious was plainly manifest.[2] After a time I noticed her place in the church was vacant, and on inquiry could learn but little of the causes which detained her at home. Pretty soon after observing her absence, however, her son came running to my house with a message for me from his mother. He told me his mother was very sick and she desired I should call at her house immediately. Being very feeble, I got my cane, and by using it, managed to hobble slowly along. As soon as I saw her, I noticed her eyes were lighted with joy.

She said, "Brother Farmer, I am glad you have come. I have heard you singing and preaching for four or five days, but it seemed too far away, and I wanted you to come closer."

I suppose her imagination was highly wrought upon in some way, and that this fancy had deluded her into the belief that she was listening to my voice.

"Now, Brother Farmer," continued the dying woman, "I shall have to die in a few days, but all is well with me. I want you to be by my bedside when the hour shall come."

I prayed with her and consoled her and encouraged her as much as possible. Telling her to send her boy for me at any time I might be needed I returned home. A day or two after this the lad returned to my house and said, "Mother is about dead, and wants you there."

As soon as I could do so, I went back to the chamber of death, where I found quite a number of the neighbors already assembled, and the sick woman was exhorting them to try to meet her in heaven. When she saw me she cried out to me, "Go on, Brother Farmer, you are killing yourself preaching, but you will soon receive your reward."

After asking me to meet her in heaven, she turned to her husband, and told him how she wanted the family raised, urging him to keep up family prayers, and to take good care of the little boys and girls, and to try and meet her in heaven.

She then touchingly addressed those of her children who were old enough to comprehend her words, addressing them one by one, in a very impressive manner, telling them how to act in order to meet her in heaven. Those who were too young to understand her remarks, were delivered up to the merciful Father, the Friend of the orphan. "Now, brother Farmer," said she, "please stand at the head of my bed, and ask God, to receive one into His 'rest for the people of God.'"

Raising her hands upward she then began praying and praising God, and thus she passed away. The scene was a solemn one.

***

I remained in Fairplay till sometime in the latter part of spring when I removed to Bloomfield. This was in 1829. I remained sometime at this place, and was sick most of the time. In order to give my self exercise it was my custom to go out into the streets surrounding the public square, and grub the stump out of the ground around the square. The people were very kind to us, and supplied us with plenty to eat. The proper authorities of the county decided at one time to make a suitable donation to me for my voluntary labors on the public square, but I have forgotten what came of the proposition; my impression is, that it died prematurely.

By the assistance of a good brother, I was enabled during the course of the summer to fix up a one horse buggy, which I afterward found very useful. I sent word to the conference, when I found my health was still feeble, to locate me; although I was improving slowly I was still unable to work. Instead of locating me they gave me Washington circuit, as a field of labor. I kept on getting better throughout the year. I went to my work as soon as I ascertained an appointment had been assigned me, and began performing my duties, performing them very feebly, moderately, and prayerfully. When I could do nothing else, I went from house to house, talking, praying, and singing among the people.

There was a physician living in Washington who was a Methodist preacher, and he told me soon after I entered upon this work that if we ever had a revival at that circuit that the Lord would have to kill off that people and people the place with a new and different creation entirely. I replied that He could convert them at His own good pleasure.

I visited all my appointments very promptly and formed a great many acquaintances.

My second child was born during this year, at Washington, the first one having been born at Fairplay.[3] *The elder child was dangerously ill at one time, soon after I moved to my new field of labor, and my family physician despaired of the little fellow's life. But my wife said the doctors did not know any thing about it, and dint of her noble efforts, the child recovered and lived to become a man. In the vigor of his young manhood, he enlisted in the United States Army at the beginning of the Slaveholders Rebellion, and fighting in defense of the union, he fell at Memphis, Tennessee, and now fills a patriot's grave.*

As I passed around my circuit, I felt like there was a great work to be done, I could see the indications of a powerful and general revival throughout my circuit and I felt greatly encouraged. One morning I left home to attend to an appointment, and after filling it I returned home to find a new addition to my family. My wife had given her second child into our keeping during my absence.

Later in the year I decided to hold a two day's meeting in what was known as "Wallace's Settlement." About this time I heard of a young preacher by the name of Arrington, a mere lad of the age of about eighteen years, whose circuit adjoined mine and I sent for him to assist me at this meeting.

He was kind enough to come to my assistance and I found him an uncommonly sprightly young man. He was singularly well qualified in every way for his sacred calling. He informed me that he commenced preaching for the Universalists, at the age of sixteen years, although of Methodist antecedents, his father being a Methodist preacher at the time of his entrance upon his clerical duties for that organization.

He attributed his change of opinions to the labors and arguments of his father. They returned home from one of his father's appointments, he said, on one occasion, and entered into an exhaustive and exciting discussion upon their differences concerning religion. The father was more than enough for his precocious son, and the result was that the young fellow abandoned his universalism, and sought an early opportunity of joining the Methodist church, and at the early age of seventeen became a Methodist preacher.

His circuit, at the time I met him, south to the Ohio River, embraced several border counties.[4] *There lived near one of his appointments, on the Ohio, a somewhat celebrated Universalist preacher, by the name of Mann. The Universalists of that section had proposed that a joint theological discussion be arranged between young Arrington and their champion Mr. Mann, and the boy accepted the challenge.*

Liberal Religion on the Indiana Frontier

Liberal religion, especially Unitarianism and Universalism, did not frequently fare well on the Indiana frontier. Liberal groups tended to be concentrated in New England among an educated and more sophisticated population. In the early 1800s Unitarianism was thriving in New England and was contending for the heart of Harvard University, as well as other established institutions. It appeared to have little interest in confronting the lawlessness of the West. Because Unitarianism denied the Trinity, a central teaching of Christian faith, most Christian groups did not consider Unitarianism as "Christian."

Universalists, on the other hand, were usually more committed to the Bible, but believed, in addition to most Christian truths, that God's grace covered all persons so that all persons would be saved in the end, denying judgment and hell. Universalists also believed in religious freedom and were for religious unity, as opposed to sectarianism. In contrast to Unitarianism (with which it eventually merged), Universalists were present on the Western frontier. While Universalism did not establish a lot of churches in Indiana, it did, consciously or unconsciously, reflect the religious beliefs of a number of people, especially those who were repelled by Methodist and Baptist emotionalism. Elmo Robinson, in an article in the *Indiana Magazine of History* (1917), offered the opinion that there were more Universalists outside the church than in it. At the same time, he recorded that in 1849 Universalists in Indiana had twenty-nine preachers, fifteen meeting houses, fifty-five societies, ten associations, and one convention.[5]

Since Universalists did not hold revival meetings, they tended to communicate their message by "discussions," "lectures," and debates. Universalists, even when not formally educated, tended to be well-read and made their case from a reasoned perspective. The Universalist mentioned in this story, E. B. Mann, later became editor of a Universalist paper, the *Western Olive Branch*, published in Indianapolis, Indiana.

Religious debates were rather common on the Western frontier. Almost all of the circuit rider biographies and autobiographies mention them. The account of this debate is instructive because it scored the religious lineup, at least in Farmer's mind, on the scale of evangelical orthodoxy. Those who supported Mann were "infidels." Those who supported the Methodist Arrington were "orthodox evangelicals." At other times Methodists on the frontier debated Presbyterians, Baptists, Calvinists, New Lights, and Campbellites, but in the confrontation with a Universalist, these groups were united as orthodox Christians. There is much more about this in the Farmer story later on, but it can be noted here that

Illustration of an early Indiana pioneer settlement. Eli Farmer lived and preached in such settlements.

this passage in Farmer's autobiography evinces the beginning of an evangelical religious culture that transcended denominational differences. Farmer continues:

The young man did not inform me of this arrangement till our meeting was over. I told him that Mann was announced to preach at Washington on the following Tuesday, telling him he would do better to stay over with me and hear him, and thereby get the drift of his arguments, so as to be better prepared to successfully combat his arguments. He succeeded in getting a minister to fill his appointments in order that he might follow my suggestions.

He stayed with me on the following day which was Monday, and on Tuesday the Universalist preacher, in obedience to the invitation of a number of infidels of Washington, arrived, and forthwith proceeded to the court house the place appointed for the meeting.

The excitement in the village was intense, and the courtroom was crowded. When Arrington and I arrived, the champion was already occupying the judge's stand for a pulpit. In a short time he began his discourse. At one point he asserted "there was no devil save calumniating man."

I was greatly astonished when the sermon was over to see Arrington advancing toward his antagonist, looking Mann sternly in the face as he advanced toward him. I confess I felt badly, for I was beginning to incline to the opinion that the fellow was insane. When he reached the steps leading to the judge's desk, he placed his hand on the railing and ascended to the platform when Mr. Mann said, "Now, my young brother, if you have anything to say, say on!"

"This afternoon at three o'clock, I will answer this sermon in the Methodist Church," the young man announced, and then added, "and for fear the people will not all turn out I will answer a few things now."

"This man says," he continued, "that there is no devil save calumniating man, and we will now try his views somewhat by way of a test. The good book says there were legions of devils in one <u>man</u>. These legions of <u>men</u>, in one <u>man</u>, were <u>cast out</u> of <u>one man</u>, and these legions of men entered the swine, now will this man please explain a little matter for me; in what manner did these men enter, did they crawl into their mouths, or into the noses, or ears, of the swine?" stepping back and waiting for a reply.

Mann advanced and said, "The young man wants me to tell whether the men went into the mouths of the swine or at the other end," and the audience fully disgusted with his obscene haggling, abruptly left the room. Amid the confusion which ensued, a certain Col. Warner, threatened to whip young Arrington.

I then said that the parties had arranged for a public discussion at another time and place, and that if they saw fit to hold it now, it was no part of his business to interfere.

He again stated that he would whip him, and I again replied, saying, "Sir, if you put your hand on that boy, I will attend to you myself, you shall not whip him."

"Would you?" he inquired.

"I certainly would," was my reply.

"The people think a great deal of you here," he replied in a patronizing way.

"I can't help that," I said, "you shall not whip that boy."

The people met at 3 o'clock in great numbers, and the excitement was intense. Members of all the evangelical orthodox churches were praying for the boy, all such denominations being considerably elated, and all anxiously hoping that the Universalist might be publicly whipped.

Young Arrington preached with great success against the sermon delivered by his adversary. Upon the conclusion of the discourse, Mann announced that he would answer the sermon at candle-lighting.

By this time I had got myself to believe the boy could manage his opponent, and I proposed to my young brother, after this meeting, to arrange for a general discussion before the public at once, and finish the debate at this time and place. After preaching at night Arrington said to Mann,—"Sir, if you are willing to consent to such an arrangement, we will meet on tomorrow morning, and draw up articles and rules for our debate, and we will go into our debate at once.

The proposition was accepted, and the preliminaries were accordingly attended to, and the moderators chosen. Judge David McDonald, who was then a somewhat noted infidel, and another infidel, Cowger, and a Methodist preacher, acted as the moderators. The result of the debate was entirely satisfactory to the friends of Arrington. I never knew a poor fellow to receive so terrible a defeat, and the job seemed so easily accomplished, by the stripling. Pretty soon after entering the discussion, Mann became so terribly dissatisfied with the articles and rules, mutually agreed upon previously he wanted to alter or modify them, and begin anew, but Arrington sternly refused to do so. The young victor then apologized for his extreme youth, yet begged to be permitted to whip his opponent, and he did it. The judge seeing how the battle was progressing requested the disputants to throw all their strength into their closing speeches and be done with it, and thereby stimulated Arrington very greatly, and he poured forth, in his closing speech, an unprecedented flood of testimony before which no adverse position could stand, and the consequence was, that Universalism was doomed in that community.

In answer to an inquiry propounded to the infidel lawyer as to what his opinion was of the discussion, he replied, "Well, my man, who will preach universalism, taking the Bible for his guide is a damned fool."

My labors were prosecuted by me with great success during the remainder of the winter. The mention of Judge McDaniels name just now recalled a little episode that occurred at about this period. The judge and I were riding out of town one day, and after we had ridden some distance, we became very communicative and confidential.

"You know," said he, "that I used to preach."

"Yes," I answered.

He then informed me that he was never called to preach, and I answered him, that he and I were entirely agreed about that matter, else he would have been a better man.

"Well," continued the judge, "nor were you ever called to preach; you may think so, but you are not called to preach."

"You may continue to think so, but I believe it, and so practice accordingly," said I, by way of a mild rebuke.

While we thus engaged in talking, as we were now riding along the edge of a strip of prairie, a body of young horses came running along in front of us, and the judge referring to them, asked me, "What will you do with these in the day of judgment?"

My reply was something like this, —"The Scriptures say, that the creature was made subject to vanity, by reason of him that subjected the same in hope, for all creation groaneth and travaileth in pain until now, waiting for the adoption of the body."

"Now," I continued, "we understand that the Scriptures say, again, that there is to be a new heaven and a new earth. It is evident that the 'new heaven' must be for man and the 'new earth' for animals, for they "were made subject to death through the fall."

"Well, well," said the judge, "I never heard the like before;" and we rode on in silence for some time, my companion seeming to be busy with thoughts my view had suggested.

Years afterward, I saw him frequently in Monroe County, and he then seemed to be seeking for light, and I am of the opinion, from several conversations had with him, that the interchange of views between us, on the occasion of our horseback ride referred to, drew his mind into a different channel of philosophic research. At a later period, he joined the M.E. Church, and after living many years a consistant and useful Christian, at length died at Indianapolis, at a good ripe old age.

I was considerably pressed during this year many times for food and clothing, for my self and family, and when my necessities pressed me so hard I had to go in debt, I would go to Bloomington, near which place I owned property, and there contract my debts for such things as I needed.

About the time the campmeeting season came on, the whole circuit seemed to be alive and in good working condition; and I appointed a campmeeting in a good location, in the valley of White River. Certain authorities of the church tried to put a stop to our preparations, thinking we could do no good, but I determined it should go on, even if I should be required to do all the work myself. The people opposing us did not understand the situation of the field, as good as I and if felt willing to take responsibility. When the time arrived I went to the campground, and preached two or three sermons before the Presiding Elder came to our assistance. There were plenty of people and provisions, and professions of religion were made on the opening evening. The Presiding Elder was in good condition, and he went into the good work with great zeal. On the Sabbath he preached with great power and acceptance. The meetings were truly times of refreshing from the presence of the Lord.

I think I counted at one time sixty young men at the altar seeking salvation. George Loon was our Presiding Elder. He was a zealous, fervent, holy and powerful man, whose sterling mental talents enabled him to accomplish much good.

10

Harvest Time, 1830 to 1832

From 1830 to 1831 Eli Farmer served the White Lick circuit. The next year he was assigned the Franklin circuit, which included Indianapolis. He talks about these years in his autobiography:

Pretty soon after this conference came on at Vincennes, on which occasion we were presided over by Bishop Roberts.[1] In order to attend this session of our conference I was compelled to sell my family cow, otherwise I could not have provided myself with means with which to pay my necessary expenses.

At this session I was appointed to what was called "White Lick" circuit, a circuit immediately south of Indianapolis ten miles, and my wife and I removed our two children to our new work at once. I was very destitute. When we arrived there we were kindly received. I was so poor, that I was shamed to tell my brethren how very poor I was, although I had exhausted all the money brought in by the sale of the cow, in moving to this circuit. After getting my family settled temporarily, I returned to Washington to try to make some arrangements for moving my household goods, I returned with an aching heart, for I was considerably indebted at Bloomington and I had nothing upon which I could remove my goods but I kept on saying to the Lord that my way might be opened up before me. On my return I met brother Wallace, a steward of that circuit and who was elected that year to a seat in the legislature and who knew my temporal condition.[2] To this gentleman I said something like this: "Brother Wallace, you know my condition. I want my goods moved to my new field and I am wholly unable to pay for it now but I think that someday I shall be able to do so. And now if you would be so kind to assist me in this matter I will pay you therefore just when I can possibly pay you. The distance of which the route lay was something like 100 miles. Said he, Brother Farmer you goods must be taken to your field of labor. I told him to start with [forth] the following morning and that in the meantime I would have everything so as to be easily thrown into a wagon and I would then go in advance of him. Leaving him up [the] street and on my return [to] work[,] pretty soon I was violently attacked of the Devil, who tempted me, "Now you have contracted debt and you will never pay," but I said, "You are a liar. The Lord will help me pay it."

Traveling out a hundred yards I was accosted by squire McDonald, a noble citizen and upon his invitation accompanied him to his house. He was not a professor of religion though his wife was. He was, however, under deep conviction. While enjoying his kind hospitality, I did what I could to benefit him in his spiritual concerns. About the time I was ready to take my departure, I exhorted him most fervently to turn to the Lord and seek salvation, informing him that perhaps I might never more see him, and that if such should be the case, I would like well for him to promise now to meet me in heaven. I gave him my hand as a token of a farewell, and as I did so he dropped into my hand enough money to pay off the debt just contracted concerning my household goods saving fifty cents.

I confess I was greatly shocked, thereby cutting off my exhortation, for it seemed very like just handing the amount to me from the good Lord. With a thankful heart I bade him farewell, again begging him to try to meet me in heaven. My heart was light as onward I rode, now that I was provided for. At such happy seasons feeling assured by such timely tokens of my acceptance, and having such eagerness of hope to benefit my kind, one could not well feel otherwise than that some in mortal favor were given to one's mind. The pure, unalloyed joy which I now felt, were enough to more than repay me, had every ensuing hour of my life thereafter been filled with sorrow, and I thought of my former wars as giants in the olden time that ne're would come again.

Upon arriving home, I left the money with my wife, telling her to pay it over to brother Wallace, and that she must ask him how much more would be required to pay him for his trouble. My wife did as I had requested her, and when she had put the question to him, in according to my wish, she was informed that fifty cents in addition to the already paid would be quite sufficient. A listener standing by said, "I will pay that amount for brother Farmer," and he accordingly handed over the amount required, and the devil was fully convicted of another black lie by a cancellation of this indebtedness.

That year was an eminently successful one in the vineyard in which I labored, and we did a good work all over my district. Three hundred and fifty new members joined our church during that year, and the people of Zion were greatly confirmed in the faith. My wife rendered great service that year at home, by spinning and knitting in exchange for clothing for her self and the children. At one season, she carried her babe in her arms to a brother's house in the neighborhood, and wove all day, day after day for some time, for leather out of which our shoes were made. At the expiration of the conference year we found ourselves in a much better condition in every way, and with a great spiritual work on our hands.

James Armstrong was again my presiding elder, and just before the conference came on he helped me hold a campmeeting. He had promised the people that as the conference was to be held at Indianapolis that year, that if they would pay of their ministers satisfactorily to all parties concerned, they might have the privilege of choosing their own pastor for the ensuing year.

Conference came on shortly after the campmeeting referred to, which meeting by the way, was a singularly powerful one, and a very interesting session was holden. This was in 1831. I attended the session, and when the appointments were about decided upon, Judge Ritchie of Indianapolis came to me with the startling intelligence that I had been selected by the church for the city of Indianapolis. In my bewildered distraction I said,—"Why judge, you are altogether mistaken in the man! You ought to have the best preacher in the conference at this point."

He replied by saying, "We've had big preachers long enough; we want to try little preachers awhile."

Well, when I heard the call read by the good Bishop, "Eli P. Farmer— Franklin Circuit;" you may be well assured I felt very weak, for that circuit meant the city of Indianapolis in that day, and I was led to my feebleness to a close proximity to the cross.

I had fallen into a very strange habit of trying to guess at the beginning of each conference year, as to the number of accessions I would gain for the church, under divine providence, during the year, and had never known my impressions in such matters to deceive me; and I now began wondering what the increase would be during this year. By some mysterious manner I became fully satisfied that the number of accessions for this year would be five hundred, and I forthwith began publishing to my congregations the impressions I had formed on this subject. Many of my brethren thought I was laboring under a very great delusion, and sought to undeceive my mind, but I told them the Lord would give me five hundred additions that year. I at once began working *for so glorious a consummation, and exerted my self without stint. Judge Ritchie a very able man every way, rendered efficient service in helping me, but his fondness for philosophical researches and his love for the beauties and graces of rhetoric, somewhat injured his usefulness among a people who needed entirely different nourishment: and I said to him one day,—"Judge, the good Lord will punish you, I am afraid in the day of judgment, for the manner in which you preach!"*

"Why so," he inquired.

"You have a sword of five talents," said I, "but you kill nobody. You wave your sword among the stars, concerning which you so often speak, but it looks pretty bad when we fail to discover that any body has been injured."

And that was the plain truth, for aiming at the stars, he would yet stumble over a straw. Seeing how well he received my honest criticism, I was persuaded to still further express my candid words of advice, and I went on,—"You must get down among the people, judge, instead of moving your trenchant blade above their heads, and then you will exercise a power to which few men can hope to attain."

He passed the matter off peculiarly, but I was glad to observe he felt what I had said.

* * *

Brother [Josiah] Strange was my Presiding Elder this year.[3] One of my early meetings this year was held at the village of Martinsville. At this meeting I received more than one hundred accessions in a very short time. Brother Strange was sick at this time with an affliction from which he never recovered, and I called upon him to ascertain whether I could secure any assistance. Judge Ritchie was with him when I visited him. When he saw me he exclaimed, "Brother Farmer, I hear you are having a great revival in Martinsville. Now, brother Farmer, I do not think myself arrogant or egotistical when I say that I believe I can preach better than you can, and I have preached there frequently. Brother Armstrong has also preached many times there, and many other better preachers than you are. That is all true, and yet, nothing has heretofore been accomplished, and now I am told you are having a wonderfull revival down there!"

Judge Ritchie, taking up the complaint where the good Elder had left off, went on with a further statement about as follows, "Farmer, here, can venture the farthest upon an open sea, and get back the easiest and safest, with a broken little bark, of any man within the range of his acquaintance."

"I think I understand the matter," I said by way of defense, "the trouble lies within your own enclosure. Now brother Strange is well aware of the fact that he is a great orator and he depends upon that, while brother Ritchie most likely depends upon his subtle philosophy and is thereby tempted to wander off among the stars, and the consequence is, no good comes of any of it. But I, knowing how very weak a vessel Eli P. Farmer is, depend upon the Lord, and He does the work and not me."

The judge acknowledged this was the safer dependence, and at once came down to a humble plain where he could the more easily reach the hearts of the people, and long before the year expired he became an eminently successful revivalist, and reformation preacher, rendering me great assistance.

Frontier Preaching

It is significant that early pioneer Methodist clergy were called "preachers" and not "ministers" or "reverends" or even "pastors." Preaching is what made Methodism grow—enthusiastic, frequent, emotional, "spirit-filled" preaching. Early Methodists scorned the kind of preaching they associated with learned ministers as cold, intellectual, and formal.

The Methodist appointment system, which in early years moved preachers to a new circuit every year, as well as the camp meetings, helped secure the reputation of the most effective preachers. Since camp meetings featured a number of preaching services daily, it was necessary to bring in preachers to help with the various services. Because of this persons were acquainted with different preachers and they tended to rank them in terms of popularity and effectiveness. Preachers whose messages would bring many to the altar were the ones with a strong reputation.

James Armstrong, the presiding elder of White Lick circuit, played a key role in developments that eventually led to Farmer's appointment to Franklin. Armstrong is recognized in all the early Indiana Methodist histories as an effective preacher and presiding elder and a leader in Indiana Methodism. He was a good example of a person who improvised to make the system work. He offered that if the circuits would pay their preachers in full, they could select their next year's appointment. This was most unusual because it was a Methodist article of polity that preachers were "sent" not "called." The Franklin circuit took Armstrong at his word, and, probably through Judge Ritchie, selected Farmer, who under normal circumstances did not have enough standing in the conference to receive such a desired appointment.

Berry Sulgrove's *History of Indianapolis and Marion County* (1884) recorded that Judge Ritchie was a local Methodist minister who was born in Kentucky and moved to Indiana in 1826. He was called Judge Ritchie because he had served as an associate judge. The account in the book states that Ritchie wore homespun jeans into the pulpit and was greatly admired for his logic and his speaking ability. When he spoke "the audience became spell-bound, fascinated by his eloquence and earnestness." He was in politics in 1840 but died in 1841.[4]

Ritchie was a "local pastor," one who usually lived within the bounds of the circuit. They were "local" because they did not "itinerate," that is, take appointments to different circuits. Often they had other employment but were used to assist the traveling elder, who was in this case Farmer. Local preachers were sometimes more educated and were often better off financially than the traveling elders. In many instances they had more standing in the community as well.

The banter between Farmer and Ritchie, and then between Farmer and the presiding elder of Franklin circuit, Josiah Strange, is informative. Despite their lack of formal education, preachers preached from personal experience, used colorful language, and made use of humor and figures of speech. They also had strong convictions as to what kind of preaching stirred the heart. Later in the Farmer story, a "preach-out" at a camp meeting in which his preaching upstages the preaching of the presiding elder will lead to a fallout between Farmer and the Methodist "authorities" and to a decline in Farmer's Methodist standing. In 1832, however, Farmer was enjoying great success:

The meetings at Martinsville were kept up, and the powerful work went on. In the absence of our afflicted Presiding Elder, I was compelled to perform his duties as well as those of the regular pastor, and was Presiding Elder and "preacher in charge," all combined. While I was preaching the customary Presiding Elder's sermon, on Sabbath morning, the Spirit of the Lord came upon me in a wonderfully powerful manner, by which I was enabled to express the following words with a peculiarly solemn and impressive emphasis and unction:—

> "Were you to live, my brethren and sisters, under the influence, and power of the Holy Spirit, God would answer your prayers, and would drive the Devil from town and country!"

The effects produced were electrical; I never witnessed such a display of divine power among a congregation in my life, before nor since. People fell down in every direction all around me, and many out cries were made, loud and piteous, for the Lord to have mercy upon them.

About the time these services were being held, there was a certain old man engaged in making sugar in his camp a short distance below town, in the bottoms. While he was thus desecrating the Sabbath, some terrible object came that way[;] his dogs, large, fierce and very courageous fellows became so badly frightened, that they precipitately fled and ran home as fast as their trembling legs would carry them. The man himself became alarmed, and thinking the Devil was after him, quickly followed his canine friends, and was soon within the barred doors of his house as wretched a man as ever suffered from mental anguish. He was afraid the Devil had come for him because he was making sugar on the Lord's day.

On the following morning, a party of gentlemen discovered a mysterious trail as if some huge monster had gone by that way, and they in turn became greatly alarmed. The trail was one well calculated to inspire the stoutest heart with terror, for it was more than two feet wide, and its bed was lined with a sickening slime all along its ghastly length, a part of which was left also on the weeds and brush over which its route lay.

This wonderful trail was followed afterward by less terror-stricken citizens for a distance of a couple of miles, till it was lost in the waters of White River. No living man or woman could account for so singular a phenomenon, and it was ever afterward, even to this day called Farmer's Devil.

Shortly after this occurrence a very wicked old man approached me one day and said,—"Sir, I have no doubt you have driven the Devil out of Martinsville, and I have a disposition I find to manifest my appreciation of your kind services. I have no money by me, but if you will accept of this silk handkerchief you are welcome to it."

I accepted his humble gift, and returned my thanks according as they were by me felt. This man's opinion was only a reflex [reflection] of that of the entire community almost; for nearly every body thought it was the Devil.

This year was, I believe, the happiest year of my life. Some time after this meeting, Judge Ritchie became involved in a difficulty with another Methodist preacher, and the Judge felt it his duty to prefer charges against his erring brother. It became my duty to look into the matter and I did so. According to my understanding of the affair, I thought the fellow guilty of the charges and I informed him he would be required to meet the investigation, before a proper committee of local preachers.

He sought an interview with the Presiding Elder, and after obtaining an audience with him, tried to persuade him to direct me to drop the charges and the proposed examination. The Presiding Elder being thus misled, urged me to do so, but I refused to listen to his suggestions. The charge related to very gross misconduct on the part of the brother in connection with certain malicious trespasses upon the lands of another, whereby a certain valuable mill race was greatly damaged. He then undertook surreptitious means to avoid having his case investigated. I felt wonderfully impressed with the fact that his case was an ugly one, and I sought an interview with one of the brethren whom I knew to be well acquainted with the facts in the case, from whom I ascertained the particulars required. He had tried to educate the people in to the belief that I was persecuting him. I again obtained an interview with my informant, who was a nephew of the party to whose conduct I had objected, and secured a written statement of the facts connected with my former interview, whereby I convicted the fellow of lying. A few days subsequently I exhibited this document to a committee of local preachers, where I told the discomfited wretch that if he would promise to cease annoying the church, and behave himself, I would permit the matter to be quietly dropped. He so promised, and the subject was never afterward revived.

All things considered, I got along better this year than I had gotten on during any of its predecessors, coming out at the end of the year, out of debt, and with enough money to purchase a two horse wagon. Investing my money thus I was enabled to remove my family home to my farm. The number taken into the church this year by me was five hundred and fifty five. Good gospel measure you see.

Methodist Growth in Indiana and the Nation

By 1831, the year Farmer served Franklin circuit, the Second Great Awakening, or the Western Revival, was in full swing. This was beginning to translate practically into some impressive church growth statistics. Farmer reported that he received 350 members during his year on the White Lick circuit and 550 members during the following year on the Franklin circuit.

These statistics need comment. Nine hundred "accessions" to the church in two years, if not a record, is in a statistical category by itself. To put it in perspective, no United Methodist Church in Indiana, including several that could be considered mega churches, has in recent years been able to report figures that come anywhere near that. However, the figures may not be everything they appear to be:

1) Preacher statistics need to be received with some caution. Methodists, among all the religious groups in America, were statistics gatherers. Since "accessions," "souls saved," or numbers "praying at the altar" were the standards by which preacher success or failure was judged, some enhancement can be suspected in the reporting of statistics. The 350 and 550 figures are rounded numbers. When the crowds at the famous 1801 camp meeting at Cane Ridge, Kentucky, were numbered "between ten and twenty-five thousand," it is pretty certain a lot of estimating was involved.

2) Methodists were also notorious for their "backsliding," which meant that there was always considerable slippage in the numbers reported. Persons who joined the church after a revival or camp meeting might never be seen again and were soon removed from membership. A person converted one year might backslide and was then converted again the next year and might be counted both years.

3) In the competition between religious groups, members circulating between churches would be counted in both churches. The Methodist figures might include thirty who left the Baptists to become Methodist. However, by the same token, Baptist figures might include thirty who left the Methodists to become Baptist. The thirty may have been counted by each group but no actual church growth was taking place.

In spite of all of the slippery numbers, it can be said that Methodist growth on the western frontier, and in Indiana specifically, was nothing less than phenomenal during the period from 1820 to 1840. The figures are even more impressive when compared with statistics in America during the period from 1790 to 1800, a time when the United States was still in religious decline. During this decade the American population grew by 35 percent, while Methodist growth was less than 13 percent.[5] But following Cane Ridge and the onslaught of the Western Revival, the statistics take a different turn. From 1810 to 1850, Indiana's population grew nearly 4,000 percent, from less than 25,000 to nearly 1 million people. During that same period, Indiana Methodism grew more than 9,000 percent, from 755 members to more than 70,000. Also, in the United States from 1800 to 1850, Methodism increased almost 2,000 percent, while the population increased less than 500 percent. Methodists were only 1.2 percent of the general population in America in 1800 but had grown to 5.4 percent in 1850.[6]

The Western Revival affected all religious bodies in Indiana. By 1860 Indiana could report (in the federal census) a total of 2,933 churches of which 1,256, or 43 percent, were Methodist.

The Place of Indiana in American Methodism

Starting in about 1840 and continuing even to the present day, the major regional divide in Methodism and in the country has been between North and South. This is because of slavery and the Civil War. Within Methodism the division occurred even before the Civil War, in 1844, when the church divided into the Methodist Episcopal Church and the Methodist Episcopal Church South. The churches did not reunite until 1939.[7]

The relations between northern Methodists and southern Methodists after 1844 were usually but not always cordial. Both churches claimed to be the inheritors of true Methodism. When Bishop Holland McTyeire wrote his *History of Methodism* in 1887, he commented that it would be a history with a southern perspective, noting, "Methodism in the South has suffered injustice from the manner in which it has been presented by learned, honest, and able writers in the North." He went on to argue: "In the South Methodism was first successfully planted, and from thence it spread North, and East, and West. If all the members claimed by all the branches be counted, there is a preponderance of American Methodism now, as at the beginning, in the South."[8]

McTyeire claimed that it was the South that was the crucible of Methodism. To make this claim he had to counteract the common assumption that it was in the East, particularly the Northeast—the region around New York, Philadelphia, and Boston—that fashioned the character of Methodism. Early Methodist notables, Thomas Webb, Richard Strawbridge, and Jesse Lee, were from the Northeast. Almost all of the early Methodist intellectuals, the editors and historians, and especially its learned men, such as Abel Stevens, Nathan Bangs, and Lee, were from the New York and Philadelphia area. Not only did these men write the histories but they edited the prestigious journals and papers: *Zion's Herald* (Boston), *The Methodist Quarterly Review* (started 1818, New York), and the *Christian Advocate* (New York), a weekly paper for Methodists authorized by the General Conference in 1826.

It was in the East that Methodism first began its transition from despised sect to respectable denomination. With this transition came predictable resistance. It was in New

York that the Wesleyan Methodist Church broke in 1842 from the Methodist Episcopal Church, in large part over populist reform. It was also in New York that the Free Methodists divided in 1859, again over issues of populist reform. A major issue for the Free Methodists was "free pews," a reaction against "respectable" New York Methodists beginning the practice of pew rental. New York was also home for the Chautauqua Movement, which was organized specifically as a substitute for outdoor camp meetings. Chautauqua organizers sought to keep the attraction of outdoor gatherings but wanted to substitute education and cultural events for the revivalism of camp meetings.[9] At the same time New York was also the home of Phoebe Palmer, who developed holiness "altar theology" and laid the foundation for the populist holiness movement. The National Holiness Camp Meeting organization was founded in New York and New Jersey in 1869.

While some would make a case that it was Easterners who set the character and ethos of Methodism, a respected historian, Russell Richey, argues for the importance of the Chesapeake Bay area: "The Chesapeake was the heart and soul of early Methodism, its center, its capital, its place of greatest strength, its site of holiest memories, its Jerusalem. There, perhaps, Methodism made its earliest significant impact." Richey argues that the assumption that there was a national church with a national vision, pulled together by a common Arminian theology, a General Conference, and a system of governance does not reflect reality. He states that historians have obscured Methodism's regional differences. According to Richey, it is true that Methodism flourished in the South and in the Northeast but the importance of these areas is overshadowed by the energy of Methodism in the Chesapeake Bay area.[10]

Between 1805 and 1815 camp meetings flourished in the Chesapeake Bay area. Charles Johnson's study, *The Frontier Camp Meeting*, drew heavily from accounts of camp meetings in this area.[11] In his PhD dissertation (1997) William Johnson explains that it is very possible that "the altar" was introduced there, as well as some of the earliest camp meeting spirituals, especially the spirituals later labeled "Negro Spirituals." To add to the speculation, it was probably in Kentucky and Tennessee and the Chesapeake area that slaves and free blacks were first significantly Christianized in America. In that process slaves and free blacks were not only influenced by but also contributed to the development of practices that became part of the camp meeting ethos. These practices included the "shout," the "circle dance," "spirit possession," processions that ran counter-clockwise, ecstatic dancing, clapping, and rhythmic singing. Some historians believe there is an uncanny resemblance between West African tribal rituals and the earliest camp meeting religious expressions.[12]

Another historian, William H. Williams, also makes a case for early Methodist success in the Delmarva Peninsula on the East Coast.[13] At the end of the Revolutionary War almost one in three Methodists lived in the Delmarva Peninsula. By 1810 one-third of the peninsula's residents were black, and by 1820 fully 20 percent of its population was Methodist.[14]

But the case must also be made for the importance of the West, or more specifically the western frontier in the period 1801 to 1840, following Cane Ridge. The western frontier not only made an indelible mark on Methodism but served in many ways to define the character of modern evangelicalism. Other religious groups were already established in the East, and Methodism grew in reaction to and alongside these groups. Methodism was defined against the Anglicans (or the Episcopalians) on the Delmarva Peninsula and along the southern seaboard. In the Northeast the prevailing religious culture was defined in large part by Presbyterians, Congregationalists, and even Unitarians and Universalists. These were groups with educated clergy and European roots. The Methodists and Baptists could not help but take on some of the flavor of those groups. In the West, however, the Methodists, along with the Baptists, with limited competition, were writing a religious ethos on a clean slate. Nathan Hatch refers to the religious phenomenon on the frontier as the democratization of American Christianity. It might also be described as the Americanization of Christianity. This way of religion was highly individualized, highly subjective, highly experiential, revivalistic, and egalitarian. And, as will be discussed later in the Farmer story, it was highly sectarian. It traded away the authority of church tradition for the authority of subjective experience. As a result it spawned groups such as the Christian church, and varieties of Baptist, Methodist, Quaker, and Presbyterian groups.

It is in the case for the importance of the Western Revival that the case for the importance of Indiana in the development of the religious culture known as evangelical Christianity can be made. The definition of the western frontier was obviously continually changing in the early 1800s. In earliest Methodist references following the Baltimore 1784 organizing conference, the "West" was the Redstone circuit that covered parts of Virginia and Pennsylvania. In 1792 the Methodists organized the Western conference, which was basically Kentucky and Tennessee. At this point most of the population west of the Appalachians was in Kentucky. In 1860 the Methodist historian Abel Stevens claimed that the western frontier line had moved across the nation at the rate of thirteen miles per year.[15] By Stevens' calculations, moving westward from the western edge of Tennessee, by 1860 the frontier line would be running north and south through the Dakotas. The Cane Ridge camp meeting did more than just launch a Great Awakening; it also identified the awakening as a western frontier revival. This is despite the fact that Methodist camp meetings had been exported to points east, and revivals in various forms were taking place in every area of what then constituted the country.

A number of Methodist historians comment that by the decade 1820 to 1830, interest in camp meetings was waning within Methodism. But this is an eastern perspective. While it is true that fewer camp meetings were being held in the East, there was a different situation in the West. It was during this very period that Farmer and his compatriots were having their greatest success in the area west of the Appalachians. The "West" now included not just Kentucky and Tennessee, but also Indiana, Ohio, Illinois, Alabama, and Mississippi. This is where the dramatic church growth was taking place, helped, of course, by a rapidly increasing population in these areas. But the church growth rate was outpacing the population growth rate.

Movement of America's Western Frontier, 1836–1854

During the 1800s, the western frontier of the United States was moving westward as this map shows. As land was opened for settlement, the frontier moved west and the Second Great Awakening, or Western Revival, moved with it, allowing Methodism and other evangelical churches to flourish.

In 1834 the Methodist General Conference, recognizing the importance of the West in Methodism, launched a second official church weekly paper, the *Western Christian Advocate*, published in Cincinnati, Ohio. This paper soon had 5,000 subscribers—one of the highest subscription numbers for newspapers in the nation. By the 1870s the *Advocate* claimed to have 20,000 subscribers. It was a regional paper, serving the annual conferences that supported it, namely, conferences in the states of Ohio, Indiana, Kentucky, Tennessee, Illinois, Mississippi, Alabama, and a conference in western Pennsylvania.

The *Advocate* was not above some regional boosterism. When the annual minutes of the conferences were printed in 1836, the *Advocate* carried a major article noting that western Methodism had grown by 64,392 members, and now had 227,700 members, or 36 percent of all Methodists, the rest being in the South, the middle states, the East, and Canada.[16] The spectacular growth and influence of Methodism in the West impressed the Methodist historian Abel Stevens. He commented that the West blended on the north with the Genesee conference (New York) through circuits in Kentucky to the mountain regions of the Holston conference in eastern Tennessee, southwestern Virginia, and northern Georgia. In the section on the "West" in his history of the Methodist Episcopal Church, when introducing the period before 1820, Stevens wrote:

> We descend, then, the western slope of the Alleghanies again to witness achievements, wonders, seldom, if ever, paralleled in religious history—great even in their faults—characters, labors, sufferings, successes which moulded young and semi-barbarous communities that have since become mighty states, empires of Christian civilization, controlling, in our day, the fate of the new world, and destined probably, before another century, to affect the destinies of the whole world.[17]

Always the New Yorker, while recognizing the importance of revivals and camp meetings, Stevens was also caught up in the movement to make Methodism respectable. It was the civilizing nature of Methodism that impressed Stevens.

Farmer and his fellow circuit riders would have understood it differently. Farmer never spoke of the importance of civilization or respectability. He was to the end an evangelist intent on saving souls. If the church was growing in Indiana it was because of camp meetings, revivals, and spirit-filled preaching. He also believed the revival was much bigger than just the Methodists. And he was correct. It was not just Methodism that was growing. All of the indigenous religious groups influenced by the Western Revival were growing: the Baptists, the Christian Churches, the United Brethren, the New Light and Cumberland Presbyterians, and the Evangelical Association.

The colonial churches—Congregationalists, Episcopalians, and Presbyterians—saw their share of the American religious market decrease. The Congregational Church, the strongest church in colonial America, could hardly make a dent in the West. In 1850, when the census reported 423 Methodist churches in Indiana, the total of Congregational churches for the entire state numbered just two. The Indiana disdain of Congregationalism and things Eastern is reflected in a caustic article that appeared in the *Northwest*

Christian Advocate (Chicago) on February 9, 1853, after a report came out that the Congregational churches in the East had raised $56,000 to establish churches "in the west." The article said:

> So you may expect to see churches going up in all directions. Of course they will be congregational churches, and after they are built, they will be used to enlighten the nations on some of the points of the old Geneva doctrine. We, in the east have long been accustomed to listen to the dreadful destitution of the Mississippi Valley and the old west. It has sometimes been represented a great moral waste, a complete "heathendom" where the people are well supplied with Methodist churches and a Methodist ministry. But the people must hear the true gospel, i.e. Calvinism.

11

Greencastle, Location, and Brown County
1833 to 1838

In the midst of Methodist success on the Indiana frontier, Eli Farmer briefly mentions spending a year at Greencastle, while trying to start a business at home:

The next year [1833–34] I rode the Green Castle circuit and it was a very successful one.[1] Paying off all my debts I had about eighty dollars left remaining. About this time I was persuaded to enter a little firm doing a small merchandize business in Bloomington, the firm being comprised of a couple of my friends. The understanding was that I was to invest my eighty dollars and they would attend to the business so as to allow me to travel my circuit.[2]

Eli Farmer—the Individual

This book examines frontier revivalism, life on the frontier, the place of camp meetings, the relationship of churches in early Indiana, and the development of an evangelical religious ethos. However, it is primarily the story of Farmer and of his adventures on the Indiana frontier as told through his autobiography. Among a number of observations that might be made about him, a comment appropriate to this point of the story is that Farmer was a restless soul who never stayed at one task for very long.

Farmer indicated himself, writing in 1872, that he knew no better year in his life than the one after his success on the Franklin circuit. In two years he had received nine hundred church members, and he was highly regarded. Furthermore, he was then given an appointment to Greencastle, considered a plum assignment. In just a few years the people of Greencastle would make the point that their community and their church should serve as the location of the first Methodist college in Indiana—Indiana Asbury (later DePauw University).

But for reasons unknown—except for mentioning that he had a very successful year at Greencastle—Farmer related no stories of what happened on the Greencastle circuit nor did he explain why it was a successful year.[3] What he wrote about instead was his sudden interest in business. Evidently Farmer originally believed he could invest in business and still travel a circuit. However, because of problems in the business, he located, giving up his preaching appointment, and without further comment indicates that he had saved eighty dollars.

At this point Farmer is in the prime of his life. But his reporting of what happens in the four years, from 1833 through 1836 is spotty:

Soon after the new firm was organized, one of my partners suspected the other of dishonesty, making known his suspicions to me. He even persuaded me to buy out the dissatisfied partner, and then all the business was entrusted to him.

The retiring member of the firm, Mr. Asner LaBerteaux, now living at Bloomington, was the gentleman who admonished me of danger. I bought out both gentlemen's interest and took upon my self all the credits and debts of the old firm, so that the other old partner, Mr. King, was now my clerk. He soon grew to be very careless with the books, and seemed to be indifferent to my interests in every way, although one of my boys was in the store as an assistant.

Watching him closely, I ascertained that LaBerteaux's fears were not groundless. In order to save my self, I was compelled to locate, and on the expiration of his [King's] year's service, I discharged him. I was now left with about five thousand dollars worth of goods, some little indebtedness at the river, and with an oil mill with about five hundred bushels of seed in it, the whole amount left on my hands reaching about eight thousand dollars; outside of three thousand dollars or more in the hands of the people. I took my boy who was about fifteen years old, into the store with me, and as he had a pretty good education, he made all my calculations for me.[4]

It was my custom to invoice about three times a year. By paying interest I could get all the money I wanted. In the course of a year I could manage the concern very nicely. The gentleman from whom I bought goods at the river in Madison, Indiana, was the cashier of the bank at that place. One day, after I had finished buying a bill of goods, he said to me, "Sir, you ought to have more capitol invested in your store for you could then sell more goods."

I agreed with him, but expressed an unwillingness to go in debt and that I wished to be careful and thus avoid disasters. He then informed me he was the cashier of the bank there, and assured me I could have as many goods as I wanted, and that he would stand good for me. I observed that he knew nothing about me, nor my business standing. He said he would risk me, and urged me to go with him to the bank. I therefore consented to add to that already purchased about five hundred dollars worth of such goods as I thought I could most readily sell, but before I took my departure, I had bought some twenty three hundred dollars worth of goods in addition to those already purchased. I returned home with a very heavy stock of goods. Making quick sales and promptly collecting the money, I was enabled to pay off my bank debt by the expiration of the fourth month after the debt was contracted. During that year I cleared about a thousand dollars; in addition to this I supported my family and ran the oil mill successfully in such a manner as to make a good interest on that concern.

My good health again returning, I concluded to go back to my life work, and I sold out my store to a couple of gentlemen, a Mr. Robinson and his father-in-law, and began actively to close up the business of the establishment. I had three thousand dollars out in the hands of the people on accounts for goods sold and delivered.

While setting up this business, I ascertained that the Salt works belonging to the State, were to be sold at public auction, together with a section of land adjoining them and I attended the sale and bought them, paying for them in installments.[5] After running the works awhile I sold three fourths of my interest to three gentlemen, each one of whom bought a fourth interest. I now formed a circuit through that region of country contiguous to the salt works and preached to the people, and yet found time to look after my business, for some five years, when I sold out all my interest at a pretty good profit.[6]

Meantime the sale of the lands came on at the place where Chicago now stands, that city being then a mere village with but one white man in it; and I attended, arriving in advance of the two ship loads of speculators from the east who also attended. I went to see the chief of the Sioux tribe of Indians with the view of ascertaining whether I could get up a school among them, but learned at his house he had gone west in search of an Indian who had helped to kill a white man a short time before.

There were four Indians engaged in the murder, and their tribes had surrendered them up to the United States government to be executed. Before the day appointed for their execution, the four condemned wretches had been granted the privilege of a short farewell visit to their friends, and as was the prevailing custom the chiefs of the tribes to which they belonged guaranteed the prompt return of their fellows. In case of a failure to do so, on the part of the condemned, then the chief, who had made the guarantee on behalf of such person, was required to bring the fugitive in for punishment. The three confederates had returned but the fellow for whom the chief was searching had failed to appear, and the chief had gone out west to arrest him and bring him back. I continued to remain there until the sales were about ready to begin. One Sunday by request I preached to the people: a large well-dressed audience with only three women in the congregation, and I have no doubt this was the first sermon ever preached in Chicago. I had taken about one thousand dollars along with me with which to buy land but found the prices as I then thought ranging so fabulously high, I declined buying.

I now made a journey further west across the country toward the Mississippi taking with me a large lot of such little gifts for the Indians as my experience taught me would be most acceptable, and with which I had provided myself before leaving home. Going directly west from

Woodland Indians, such as those Eli Farmer met in Indiana and Illinois, lived in wigwams such as these. They might also have built cabins and longhouses in their villages.

Chicago, I traveled about forty or fifty miles the first day, crossing a wide prairie whose every scene was a stranger to me.

Late in the afternoon we observed a large grove of timber in front of us, and believing we would find water there we drew near to it. Just before we reached the timber, our ears were saluted by a wonderful series of loud yells and cries, and we concluded they were human voices. Riding a little way further on, we came to the Fox River, at which place we found some 25 or 30 Indians engaged in driving a large body of fish up that beautiful stream. They would now and then use their bows and arrows in taking up an occasional fish. Crossing the river we rode up to their Indian village, the squaws disappearing with their children at our approach, and we remained some time among them engaged in a friendly talk with several big, rough fellows, who were reclining upon some robes within their wig-wams. By and by we distributed our little gifts among them. This occasioned them to be very friendly with us.

We pursued our journey some distance further west, but at length Mr. West who was my brother-in-law, prevailed upon me to return home. In returning we had to exercise a great deal of prudence in selecting a route, as we were wholly unacquainted with the country we were now traversing. Crossing at length the Kankakee River, we struck the main road leading from Chicago down to Danville.

I had traded off my horse at Chicago for a very large horse and I was now riding him while his back was sore under the saddle. Soon after striking the road mentioned, a prairie wolf jumped up along side of the road, and ran scampering off away from us as rapidly as possible. I cried out that we must catch him, and we then gave him a fine chase. During the pursuit my brother-in-law lost his blanket, and returned to get it, while I rose on closely following the fleeing beast.

Following the animal about a mile, I succeeded in overhauling him, and began whipping him savagely as onward we rushed, till he finally squatted down in the grass. My brother-in-law

Sawmill at Kossuth, Indiana, ca. 1885. Sawmills were common in Indiana, and Eli Farmer's sawmill may have been much like this one.

rode up, and, dismounting, got ready to dispatch him with the butt end of his whip, but the wolf became again badly frightened and ran off, thus affording us another and more successful chase. After killing him, I concluded to use his hide for a sale blanket for my crippled horse. I prepared the skin as best I could for that purpose and put it under my saddle, after which we returned to the road and resumed our homeward journey.

Pretty soon we were troubled somewhat by the green flies, and bees, that were following up our trophy, for the hid[e] of the wolf had already began to be tainted. A little further on I was compelled to throw it away to get rid of their presence. The annoyance however did not cease, even now that the hide had been thrown away, for the pests persisted in following up the odor left on the horses' back, so that we were surrounded by swarms of green flies all the day long.

We arrived home in due time, and now felt satisfied with our own country.

I now resolved to improve my farm. About this time the state was committed to a wild improvement system, and numerous roads and canals were agitating the minds of the people of the young commonwealth. Believing that this system would prove to be a ruinous one, by bringing the state into competition with herself thus raising the price of labor beyond the ability of employers throughout the state, I was greatly opposed to such a policy. Fearing that the improvement system was yet to assume more gigantic proportions, I hired six or seven men to assist me in clearing a considerable portion of my land, in advance of the anticipated rise in the daily wages of laborers.

These laborers worked for me about a year, cutting off a great deal of timber, and preparing the land for meadows, building a barn, and fencing in a quarter section of land for a pasture. I took good care to show my employees where my farm lines ran, so as to prevent any trespassing on their part on the lands of my neighbors. While the greater part of the work was progressing, I was busily engaged collecting my outstanding debts, and occasionally preaching a funeral, or uniting in marriage some of my matrimonially inclined friends.

Notwithstanding my precautions, one of my hands inadvertently trespassed upon the land of one of my neighbors and cut up some of his tim[b]er, cutting down a little tree out of which he made twenty rails. On my return home I heard of the matter, and told the man who did it to be more careful in the future, for my injured neighbor was a very close and exacting man, assuring him I would call upon him and either replace the time or pay for the damage done.

The first opportunity that presented itself, was some time afterwards, and occurred at the big log-rolling upon my own premises, at which I had four companies of hands. Thinking this a good time, I informed my neighbor, Mr. Phillip Bunger of what my employee had done. He became very angry, and finding he had no control whatever of his angry passions, I left him and went to another company and joined their ranks, as I did not wish to have any difficulty with any man at or about my own house.

After the rolling was over, we began getting out some timbers again. Mr. Bunger came to me where we were at work and abused us considerably but would not accept of the money proffered him by me, to pay for what we had damaged him. Some of the young men wished to whip him then, but I would not suffer it. This happened I remember on Friday.

On the following day I went to town, with a view of attending to a lot of unfinished business connected with the store, and while thus engaged, I was attacked for the fourth time by Mr. Bunger, who now threatened to whip me. He abused me roughly offering me many gross intemperate insults. Some of my neighbors wanted me to whip him, but I refused to do so, when others of my friends interfered in my behalf and made him cease his abuse and threatenings.

He next provided himself with a cowhide with a view to chastise and degrade me, and coming up to me, informed me very coldly he had gotten it for me and proposed to use it. Said I, "Sir, were you to pause for a moment and give yourself up to sober reflections, you would abandon your designs."

He still persisted in his rashness, saying he would whip me.

A very powerful man who was a friend of mine, caught hold of his throat and pushing him roughly ejected him from the room. Another neighbor came to me now with the advice that I would better slip off home as Mr. Bunger had avowed his purpose to whip me out before him, before night fall of that day, but he added after a moment's hesitation, that he did not think I would drive well. In order to get rid of him I slipped off from town and went home where I studied over the matter calmly, and where I made up my mind that if he attacked me the fifth time I would cure him, and yet I prayed that the whole matter might be directed of the Lord.

When I arrived home I said to my wife that I desired her also to pray over the matter, telling her that if my enemy came to me again with his swaggering threats I would take that fact that he had been providentially sent to me to receive a whipping. She smiled as she said that "that was a difficult way of settling such affairs."

Sure enough he came to my house early next morning, bearing in his hand a large cudgel, and was fully prepared to whip me, as he supposed. Fully settled in my purpose, I took down my wagon whip, and calmly awaited his attack. As he came up I spoke to him in a friendly way, and after we had talked a moment, he began to abuse me again, in an exceedingly coarse manner. I went close up to him, having my whip conveniently arranged for my purpose, and gave him a fine opportunity to strike me if he wished to do so, and yet tried to pacify him, but he grew more demonstrative. He was sitting on his horse, and soon became so nervously excited he could scarcely remain in his saddle. I watched him closely to ascertain when he intended to strike me. In a moment he raised in his stirrups to strike and as he did so, I caught him by his collar and pulled him off of his horse, and catching him now by the breast, I managed to get so close to him that his lick missed me. Our struggle frightened the horse and he broke away from us. We at once became involved in the fight, in which I managed to throw my adversary. I now laid the lash to him in a lively manner, and punished him so sharply he tried to run away, but at every jump I hit him a severe lick, so that he soon found he could not escape me. Running along thus for about a hundred yards, he grabbed at a club, and as he stooped over I gave him a good cut across his rear. He sprang up with the club in his hand, but as he raised I took a firm hold upon him and bade him throw his club down [---] would tear him to pieces. My hands were amused spectators of the fight.

After disarming him I ordered him to return to the stable where his horse now was, but he said —"No, I will go home."

"But you shall not, sir, go back and get your horse, or I will give you the lash again."

After I had made him go back for his horse, I said to him, "now if you have not received enough of this just let me know, and as you compelled me to take upon myself this unpleasant duty, I will try to accommodate you at any time."

He promised to do so no more. As he rose out toward his home I accompanied him, talking with him as we journeyed along. When we arrived near a certain woods pasture he began to grow insulting again, and I caught him by the throat and running him against a fence choked him til his tongue protruded and he began to try to beg. "Get down on your knees, you rascal" I cried, and I made him kneel down, for I thought he was exhausting my patience.

"Now sir," said I "stand out here"—indicating the position I wished him to take, and he did as I had bidden him. I did this to let him know I had conquered him. I now informed him we would go down and look at the timber about which he pretended to feel affronted, telling him again I would pay him whatever it was worth. He told me he would take whatever any body would say it was worth, and I permitted him to return home. As I returned I found one of my hired hands in the grove but I didn't suppose he had heard what had passed between Mr. Bunger and myself and so kept silent.

On the next day I divided out my hands and then [sent] them to different localities to attend to different "rollings" in the neighborhood to pay back similar work done for me by my neighbors. Mr. Bunger and I were thrown together at the same rolling, and I worked with him till noon, by which time I ascertained the news had been made known to the public through those who had witnessed the affair, and I went to town to report the matter in advance of the court. Going to the magistrate's office, I informed squire Butler I had horse-whipped a man and I wanted to know what sort of a crime I had committed.

Said he, "I am no woman's priest, I do not forgive sins."

He then assured me, after he had been made acquainted with the facts, that I "ought to have whipped him the other day."

But I told him I thought differently as he was now cured.

"Well," said he, "can you prove you whipped him?"

"Yes," said I, "here is a witness."

After the witness was sworn and examined[,] the magistrate had Bunger brought into court where he was fined three dollars and amerced in the cost of the proceedings. Ever afterward Mr. B was a civil law-abiding citizen, and at length came to be a good friend of mine.

* * *

1835

A short time after my return home I began laboring in my field in Brown County again, where I labored zealously and with good success till about the time of the sitting of conference at New Albany. I attended the session, and told the conference they must send a preacher to supply the work I had organized out in Brown County, telling that body that in case they failed to do so, I would institute a system of my own, and supply the work, developing my ideas pretty fully, at which they seemed to be greatly amused. They told me I was just the man to send out there, and that I must come back into the conference and be sent there myself. I was loath to re-enter the conference for I experienced even then a great aversion for their tyrannical powers, and I hesitated some time before I assented to their wish. I was sent back to Brown County to the work I had formed. I had a few appointments in two other counties.

My Presiding Elder this year was Dr. Tolbert. During the year [1837–38] I formed other churches, some of which were established under unusually adverse circumstances.

A certain region of the county was known all through that section by the undignified appellation of "Big Hog Thief Settlement," while another settlement was distinguished by the vulgar sobriquet of "Little Hog Thief." A great many vicious bad men lived in both neighborhoods, but I resolved to see nevertheless what could be done toward benefiting them, by carrying the gospel into their settlements. In some instances it reformed some very bad men, but seemed to fail upon various bad men who were leaders in all manner of evil practices, such as gambling, fighting, stealing horses and the like. These fellows became so desperately wicked and audacious that they absolutely stole every good horse in a wide circuit, extending out into the adjoining counties. They became so bold and powerful that good citizens were compelled to organize a band of "Regulators." A fellow by the name of John Holland, whom I had taken into the church, was the captain of the company. Many others of the organization had also joined the M.E. Church under my ministrations, for the company was one hundred strong. Besides this effort upon the side of peace, many citizens in the adjoining counties raised more than five hundred dollars by private subscription to assist in breaking up the den of ["Hootings"?]—as the robbers and thieves were called using the slang of Black Masons. So unsettled had affairs become in consequence of the insecurity of property by reasons of these Hootings that attorneys agreed to refuse an employment from any of the gang, promising further to decline accepting a fee or appearing as counsel against any of the Regulators, in case they would scatter and disband the desperate clan.

I was generally apprized by the boys as they were passing around in furtherance of their common design, as to what was being done towards contributing to so happy a consummation. Pretty soon they began to have trouble, many of their number being required to defend themselves in court against charges lodged against them by the grand juries.

A sort of a jack-leg petty logger Stephens by name, was the only person characterless enough to advocate their cause. Being unscrupulous and utterly depraved, they did not hesitate in swearing each other out of trouble. During one of my visits to that section, they stole a horse belonging to a Methodist Presiding Elder living in Boone County and ran the horse into Brown County, after which all trace of the animal was lost. The regulators kept pressing them on all sides, and by dint of much litigation, and some violence, by and by began to drive the stubborn rascals out of the county. Stephens became such a troublesome meddlesome auxiliary of the guilty felons, that orders were sent to him requiring his departure, and warning him of trouble in case he stood an hour on the order of his going, after the expiration of sixty days allowed him in which to settle his business affairs. He swore he would not leave.

About the expiration of the time specified, the captain of the Regulators marshaled, as I afterward learned from one of the participants, about sixty men, at Bedford and rode over into Brown County, and about daylight surrounded Stephens' house, the party being well armed, and succeeded in capturing the fellow. After securing his hands so as to render him entirely helpless, they conveyed him up a little hollow and proceeded to prepare a suitable punishment for him. The graceless scamp manifested great bravery and independence, flopping his arms and crowing in imitation of a game-fighting cock.

This captain now formed a circle around him, each man turning his face away from the victim, save the one with the chastening rod, so as to have no eye-witness to the scene that followed. John Winfrey, then, stepped out of the ranks and began whipping him, and applied the lash to him until he supposed it would be about all the fellow would do to crawl of[f] home, and then stopped as he didn't wish to kill him. Just after Winfrey had released him he turned to Winfrey, who was a leading Methodist in his section, and looking him angrily in the eye scornfully and even bravely said, "We will return thanks to the Lord and be dismissed!" He hobbled off home, but afterwards was careful to not allow any of his old patrons to hang about him, and he was never again molested.

About this time my Presiding Elder Mr. Tolbert came around to attend our first Quarterly meeting, and in a conversation with him concerning the recent stealing of a Presiding Elder's horse, on the part of these fellows I remarked that I believed I felt like giving ten dollars toward bringing the guilty parties to justice, when he, assuming an important air, indignantly replied, "Never let me hear you say anything of that kind again." I bore his unjust rebuke so meekly that he felt encouraged to go on with it, and he now began to abuse me in a very insulting manner. Feeling deeply wounded in my feelings, I said, "Sir, I am a Methodist preacher, and I will let you know right now that you shall not talk so to me, notwithstanding you are my Presiding Elder; I am not a dog, nor a slave, that I should bear this insolent abuse on your part."

My plain defense caused him to change his manner entirely, and he now became very sullen. He went to the Quarterly meeting which was held in an adjoining settlement, and he still treated me with a dogged indifference. After preaching one sermon he went away, leaving all the work on my hands. He seemed afraid to preach in the neighborhood.

The second Quarterly meeting was held near the same locality. He brought another preacher with him to preach for him as we afterward learned, on the Sabbath. He preached only one sermon, a bitter, violent, and insulting sermon, on Saturday morning, which affronted the entire congregation. He called on me to preach on Saturday night and I did so. My sermon had a powerful effect upon the audience and the result was we had a good meeting, at which two very clear conversions were made.

When I had finished my sermon he said to me, "Sir, you cannot preach!" I replied to his very gracious and gratuitous assurance by saying, "Well, sir, if I have but one talent and am instrumental in doing good, and saving souls, and you have five talents and yet do no good, accomplish nothing, God will damn you, sir, for a misimprovement of all your wonderful talents.

My brethren now took the fight off my hands, and scared him till he finally became very angry.

I accompanied him to the next Quarterly meeting, but he would not allow me to preach. We were holding the meeting at a point where I had formally been very successful in making accessions to the church, and it was but natural that my old friends should want to hear me preach. He was so cruel to me here, that he caused very many members of the church to become disgusted and angry with him. Anxious for peace I proposed at one time that we get down on our knees and pray away the coldness existing between us, but he refused, but on the contrary, he bore down on me the more heavily as opportunities offered themselves.

The last Quarter meeting was held at what was called "Leatherwood Camp Ground." Previous to this meeting I had taken into the church three hundred persons at this place, and of course, had many friends among the people there. The Quarterly meeting was held here, on this occasion in connection with a campmeeting. I attended these meetings in order to meet my friends in that locality once more. Tolbert was yet angry, and his actions toward me were of a very insulting character.

A young brother stationed at Bedford came out on Saturday by previous arrangements, to preach the customary Elder's sermon on the Sabbath. A great many people came to me and said, "Brother Farmer, you must preach for us. The work, you see, is dying on the hands of these other men." I told them it was not my meeting, that it was in the hands of Tolbert, and that he would not permit me to preach. They then sought an interview with Tolbert, and urged in vain, their desires upon him. The young Bedford preacher, the Rev. Amsa Johnson, preached at 11 o'clock. This enterprising young man understood a big job on this occasion, by trying to prove that Adam was as originally created, a huge fellow physically, some four feet, I believe, between the shoulders, and eight or ten feet high, according to this lad's measurements, and as might reasonably have been expected, broke down under the gigantic enterprise. His wretched blundering destroyed also, the devotional feelings of the audience, pretty generally, they derided him not a little by their manifestations of skepticism on the subject.

After he had come down out of the stand, I inquired of the young man, "Amsa, where on this earth did you get that new revelation?"

Tobert interfered, and renewed his abusive attacks, telling me I was a meddlesome fellow.

The Rev. John McCrea was announced to preach at 3 o'clock in the afternoon, and that gentleman was persuaded by Tolbert [and] a few others to believe that he would succeed in getting up a powerful feeling among the people. The vast audience was particularly requested to arrange their engagements so as to be in readiness of this great work, to be inaugurated at that hour. I was sitting in the preacher's tent, just in the rear of the preachers' stand, when this announcement was made by Col. McCrea, and although I knew the Col to be a very able assistant upon such occasions, I yet felt constrained, to doubt their promises, and I said, "He will miss the world, he will touch neither side, edge, top nor bottom, as touching the matter of getting up a revival."

"How know you this?" said Tolbert, adding "you are always intermeddling." He then abused me roundly again, all of which I meekly bore in great good humor. The splendid effort even of Col. McCrea failed—his truly excellent sermon falling flat, and his terse fervid and eloquent exhortations accomplished nothing. The ears of sinner and saint seemed heavy, and their hearts hardened. Four or five other efforts were made subsequently but the clouds lowering over the congregation seemed to become only darker and denser. A local preacher came running to me and crying, "Farmer, you must come into the grounds and help us."

"I cannot go, sir," said I, "for if they will kill the people, they must also bury them themselves."

I was then lying down in the preachers' tent. They came for me the second and third times, urging me to preach. Tolbert had been in the tent a portion of the time the people were urging me to preach, and when he had gone out I rolled under a bed and covered myself with straw so as to hide from those who were importuning me. As I lay there under the bed in my place of concealment I heard the brethren mournfully lamenting over the sad condition of affairs, and I knew they were seeking me again. By and by I was discovered, and was again and again begged to preach. I told them the meeting was not of my appointment, but was in the hands of Tolbert, and besides Tolbert was opposed to my preaching and in thus trifling with them I backslid in feeling, and seemed to have lost the power of preaching.

About the time preparations were all made for the night meeting, Tolbert came to me and said, "Sir, you will have to preach and we will see what you shall do." I felt shocked, knowing that by my trifling I had lost a preaching spirit, and for a time I was undecided as to what I ought to do.

I at length got a number of my brethren and a few local preachers, to accompany me a short distance into the woods adjoining to hold a little prayer meeting. My thoughts were so unsettled that I found it impossible to decide upon a subject for a sermon. About the time I got down on my knees to pray, the bugle sounded the second and last call for services. While kneeling there I asked the Lord to forgive me for my ugliness, after which I exhorted the official members and the exhorters present to pray God to forgive me for my miserable bitterness of soul, and deliver me from all kinds of sins and evils. My brethren seemed anxious in my behalf, and prayed for me most fervently and we then returned to the meeting.

I chose for my text: "Awake thou that sleepest, and arise from the dead, and Christ shall give the light." I tried to open up my subject four or five times, failing sadly each time before I felt the right kind of a disposition to "preach." I experienced so many difficulties at the beginning that I felt almost persuaded to abandon the sermon. By and by the Lord touched my heart very sensibly, and forthwith began to feel the preaching effort come upon me, and my difficulties fled away like timid doves, and there was not jot nor hindrance in my pathway.

As I progressed with the discourse the power and unction of the Holy Spirit perceptibly increased till they became a mighty volume, and my words came to me as easily as birds cleave the air. As I looked over my congregation I saw the tears of sympathy and joy glistening in the eyes of my brethren and sisters, while sinners were tremblingly receiving my exhortations with deeply stricken hearts. By and by the joyful gladsome emotions of the Christians arose to loud acclaim unto the blessed redeemer, who had done such wonderful things for us, and then there was a long continued season of hand shaking, clapping of hands, and triumphant shouting. About the time the meeting had reached its acme, a characterless fellow by the name of Thomas Whitehead who had come to the meeting with a view of breaking it up, fired off a pistol, close to the rear of the stand, and I immediately shouted out to him, "Come in devil; we are not afraid of you, and are ready for you!"

After this I now jumped over the rear railing of the preacher's stand and extended a general and pressing invitation for sinners and backsliders to come forward to the altar and seek forgiveness for sins, and there was a general rush to the altar. They came by platoons, yea, came by companies, and even battalions, and among them Whitehead, who was about the first one to reach the altar. The laborers at the altar were divided now with my brethren excepting the traveling preachers, all of whom stood aloof, refusing to lend a helping hand. More than fifty persons professed religion, including Whitehead, before leaving the altar, all of whom joined the church that night. The father of Whitehead was a New Light preacher, and a most excellent man. When he saw what his son had done, he became very happy for he had long since given his son over as an incorrigible outlaw and ruffian, and came running to me, and throwing his arms about my neck cried, and even shouted for joy. The new convert soon became a Methodist preacher, and was a useful man ever afterward. He continued to faithfully perform his arduous duties as a minister of the gospel till death released him about one year from this writing, from labor he was called to a higher and brighter place of usefulness. His death was one of the happiest ever known in his section of country. He died as [he] had lived, a consistent Christian. Sweetly resting in Jesus he awaits the call of the bridegroom, bidding him enter the marriage feast far beyond the skies.

After repeated efforts I failed to effect a reconciliation with my Presiding Elder. Conference came on in the fall, and I again went to Tolbert and said, "Brother Tolbert, if you think you cannot forgive me, I want you to let me know it now, in advance of the setting of the conference, and I will locate, for I am well aware of the powers you may exercise in controlling my appointments in the future, and I do not wish to be thrown out into some unsettled locality, where I cannot support my family. I have given up the great part of my life upon waste places, laboring hard to build up the church, and making nothing except barely enough for our frugal meals. "Now I am willing to work longer if you can provide me a small field of labor where I can have some time during the year for reading and studying and in otherwise improving myself. If I neglect this matter a little while longer, it will then be too late for improvement."

Said he, "What place would suit you?"

I mentioned the names of four or five places as being agreeable ones for me in every way, and I again urged him to advise me in time, in case he concluded to refuse my request.

12

Danville, Christian Union, and Sectarianism
1838 to 1842

As he had feared, Eli Farmer was disappointed in the response from Presiding Elder Tolbert as he relates below:

1838
We went to the conference.[1] When the appointments were read out I anxiously awaited to hear from my fate, and finally heard with a saddened heart my name read out in connection with Danville Circuit. This circuit had given eighty dollars to its preacher the year previous, and yet, this work was cut in two and the big end thereof assigned to me. Thus was I trapped again by my designing and cruel enemy, but with a brave heart I went to my appointment, but my already strong aversion for the arbitrary character of some of the ecclesiastical powers connected with the church government was only strengthened by this cruel exercise of power, on the part of my superiors, the greater part of whom were conversant with the facts relative to the case. I began to loath the tyranny of my church government. Aching for a drop of water, a poisonous liquid had been offered me instead. My conference had become—shall I speak the hated word—yes, had become a tyrant: Oh: my church a tyrant.

"Tyrant! It irks me so to call my prince: But just resentment and hard usage joined the unwilling ward: and grating so it is. Take if for it is thy due!"

For how would my revered superiors say are their inferiors in official positions, were free from fetters, when they laid whom they pleased in basest bonds, and brought whom they pleased to poverty and sorrow—empowered too as they were, to drive us, as I was driven, "like wretches down the rough tide of power." Could a free man, a minister of God's full gospel long bear such petty violence and not be aroused at the great call of nature to check the growth of such evangelical spoilers who fain would have made me a slave, and then peradventure have told me afterwards it was my character." By whatsoever name such oppressions come disguised, yet, one cannot fail to see that they are oppressions and oppressions of so mild though terrible character as would, if unchecked, turn nature's bright plains into putrid pens, as rapidly and severely as though the rapacious hand of the despoiler were to blight them with the pestilence of rugged horrid war! I humbly felt that "Power is a curse in a despot's hands, but in a bigot tyrant, a terrible curse."

Injured and unredressed—having asked for bread, to receive a stone, I turned away with a sad heart, to take upon myself this heavy load, disgusted with the wicked cruel, foul wrong done me, a degrading, defiling wrong whose kindred tyrannies have many a time dethroned kings.

I found on going to my new field of labor, that it would be utterly impossible to support my family there, and so decided to remove to Bloomington to my farm, fully determined as I told my wife at the time, to locate at the expiration of the year, but my wife objected to a removal just then. I argued we could not support ourselves in that barren region. But she said, "We have never abandoned a work assigned us till our labors were finished." "Do you go on with your work" she continued, "and I will teach school in order to help support the family."

By the assistance of the clerk of Hendrix County my wife succeeded in organizing a pretty large school, for that day, and she got along with it in good manner for three months.

The following winter was an uncommonly unpleasant one, especially so for traveling. The roads were covered all the winter through pretty much with deep mud. My friends did all they could for me in every way and we met with good success in reviving the hearts of the Christians and causing sinners to turn to Christ. During the winter I wore out my cloth[e]s, and also wore out three horses. All of the horses were broken down by having their legs skinned and barked in a fearful manner.

One day during the winter, I was called to the bedside of a dying man. I found him ready for the great and solemn transition from time to eternity. He told me he had been a member of the church forty years, and that God was sustaining him in his hour of affliction, and then told me he wished me to be present when he died.

I addressed him somewhat as follows, "Now brother, as you are about passing over, I want you to leave us messages at as late a period as possible, so when I ask you a question as to whether all is well, in case you are unable to reply verbally, and cannot talk, please raise your fingers, and we will know by that you are at peace with God.

The old veteran gave us the signal as he went over the streams of "Jordan" and we knew that "all was well" with him.

The religious interests grew stronger and stronger during the winter among my little flock. Towards spring we began to make some inroads upon the Presbyterians at Danville, greatly to the indignation of the pastor of that church, a Mr. Chase. This minister became so angry at me that he abused me roundly to many of the citizens of the community.[2]

A short time after this my wife and I held a two days meeting at a little town by the name of Winchester, about seven miles west of Danville, where we had a few Methodist friends. I preached there on Saturday and Sunday. The work broke out in a powerful manner. Feeling greatly encouraged we tarried there some seven days, taking into the church about forty persons, all of whom professed religion before the meeting broke.

In addition to these accessions, some forty others, Baptist and Presbyterians, professed religion. I sent out for assistance to my Methodist brethren who were my neighbors at the time, but could get no help. Failing in this I concluded I would try my Christian union plan, which I had long contemplated, and so I sent a message for help to the Presbyterian preacher at Danville; I also sent for a Cumberland Presbyterian preacher by the name of Somers, a warm hearted zealous Christian; and also for a Baptist preacher whom I knew to be a good man! These good people all came to my assistance.[3]

Taking them into a private room I thus addressed them, "Now brethren, the Lord is working wonderfully among the people here, about forty persons having joined our church and some forty others have professed religion whose parents are members of other churches, and have not united with any denomination. I suppose that these who have not yet joined the church, will most likely wish to join the church to which their parents belong. Now I want you to divest yourself, as I have done, of your own private opinions, and prejudices, and come into our meeting and sing, and pray and preach with us for a revival. I promised them that at the proper time they should have opportunity to open the doors of their churches to receive such of the converts as wished, to unite with their respective denominations."

Brother Chase said, "But I cannot work as you Methodist[s] do." "We do not wish you to work like Methodist[s] do, work just like a man of God," was my reply. To that he said, "Well, I rec[k]on that will do." Mr. Somers preached a good, warm sermon, and called for mourners, with good success, and we all went into the work, excepting Mr. Chase who held back. Towards the close of the meeting, I went out into the congregation in search of Mr. Chase and found him beleaguering a weeping sinner in one corner of the room, whom he was exhorting to be converted. He labored here until he got warmed up, and then went forward where the good people were singing and shouting and praying, and called out to us. "Stop, brethren, stop. I want to talk awhile," but the brethren were so engaged they paid no attention to him. He finally opened his mouth as loud as any of us, and thus got rid of his timidity and his prejudices.

Just before dismissing the congregation, we opened the doors of the church, the Baptist minister stationed in one corner of the church to receive at that point and as wished to join that denomination, the Presbyterian clergymen stationed in another corner to receive into that church such as wished to become Presbyterians, while I occupied a third corner to welcome to the Methodist church, such as desired to commit themselves with that denomination. I then explained to the converts the arrangements thus provided for them and in compliances with my request, each denomination then began to receive its own converts, the converts going to the preacher representing the church to which they desired to join, and giving him their hands and names.[4]

The work went on after this Christ-union plan, working with eminent satisfaction all around. All prejudices gave way, every heart was filled with love and union sentiments and all were happy and joyous. We scarcely knew the difference between Baptists, Presbyterians, Methodist[s], for we had indeed become, "one in Christ Jesus."

The meeting was continued for five weeks. Immediately following this meeting we held a joint campmeeting at a point about seven miles distant, which was kept up some two weeks, and at which many others were added to each of the churches represented therein. Seven young men of the number taken in to church at this place afterward became ministers of the gospel. It was a mighty work. The whole country for many miles seemed to be lighted up with the bright and blessed beams shining forth with a heavenly radiance from the Sun of Righteousness. The power of God was sensibly among us. These union meetings were continued at stated times, for more than three years successively.

1839

Conference came on this year at Lawrenceburg, and although my cloth[e]s were worn out, and I had no money where with to defray my expenses, I determined, nevertheless to attend it, for I was wholly fixed in my purpose to locate. Besides, I was more than ever before, anxious to test further my Christian union plan. About this time a merchant in Danville called me into his store, one day, and gave me a suit of cloth[e]s. I took my family home, and then went on to conference.

Bishop Simpson preached the initiatory sermon at this session of the conference.[5] I had now become fully satisfied, the M.E. Church had abandoned her ancient simplicity and her ancient faith in a great measure, and had become too nearly assimilated to the things of this world, so as to become fashionable, and I concluded she had reached her growth.[6] She was now, according to Bishop Simpson on this occasion just a century old.[7]

In pursuance of my plan above mentioned, I asked permission to locate. My request was opposed by most of my brethren who offered all sorts of objections to my locating. They offered me better work if I would remain with them. I told them my word had gone out and I would not

An 1833 painting by Cornelius Pering of Indiana Seminary (left) and the first college building in what became Indiana University in Bloomington, Indiana (right). The college building held a chapel that Eli Farmer preached in.

retract it, and I was finally given my papers of withdrawal, whereby I was shown to be in good standing among them.

On the day of my withdrawal, I wrote on the "Fly leaf" of a book, which I had purchased at that period, these words, "This day Methodism is one hundred years old; and this day begins a new era with Eli P. Farmer."

* * *

Many of [my] friends urged me to hold a campmeeting about this time, and we went for that purpose at the specified time and place. While this meeting was well under way, my Presiding Elder sent a Methodist preacher to us, to manage the meeting, and to take it out of my hands. He claimed the power to control the meeting by authority vested in him by the Presiding Elder. I informed him that it was my meeting, and as I had not sent for him, he had better leave, especially so, since he was too green to manage any sort of a meeting.

My action was endorsed by my local preachers and the lay members of the Methodist church, but the traveling preachers were opposed to me.[8] I continued to preach my Christian union doctrines, but remained in the M.E. church, for I believed by so remaining therein I could have more influence with my Methodist friends.

About this period I was greatly in need of means upon which to support my family, but by burning a couple of brick kilns pretty successfully, I managed to provide for my family's wants, and also to build a brick house. While engaged in watching with jealous eye my struggling child of Christian Union, many times wondering whether the frail, feeble infant would survive the gross and bitter attacks of Sectarianism.[9] One Phillip May, the then stationed preacher at Bloomington, for the Methodists, preached a sermon on the subject of Baptism.[10] In this dis-

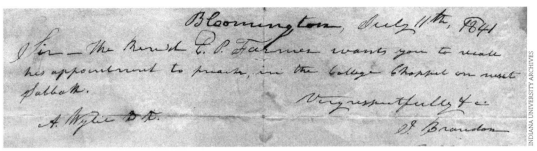

Eli Farmer and Indiana University president Andrew Wylie both believed in a union of Christian denominations. Wylie had even invited Farmer to preach in the college chapel with this idea in mind. This angered Methodist authorities, so Farmer decided to cancel his preaching engagements at the chapel. This note is that cancellation. It is from J. Brandon (for Farmer) to Wylie, dated July 11, 1841, and is kept in the IU President's Office Records. The note reads as follows:

Sir—The Rev'd E. P. Farmer wants you to recall his appointment to preach, in the College Chappel on next Sabbath.
Very respectfully &c.
J. Brandon
A. Wylie D D.

course he tried to destroy immersion altogether. The Campbellites took up the glove at once, and renewed the fight with great force, and of course succeeded in gaining the victory routing their adversary on all sides.[11]

During May's absence, they got up a water revival, and were about to steal a number of May's best members.[12] The Methodist[s] held a council to decide what was best to be done. They failed to suggest any remedy, and I now suggested that I bring up my Christian Union plan and get up an excitement about that system, so as to supercede their water baptism excitement, and they consented to my proposition.

Our first meeting was announced for the 4th of July, at the courthouse, the 4th coming round that year on Sunday. On the return of brother May he consented to assist me if I would change the place of meeting from the courthouse to the College chapel. We obtained permission from the resident Trustees of the College to hold the meeting in the chapel.

Dr Andrew Wylie who was then President of the institution, and who was one of the wisest and most learned men of the west, at that time, received us cordially. I reasonably counted on the assistance of brother May, for that was the arrangement between us. I continued the meetings every Sabbath for six weeks, notwithstanding I was abandoned by brother May, about the time of the first meeting, who became insulted on account of some imaginary slight, and withdrew, taking with him five or six Methodists, all of whom went to the Methodist church and held opposition meetings.

Dr Wylie paid me great respect, cheerfully yielding up his Sabbath lecture hour to me. He was very anxious that the meetings should be kept up, but I was compelled to abandon them by reason of the difficulties engendered by a Quarterly meeting held in the M.E Church a short time before we gave them up. The Quarterly meeting got up a fuss with me, by spreading it about that "Farmer was about to divide the Methodist church." So I was compelled to abandon these meetings in order to see what the result of the before mentioned disturbance would be.

When asked in the Quarterly meeting Presiding Elder John Miller what I meant by the Public Square religion, and in answering him, I took occasion to defend my positions, and succeeded so well in so doing, the Elder let me off very pleasantly.[13]

In the year 1842, Rev. Isaac Owen was stationed in Bloomington.[14] *During the year he undertook to build a Methodist church, and he pressed me very closely to donate a large amount of money for that purpose. I told him if he would demean himself aright I would help him a little; otherwise I would not help him any at all. He was a very strict sectarian and watched closely. At the proper time for doing so, he wrote to a minister then living at Terre Haute, to consent to deliver the sermon at the laying of the cornerstone of the new church, and the man assented to the request. When the appointment arrived the fellow came not, but, on the contrary disappointed the people. At the request of my brethren I was asked to make the address, and mounting the stone in which was deposited a Bible, a Methodist Discipline; a hymn book and fifty cents in silver, I delivered an extempore sermon. During this period every where I gave my audience same broken doses of my Christian union even upon this occasion.*

Sectarianism in Indiana in the 1840s

Farmer's account of the events of 1839 to 1842 in Bloomington serves as an opening to examine an important theme of this study: sectarianism in Indiana in the 1840s. Persons who study religion in Indiana or, for that matter, religion in the West, cannot but be overwhelmed with the multiplying of various denominations, sects, assemblies, associations, conventions, and brotherhoods during this period.

In his two volume history *The Old Northwest Pioneer Period: 1815–1840*, R. Carlyle Buley describes what was happening in the religious field on the western frontier:

> No chapter in the history of religion in our country offers more complexities or more interest than that which deals with the Middle West in the first half of the nineteenth century. . . . Although revivalism and the question of freedom of the will precipitated sectarian difference, there were really dozens of matters of dogma and church organization and government which caused fission. Denominations split along one line on one issue, along another line on another. So numerous and complex were the schisms and crossings over and so illogical were many of them, that groups and sects not infrequently found themselves back in the fold whence they had started. So confusing did the history of the Protestant sects become that no historian, church or lay, has been able to make a clear and organized presentation of its course.[15]

While it is true, as Buley suggests, that many of the "schisms and crossings over" were illogical, it is also true that changes within the evangelicalism of the time, much of it brought about by revivalism, offer insight into Indiana sectarianism. Farmer's own story should help in understanding these changes.

One key change is how the idea of "republicanism," as understood by Farmer, is related to evangelical sectarianism. In Farmer's day and also today the word "sectarian" is used in several ways. For theologians and sociologists studying religion, the word "sectarian," signifying a tendency to break into separate groups, can be used to contrast with the word "catholic," meaning universal membership in a Christian body, in understanding doctrines of churches.[16] When comparing sectarianism on the frontier with catholicism, however, the differences can best be understood by the following series of statements representing contrasting tendencies. It is possible to put different groups on a scale—with Roman Catholics, Orthodox, and Anglican being the truest example of a catholic understanding, and American Quakers, Mennonites, and Baptists the truest examples of a sectarian understanding:

Catholic: The Church tends to be identified with the State.
Sectarian: The Church is separate from the state and often views the state as part of the world.

Catholic: Religion tends to be culture-affirming, believing that faith can change the culture. Christianity is often linked with western civilization.
Sectarian: The Church is to be separated from the fallen world. There is a suspicion of culture.

Catholic: Tradition is important in interpreting the Bible. Following the liturgical year is an example of the use of tradition.
Sectarian: Conscience–Spirit–Experience is used to interpret the Bible; there is no emphasis on the liturgical year.

Catholic: Religious authority is vested in the institutional church body.
Sectarian: Religious authority is vested in the local fellowship of believers.

Catholic: There is an elevated view of clergy; clergy are intermediaries between God and humanity; the education of clergy is essential.
Sectarian: There is a radical understanding of the priesthood of all believers. This radical understanding leads to an egalitarianism in which there is no special power or authority in the clergy. The education of clergy is not essential.

Catholic: The true Church is where the sacraments are rightly administered.
Sectarian: The true Church is where two or three believers are gathered in Jesus' name.

Catholic: Infants are baptized and are considered church members.
Sectarian: A believer's baptism is a symbol or sign of conversion; church membership is by voluntary decision.

Catholic: The unity of the Church is more important than the purity of the Church.
Sectarian: The purity of the Church is more important than the unity of the Church.

Catholic: The worship setting is based on the Old Testament temple with a center altar table.
Sectarian: The worship setting is based on the Old Testament synagogue with the pulpit and Bible center with no altar until revivalism introduced an altar area in front of the pulpit.

Catholic: The Kingdom of God is advanced by civilization and education.
Sectarian: The Kingdom is advanced by growing the church (revival).

As a general rule, all church schisms, whatever their reason, have been accompanied by the tendency to view the church in a more sectarian way than the original group. At the same time the groups that withdraw from the larger denominations grow more catholic in their understanding of the church as they mature.[17]

Through all of its history the established Christian churches in Europe—whether Roman Catholic, Orthodox, Reformed, Lutheran, Anglican, or Presbyterian—have been characterized by an understanding of the Church more catholic than sectarian. Sectarian groups—Anabaptists, Quakers, Moravians, and Puritan separatists—have been religious subgroups or minorities within an established catholic church culture. John Wesley in England launched a sectarian Methodist movement, but so feared sectarianism that he played ecclesiastical games to pretend that Methodists were really catholic Anglicans and not sectarian Methodists.

Colonial America, dominated by Congregationalists, Anglicans, Reformed, and Presbyterian churches, was religiously pluralistic, but the religious culture carried with it the European and catholic understandings of the Church. The major denominations baptized infants, honored the sacraments, elevated the office of clergy, and desired church unity rather than purity. Even the Baptists in New England, for all of their emphasis on religious freedom (and believers' baptism), were becoming institutionalized by the time of the Revolutionary War. Some of the denominations, at the writing of the U.S. Constitution, would have joined church and state.

The frontier experience, and especially camp meeting revivalism, changed much of that. On the frontier there was no established religious culture. The West was a religious clean slate ready to be written on. The first groups that wrote on it were the revivalists, who leaned strongly toward a sectarian understanding of the Church/Christianity. Because of their influence, religious sectarianism became a strong underpinning of a new religious culture. Thus, a different understanding of the doctrine of Christianity set American religious culture apart from European—or even eastern American—religious culture.

Farmer could serve as exhibit number one. Even though one of the purposes of the Methodist quarterly conference was to offer the Lord's Supper, Farmer never mentions that sacrament in his autobiography. He never mentions any Catholic church traditions, including the liturgical church year, or any Christian holy days, such as Christmas or Easter. Farmer never mentions Wesley's Sunday Service; he rarely mentions baptism; he receives members on the basis of their testimony, and there is no indication he ever required any of them to be baptized or instructed (although eventually, he does commit himself to believers' baptism); he rails against the trappings of culture including fashion, dancing, alcohol, and expensive church buildings; and when he leaves Methodism it is because he feels it has become too worldly.

Farmer is not an anomaly in these matters. If anything, he represents characteristics that were becoming widespread among Christian groups on the frontier: egalitarian, individualistic, suspicious of outside authority, and republican. Farmer was part of a seismic shift in America on how to do religion. Sectarian bodies had always operated on the fringes. Now, suddenly, on the American western frontier, these groups were becoming the dominant religious force. Minority religious tendencies were becoming majority religious tendencies. This is seen among Methodists, in the rapid rise of the Christian

Church, among the Baptists and Presbyterians, and then among the various splinters off these main denominations.

It is no wonder that by the mid-1840s even the Presbyterians were dividing: into Old School and New School, Cumberland, and New Lights. In Bloomington during this time there were four different groups of Presbyterians: Presbyterians, Associated Presbyterians (Seceders), Associated Reformed (Union) Presbyterians, and Reformed Presbyterians.[18]

Presbyterians were not alone. Methodists would suffer the O'Kelly (republican) split in Virginia in 1795, and then the Methodist Protestant split in 1822, followed by the Wesleyan Methodist split in 1844, and the Free Methodist split in 1859, with seeds of many more groups in the making. Baptists would divide into Separate Baptists and United Baptists and then, a group known as United Separate Baptists. They also further divided into Regular and Primitive Baptists, Missionary and anti-Missionary Baptists, and Free Will Baptists. Along the way they took the names of Particular Baptists and Hardshell Baptists.

These various splintering groups all exhibited sectarian understandings of the church: a disdaining of church tradition, authority apart from a centralized institution, egalitarianism, and membership on the basis of conversion and voluntary association. For the most part, except for the Quakers, this was happening even before the historically sectarian groups, such as the Brethren and Mennonites, were in Indiana. These latter groups found religious freedom and acceptance in Indiana. But the Indiana religious climate also fed their sectarian tendencies. Mennonites would divide into Conservative Mennonites, Old Order Evangelical Mennonites, General Conference Mennonites, the Missionary Church Association, the Woodland Amish Mennonites, Nonconference Conservative Mennonites, and several Amish divisions. The Brethren divided into Old German Baptists, Old Order German Baptists, Old Brethren, Dunkard Brethren, Brethren Church Ashland, Brethren Church Winona Lake (Grace Brethren), Brethren in Christ, and Apostolic Christian.[19]

By the 1840s the Quakers were dividing into Hicksites and Querneyites, and within a few years, they divided into the Indiana Yearly Meeting, the Friends General Conference, the Western Five Years Meeting, the Friends World Committee, the Western Conservative Meeting, and the Central Yearly Meeting. To add more complexity, the Millerites or Adventists were thriving in Indiana in the 1840s. There were also Mormons and Shakers.

Did all of the wrangling hurt the cause of religion on the western frontier and in America? Conventional wisdom would say yes. Sophisticated religious leaders despise religious wars and the wrangling that accompanies them. All groups, supposedly, lose in religious wars, and the cause of religion suffers. In the case of America on the western frontier, however, statistics argue against the conventional wisdom. The First Great Awakening in New England lasted perhaps twenty years. The Second Great Awakening, or the Western Revival lasted a hundred years. The First Great Awakening was cooled by the criticism and cynicism of New England church leaders.[20] There was no similar moderating voice on the frontier. Religion there thrived under the competition and the multiplicity of sects. Nathan Hatch points out that mainstream Protestant church historians in the twentieth century tended to interpret the frontier religious experience as a civilizing force, taming the frontier and leading to a kind of Protestant solidarity and the overcoming of sectarianism.[21] These historians often fail to see the other side of the frontier religious experience: egalitarianism, populism, division into many religious groups, anti-intellectualism, and—to put it in Hatch's words—the "democratization of American Christianity." Nearly 140 years after Farmer lived, the number of religious groups in America has increased tenfold, with a myriad of independent churches, Pentecostal churches, fundamentalist groups, as well as African American denominations, and many others.

In 1800 there was one church in America for every 1,122 inhabitants. The heaviest concentration of those churches was in New England. In 1870, according to census figures, there was a church in America for about every 600 persons (roughly twice as many churches per capita than ninety years before). Moreover, there were five states with many more churches than the others. Ohio, Indiana, Kentucky, Tennessee, and Mississippi as a group averaged a church for every 432 inhabitants.[22] If one were to take these five states with the most churches per capita and find the geographical center of that area, it would rest at Cane Ridge, Kentucky, home of the famous 1801 camp meeting that many historians credit with kicking off the Western Revival era.

It is safe to say that Farmer and his contemporaries thought very little about an analysis of sectarian and catholic tendencies of churches. For them the word sectarian was a much less theological and technical word and a much more a common, everyday word, referring to any group that acted out of bias, prejudice, opinion, or self-interest. The word almost always carried a pejorative meaning; thus groups often attributed the label nonsectarian to themselves and sectarian to others. Often the word was used simply to refer to denominationalism.

In the 1830s and 1840s the conflicts between churches led to heated debates about which were the most sectarian. The newly established Indiana College could not avoid this controversy. Soon to be Indiana University, the college was founded in 1828 and was the first institution of higher education sponsored by the state. However, since the Presbyterians were initially the only group present in the state advancing higher education, it was natural that Presbyterians would be the most involved in the new school. Two other institutions of higher education had already come into existence at that time, Hanover and Wabash, both founded by Presbyterians. When it turned out that the president of the trustees at Indiana College, David Maxwell, was a Presbyterian, and the president of the school (from 1829 to 1851), Andrew Wylie, was a Presbyterian, and three of the first professors were Presbyterian, it was understandable that the Presbyterians were accused of making the college just another sectarian school.

Before this time the Methodists had very little inclination to found a school. It might be argued that the Presbyterian dominance of the new school energized Methodists as much as anything for the cause of higher education. Why should Presbyterians, who had only 5,000 members in the state, have three schools while the Methodists, who had 24,000 members, have no schools? It did not help matters that when Methodists petitioned to have a Methodist professor at the school in 1831, Samuel Bigger, a trustee (and later state governor), laid the petition on the table with the remark that there were no Methodists in the state that would be qualified.[23]

Farmer joined the argument. He presented a petition to the Methodist annual conference accusing Indiana College of sectarianism. By 1841 Farmer was accusing the Methodists themselves of being sectarian. In the meantime, Indiana University worked hard to establish its reputation as nonsectarian, and suddenly Farmer, in a strange turn of events, found himself not an opponent but a friend of the university:

Doctor Wylie again and again besought me most earnestly to continue holding union meetings in the chapel, assuring me, I was doing a good work; but for good and sufficient reasons, I reluctantly declined doing so. He became so deeply interested in the subject, that he wrote a book call[ed] "Sectarian Heresies," and was an able defender of Christian Union.

Wylie bore the brunt of the sectarian controversy.[24] He had originally served as pastor at the Presbyterian Church in Bloomington, but during the course of that pastorate he had sided with the New School Presbyterians rather than with the Old School. Wylie was soon being criticized from all sides: within the Presbyterian Church and from the Methodists and the Campbellites. The issue became so consuming that in 1840 Wylie, as reported by Farmer, published a book *Sectarianism Is Heresy*.

Wylie must have seen Farmer as an ally in the cause. Gayle Williams, in an article on Wylie and sectarianism, suggests that Wylie's most troubled years on the issue of sectarianism were in the late 1830s and early 1840s, at the very time Farmer was on the scene. Wylie wrote his book in 1840. He became an Episcopalian in 1842. At the time Farmer, still a Methodist, and evidently fairly well regarded, at least among rank-and-file Methodists, was himself beating a drum for nonsectarianism. So Wylie does what must have been a rather unusual thing: he makes available the university's chapel for nonsectarian meetings. Not only that, he invites Farmer to share with him the Sunday lecture hour. This is evidently the basis for Farmer's use of the phrase "public square religion."

What is unusual is that ordinarily Farmer would not be attracted to the Wylie types of that time. Farmer was suspicious of persons in authority, especially if the authority was based on education, position, and sophistication. Ordinarily, Wylie would not be attracted to the Farmer types of the time. Farmer was a camp-meeting preacher whose religious services were characterized by "enthusiasm" (emotionalism). He represented that part of Indiana that the Wylies of the time were trying to educate and civilize.

Farmer suggests that his involvement with Wylie and the preaching at the IU chapel did not go down well with the Methodists, and he actually called off his involvement after he had difficulties with questioning at the quarterly conference. As will be seen as the Farmer narrative continues, it is probably not possible to be nonsectarian, at least not in the way Farmer and Wylie envisioned it. To be nonsectarian implies a kind of tolerance and neutrality that leads either on the one hand to secularism, or on the other hand, to further sectarianism when the issues behind nonsectarianism lead to ideology.

Wylie believed in nonsectarian education, which he understood to be on a religious but nondenominational basis. Ultimately, that proved to be an impossible position. Williams, in the article on Wylie and nonsectarianism, observes: "Nonsectarian education was an important component of Indiana University's mission during the early years. Throughout that period, the university's faculty and supporters believed that it could be both [religious but nonsectarian]. Nonsectarianism, however, set the stage for the gradual secularization of the institution that would take place at Indiana University in the second half of the nineteenth century."[25]

Farmer's nonsectarianism went in a different direction. For him and preachers of other evangelical churches, "union meetings" meant revival meetings. The key to unity was a conversion experience; this one important event transcended other religious differences. However, there could be no such thing as nonsectarian revival meetings. The phrase itself is an oxymoron. As ensuing chapters will show, when Farmer tried to rise above denominationalism with his Christian Union plan, he discovered that because it was an ideology based on criticism of those who did not agree, it became just another denominational sect.

One more voice deserves a hearing. It was Indiana's sectarian controversies that played at least some part in the founding of Indiana's first Methodist college, Indiana Asbury (today DePauw University). In his inauguration speech, Matthew Simpson addressed the problem of sectarianism at the new institution:

> But the startling cry of "Sectarianism" may perhaps by others be echoed throughout the land. Nay, we expect it, because it has always been the favorite resort of infidelity. Eighteen hundred years ago Christianity was the sect everywhere spoken against, and from that period to this "Schism and Sectarianism" have ever been the cry of its relentless opponents.
>
> If by sectarianism be meant that any privilege shall be extended to youth of one denomination more than another—or that the faculty shall . . . dwell upon the minor points controverted between branches of the great Christian family—then there is not, and we hope there never will be, sectarianism here. . . . But if by sectarianism be meant that the professors are religious men, and that they have settled views upon Christian character and duty, then we ever hope to be sectarian. . . . If it be sectarian to differ from one man's religion, then it is equally sectarian to differ from that of another. Where shall we pause? We must not believe in a future state of rewards and punishments, for that is sectarian. We must not teach that the Messiah has appeared, or that is sectarian, or the Jew cries out "sectarian." We must not claim the Bible as inspiration, or the Deist is shocked at our illiberality. We must not deny the existence of pagan gods, or Nero's torch is the brilliant argument against sectarianism. Nay, we must not admit the existence of a God, or the Atheist will rail at our want of liberal feeling and sentiment. What then shall we do? Whether professors are Pagans or Atheists, Mohammadans or Jews, Deists or Christians, still they are sectarian. The only persons who are properly free from sectarianism are those who either believe all things, or who believe nothing.[26]

13

Politics, 1830s to 1845

Religion was not the only arena in which there was division on the Indiana frontier. The political field was also one of division. Eli Farmer held strong opinions about what was going on in Indiana politics, so he became a politician. He tells the story in his autobiography, beginning with his fight against Indiana College being run by Presbyterians:

The county was very strong democratic, and was controlled by Dunning.[1] The lamented George G. Dunn, by far the most eloquent orator in the state in his day, and his uncle, Doctor Maxwell, long since deceased, headed the old Whig party. These persons had become angry with me about some matter of trifling importance, and fell on me at all convenient seasons whenever there was an opportunity offered them to injure me, with great [virulence?] and severity so that I was between a very dangerous crossfire. My enemies were intermarried over and over with each other in almost all manner of ways, and were of course very clannish and jealous. I had incurred their displeasure originally by my opposition to the attempt made on the part of the old Doctor Maxwell by which he sought to make a sectarian institution out of the State University. The Dr was a member of the board of trustees. He had also been a member of the convention which located the institution at Bloomington, taking a prominent part in the proceedings connected therewith.

After the location had been decided upon, he very adroitly manipulated the selection of the Faculty by his action before the Board, and thus secured the appointment of a majority of the chairs in the Faculty, for his ecclesiastical friends among Presbyterian clergymen. He did greater things than this for his church, he even so arranged the affairs of the college, that in case of a vacancy in the Faculty, such vacancy was to be filled by appointing persons of a similar faith. As I was greatly opposed to this improper manifestation of sectarianism, I prepared and circulated a petition among the members of our conference in opposition to the management of the college as above described, and succeeded in getting my brother ministers to pledge themselves to get signers to similar petitions among their parishioners and friends, during the succeeding year, and thus petition the Legislature to no longer permit the college to be made a sectarian institution. I did my work so thoroughly, that I thereby incurred the displeasure of the Maxwell Dunn faction as before mentioned.

* * *

As a matter in course this agitation created considerable excitement among all classes of people pretty much throughout the state. Governor Bigler [Samuel Bigger] thought he was abundantly able to overcome our opposition and he linked his fortunes with those of the Presbyterian faction, and we snowed him under at the first opportunity in his candidacy for gubernatorial honors, notwithstanding we believed him to be a good governor.[2]

In [t]his way I had stirred up quite a formidable combination against me, all of whom exhorted them selves to put me down. I had hosts of friends however among the people, for the masses were beginning to realize that I was pretty well acquainted with the political affairs of the state, and was especially versed in the new financial and improvement systems then being foisted upon the people, and I was encouraged to persevere. I became so zealously wedded to my political views, that I soon came to believe that part of my mission in life was to combat these things which I plainly foresaw would, if carried out, prove destructive of the rights of the people. I was again brought into a fight with my old enemies the Maxwells and Dunns, by reason of my political opinions. In a short time my oft repeated forebodings of danger and disaster began to be realized, and the people then saw that my counsels had been the safer ones.

The Preacher as Politician

If it is difficult to sort out Farmer's religious alliances and his attitudes toward sectarianism, it is equally difficult to sort out his political alliances. We know that Farmer was strongly opposed to Indiana's Internal Improvements Act of 1836, which sought to build roads and canals throughout the state. We know Farmer was a Whig but was in conflict with some of the state leaders of the Whig Party, namely George G. Dunn. He was opposed to what he referred to as the Presbyterian domination of Indiana University. Farmer was strongly anti-slavery and was opposed to anyone with southern sympathies. He supported the Mexican War. He was an antagonist of Paris C. Dunning, who served as state representative from 1833 to 1836 and as state senator from 1836 to 1840 and again from 1861 to 1867. Dunning also was lieutenant governor from 1846 to 1848, and then governor from 1848 to 1849. Adding to the confusion is that in his autobiography, Farmer mixes up the timing of events somewhat, referring to things that took place in the 1830s when he is speaking of the 1840s or even later. In the next part of his narrative, Farmer is referring to his candidacy for the Indiana State legislature in 1836. Thereafter, he gives an account of his political activities during the 1840s.

Taking the field after Dunning, I began canvassing actively, and succeeded in securing an advantage over my competitor. He had boasted in his speeches that he had helped to establish the new banking system of the year previous in the Legislature. By some happy chance I had gotten an opportunity of making an examination of the charter and did so, whereby I was able to prove that the whole matter was a swindling concern.

Taking it up as such I proved conclusively its character by showing the banks were charging from 25 to 37 percent for monies loaned, which thing I denounced as an iniquity and a grievous wrong inflicted upon the commonwealth.

My competitor jumped to his feet and swore it was a damned lie, and drew his knife in a menacing attitude. The people were evidently in harmony with my views and I did not allow myself to become angry. I told them I would not get angry because of the disposition manifested by my competitor to resort to violence, but if he attempted to use that villainous looking blade on me I would not hesitate a moment to cure him. I then went on good humouredly with my argument.

There happened to be present quite a number of good citizens of parties who knew by experience that my statements were true to the letter, for they had had dealings with some of the banks, and I had no trouble in establishing my propositions. Before I sat down I made up my mind to twit my opponent a little, and I asserted that he had as an attorney sworn that he would lie and I was not at all surprised to find him doing so. After the speech was concluded, we all went to the house at which dinner had been prepared for us, and I was seated at the table directly opposite from my worthy antagonist. As he now and then choked up with anger, I laughed at his discomfiture, till he finally declared "it was too much for a man to state before a public audience that he had sworn he would lie and had done so."

Political ads from the Bloomington Post of 1836 promoting Eli Farmer's candidacy for the Indiana State Senate. Although he lost this election, he later won a seat in this body, where he served from 1843 to 1845.

"Then," said I, "it is your child, and a black one at that, and you shall have it," and I annoyed him not a little about his black child, till I by and by succeeded in getting him in a good humor when he desired me to take it back, but I now refused to do so.

He then proposed if I would abandon the track he would do so too, but I dismissed his proposition by saying, "No, no, Paris, I cannot consent to do that, now that my hands are at the plow I dare not even look back."

I had him badly beaten in advance of the election. On the day of the election my competitor rolled out a couple of barrels of whisky and invited all to come out and help dispose of it, and as there were many topers close by there was no dearth of assistance in helping to get the fiery liquid out of the way. As I was opposed to liquor, of course, I lost these votes, for as soon as the elector was made drunken he was hurried off to the precinct by the governor's toadies and other local politicians. The results disclosed the fact that I was beaten by a few votes. The now jubilant governor, proposed to give a great feast at an early day, and invited me to attend as one of his guests, and I did so and we got along pleasantly.

My defeat didn't cool the ardor of my enthusiastic feelings against the internal improvement system, on the contrary I fought against it whenever an opportunity offered while I continued to settle up the unfinished business of the store.

* * *

1843–45
The internal improvement system, as I had anticipated, was increasing in strength day by day and was now assuming fearful dimensions. Governor Dunning had been our representative and had helped to form a great many bonds and he was now standing again before the people as a candidate for the same office.[3] His speeches were very plausible and popular, as the governor gave out many spacious promises, and left the impression where he went that the legislature by continuing the improvement system would make all the citizens of the state rich.

Many of my fellow citizens whose views coincided with my own views, and who were opposed to such a gigantic system of improvements, besought me earnestly to contest the matter with the governor before the people. Dunning had run several men off the track, and now I was surrounded by friends who were clamorously demanding I should enter upon the contest, but I refused to do so for some time. Politics were extremely distasteful to me, but as I had been in the habit of fighting intemperance, I at length concluded by accepting the position I would have a good opportunity of keeping up that warfare anyhow.

While surrounded one day by a large body of my friends, who were urging me to make the race, I observed my old adversary Mr. Bunger among them, and addressing myself to him, I inquired, "Shall I be a candidate?"

"O yes," said he, "by all means!"

* * *

Solicitations to run for a seat in the Legislature now came rushing in upon me like a mountain torrent, and I again entered the field [1842]. I assured my friends that the harvest was fully ripened, and I wished to reap and gather in my crop. I was now running for a seat in the state senate, my claims being contested by Gen. Lowe and Col. Berry. During a previous canvass on the part of General Lowe, while he was running for the Legislature against a Democrat Gen. Willis A. Gorman, he had carried with him to the country of Brown a number of certificates to the effect that he (Lowe) was veritable democrat, and these he industriously circulated among his constituents of the county in order to break down his opponent as greatly as possible.

Soon after I announced myself a candidate I ascertained that Gorman was on the track for the House. My competitors for a seat in the Senate were Col. Berry and Gen. Lowe. I soon became satisfied the people were for me, notwithstanding the opposition of my competitors, aided and abetted by Dunning and Gorman, and backed by the factions heretofore referred to as being led on by Maxwell and Dunn. My confederated enemies soon saw I was running away from my opponents and a convention was called by them to assemble at Bloomington at which one or two of my competitors was to be taken out of the fight, so as to consolidate their strength and give it to one man against me, thus uniting the Whig and Democratic parties.

An old line Democrat by the name of Wm Foster, a physician of Bloomington was one of the principle actors in the convention. Dr. Foster called Gen. Lowe before the convention and thus questioned him, "Genl. Lowe, will you leave the track in case your friends say so?" "Yes," said Genl. Lowe, "I will." I was an amused spectator of the sublime scene. Genl. Lowe's friends now cried out, "If Lowe leaves the track we will go to Farmer; we cannot go for Berry." The same question was propounded to Berry, and a similar answer was returned thereto by the Col., but his friends were quite as obdurate as Lowe's friends had been, and they also threatened to come to me. The withdrawal of either of these gentlemen then would strengthen me, instead of weakening me. The only choice left them was to run both men and strengthen, as far as possible, the strongest man.

General Howard was a candidate that year for a seat in the United States Senate. He was a son-in-law of the Maxwells, but I always regarded him as a very able statesman, and I was somewhat afraid of the strength of the Gen. He was a strong Democrat, and the counties in which I was seeking an election w[ere] strongly Democratic, and I proposed to the friends of Genl Howard that if he would not use his strength against me, I would in case of an election, support him for the United States Senate, in case I received an instruction of that sort from a majority of the two counties, at the same time declaring that in case they threw his strength again[st] me at the ballot box, I would cripple him as badly as I might be able to do in the Legislature in case I should get there. Feeling themselves to be masters of the situation, my proposition was rejected, and Howard's candidacy was urged as a special objection to my election, and his influence was thrown against me. On the day of the election, both factions became apprehensive that the other would succeed, and the result was they all came to me, and I was elected by an overwhelming majority to a three years term in the state senate.

Dr. Maxwell and other friends of Genl Howard now sought to arrange a compromise between us, but I told them they were too late in their overtures, that as I had whipped them I intended to keep them whipped. I reminded them of the fact that I had tried in vain to make a compromise at one time but my advances had been cruelly spurned by them in their hour of supposed might, and that such propositions came with a bad grace at such a tardy hour from the over-zealous friends of Genl Howard. After I became a member of the Legislature, General Howard came to me and made several efforts to effect a reconciliation, but I told him it was too late a period for compromise and therefore I could do nothing for him. He offered to meet me on half way grounds, but I refused every overture. Subsequently by money, other persons in the interest of Howard tried me, but I inclined not any ears to their entreaties.

The election of a senator drew near, and we counted our votes very closely to see whose chances seemed most flattering, and we saw we were lacking one vote to defeat General Howard. I suggested that we delay the election in order to give us time to come to Monroe and Brown counties and get counter instructions for John M Sluss, one of the representatives in the lower House from these counties. We deferred the election a few days. Meantime Mr. Sluss and I returned home, arriving at Bloomington Saturday night. Calling the people together at the courthouse, we made our speeches to them, in which we made known our plan of getting a counter instruction from the people for John M. Sluss, who had been instructed to vote for General Howard. Mr. Sluss was a Whig, and was not very friendly to Howard anyhow. The counties composing the district were canvassed and a new instruction given within two days, and by it Mr. Sluss was directed to vote for measures and not for men. Joseph Howe brought up a new instruction in the interest of Howard, on I think the third day. The Howard party became very angry when they ascertained we had saved Sluss's vote. We went into an election and elected a middle man, a Tyler man (Hannigan) at last, but this was accomplished by their buying up one of our votes. We succeeded however in defeating General Howard. Howard was afterward sent by the President to Texas as American minister.

On the night succeeding the senatorial election, the successful senatorial aspirant treated to a barrel of wine, and his friends held a grand jubilee at the State House, where many of the party became very drunk. I refused to go, but a friend of mine, a Christian preacher, who did attend, returned from the jollification with a report that the speaker of the house, a man by the name of Jefferson Hensley [Thomas Jefferson Henley] had stated at the meeting in a speech, that there were two members of the legislature, two ministers of the gospel, who had stolen the livery of heaven to serve the devil in, and in which to deceive their constituency.[4] Mr. Sluss and I were in our room when this message was brought to me. My informant also stated that he believed I was one of the ministers referred to by speaker Hensley. Upon receiving the last statement Mr. Sluss said I turned over in my bed and solemnly wailed forth something like this, "I wish that it might be a religious act and I would whip the fellow," but I have no recollection of having made such a statement, notwithstanding I have no doubt I felt just that way.

Early next morning, I went out in search of the gentleman, and found him at last in the consultation room of the Democratic party, a room in the Palmer House. Entering the room I engaged in an interchange of the customary morning salutation, after which I said, "A word with you Mr. Hensley, aside if you please." We slipped into an adjourning room and as we went thither I saw several of his friends exchange significant winks and nods. When we were alone I told Hensley I had been informed he had said certain things concerning me, and repeated them according to the foregoing narration, and was told by him that he had uttered the remarks ascribed to him.

"My friends suppose," I continued, "that you intended a part of your denunciation for me."

"So I did," was his answer.

"Mr. Hensley," said I, "I think this a small matter, although my opinion is that nobody has any sort of right to intermeddle with those things which are purely in the keeping of myself and Maker; nobody will be required to answer for my own acts save myself. If I have done wrong, or in any manner wronged my constituents, they will be swift witnesses against me, and will scarcely hesitate to correct that wrong, and now I ask of you to do, as under similar circumstances do by you, and that is to retract what you have said, so far as it relates to me, I ask this of you as a gentleman."

"Damned if I do either," was his course rejoinder.

I now offered to submit the matter to his own personal friends for their arbitration, but his answer to my proposition was much the same as the one mentioned above.

"Well, sir," said I, "if you will not reason with me, nor yet submit it to your own personal friends, then I shall not talk to you."

By this time he became boisterous, and now cried out passionately, "Damn you I will make you talk!"

But I stood firm and calm, opening not my mouth for some thirty or so minutes. During those thirty minutes I studied my case pretty closely. I was a preacher of the gospel and a sworn officer of the state, and of course was utterly opposed to engaging in a fuss. I did not wish to do wrong. The boisterousness of my raging adversary soon collected quite a crowd around us, but I stood dumb and motionless as a statue. He became so furiously enraged that he danced around a great deal, and beat the air wildly, and was indeed remarkably demonstrative, as well as provokingly insulting.

He finally swore again that he would make me talk, and I now began to feel a spirit of resentment seizing hold of me, and I determined I would speak, and speak in such a way as to test his manhood, of which he had so often boasted, and I said, "Sir, I cannot condescend to kick with a jack ass!"

"G-d d-m you," cried he, livid with rage as he jumped at me. As he came toward me I braced myself to receive him, and doubled him up quickly by a deftly directed blow, and he laid down at my feet as a limp wash rag. Two of the by-standers caught my lick in such a manner as to destroy in some measure its force. Another man caught hold of me and said, "Come let us go down stairs."

Leaving the room I stepped out into a hall leading to the stairway and walked off down the hall towards the stairway and had just made one step in my descent thereof, when my ears were saluted by the cries of a mob at my heels, "Kill him, d-m him, kill him!!" Turning around at the head of the stairs I faced the excited crowd, not knowing whether they were all enemies or not; and I threw my gold-headed cane up in a defensive attitude. By a quick jerk, Doctor Norvall, of Springville, succeeded in wrenching the cane out of my hands, and I cried out, "Gentlemen, a fair chance is all I ask." About this time the crowd pushed Hensley on me, my adversary striking at me with all his might as he came up, but I succeeded in evading his blow by throwing up one arm in such a manner as to ward it off, at the same time planting a square blow just under his uplifted arm, knocking him down. He tried to recover himself as soon as he fell, but I threw him back on the floor time after time, and in this manner I so worried him, that he by and by became exhausted, and could do nothing at all. I had him in my arms and was about ready to throw him upon the floor the fourth or fifth time, and he was as limber as a piece of cloth, when a party of bystanders interfered and begged for him, and tried in vain to get him out of my grasp.

I kept crying out, "Give me room, give me room." The first friendly voice and face I recognized in the crowd was that of John Sluss, who made his way to me, and observing that Hensley was considerably mashed up, he also begged for him, and I then released my hold and his friends carried him away.

Immediately after the fight was over the Hon Jesse D. Bright, a good friend of mine, and who was the President of the Senate, came up to me, and taking me by the hand said, "Mr. Farmer, you can whip two such men as Hensely, at one engagement." The intelligence ran quickly all around the city that Farmer was being whipped at the Palmer House, and my friends came rushing in by companies. Among the earliest arrivals was a very large man by the name of Lasley, whose seat in the senate chamber was next to mine, and he anxiously asked me if I was hurt.

"Not a hair of my head is injured; I am whole," was my good-natured reply. The house was densely packed by my friends in a few minutes, many of whom were like Mr. Lasley, anxious to renew the fight with our political opponents. As they would come in, I would have to answer them I was not injured. A representative from Danville, an excellent lawyer and a warm friend of mine, walked up the street swearing he himself could whip any man in the government. So great was his excitement, and the fact is we Whigs had every thing pretty much our own way during the remainder of that day.

* * *

Two days after the events narrated in the last chapter, Hon John Ewing, from Vincennes, became involved in a protracted and exciting debate in the senate, with a couple of members upon some questions relating to the Wabash and Erie Canal. I was inclined to favor "Old John's" side of the issue, and sympathized actively with him in his unequal contest, numerically speaking. Now and then, as the argument progressed, a member from Franklin County by the name of Ritchie, would jump up and take a part against my old friend Ewing. The discussion extended over the greater part of two days. Mr. Ewing meanwhile manifesting a great deal of sarcasm, before which his opponent would stagger every time, for, like the famous Damascus Blade, his sarcasm cut both ways, and cut like a sharp knife. About the close of the debate Mr. Ritchie interrupted Mr. Ewing, and received a dangerous wound from which he found it difficult to recover, and in his confusion he cried out that if he could not get satisfaction on the floor of the senate, he would seek it outside, adding with a show of mock manliness "nothing but your gray hairs saves you!" To this venerable old John replied, "Well, sir, you are excused from any such considerations on my part," and Ritchie attacked there in the senate chamber. Jumping in between them, I cried out, "Sir, I will take this whipping upon myself, and you shall not touch a hair of this old gray head, you shall not lay your hand on the old man." The warlike hero reconsidered the matter and retired amid very great confusion.

The secular papers throughout the state now took up the affair between Mr. Hensely and myself and by putting it as favorably as possible for me, gave me a great amount of free advertising. They stated that my adversary had been a member of the legislature for nine years and that he had always been noted for his propensity for violence, and that his conduct had been condemned by his own party while my action had been approved. This fact made a great many friends for me, and the affair was magnified as to give both of us a national reputation for a time.

Before we adjourn the session a distinguished representative in congress from New York [Charles Butler?] paid the capital city a visit and we vied with each other in doing him honor.[5] On one occasion he was called in for a speech during the delivery of which he gave a humorous description of the fight and how the story reached him in his distant home, in which connection he was reminded of the story of a couple of Yankee laborers who were in the field at work together when one of them cried out to his comrade, "Bill, did you see that little bull over the way, just now trying to fight that locomotive!"

"Well, what of it?" inquired the other.

O, nothing, only he got smashed all to pieces, and was just admiring his courage," and then after a moment's hesitation he added, "But d-m his judgment." This was told in such an apt and droll manner by the Yankee congressman, as we called him, that the audience was convulsed with laughter.

Before the adjournment of the legislature I provided myself documentary, and other wise, pro and con, upon which to demand an investigation on my return home in case the church to which I belonged saw fit to inquire into the affair. A great number of persons voluntarily furnished me written certificates vindicating my character in every particular. On my return home I handed in the papers relating to the difficulty to my pastor, the Rev. Isaac Owen, and asked that the matter be investigated.[6] He organized a committee of local preachers to whom my case was referred. During the trial brother Owens said to me—"Brother Farmer, are you not sorry you did it?"

"I am not" I answered, "I am only sorry I felt compelled to do it."

"Don't say that!" implored the good pastor.

"But I will say it," said I firmly.

The committee decided that I should receive a mild rebuke by the mouth of the Presiding Elder, Rev. John Miller. Mr. Owen now asked whether I did not have other papers relating to the matter in my possession, and was informed by me that I had some of my own private papers *which were my own property. He asked to be permitted to examine them, and I gave him permission. Looking them over hurriedly, he then declared he would file them away with the Quarterly meeting papers.*

"They are not your property," said I protestingly, but he still refused to surrender them up. "When we arrive in Bloomington," said I, for the investigation had been held six miles west of that town, at a place called the "Cross-roads," "I will get them back again." When I arrived at that place I told Mr. Owen he was trifling with the wrong man, and that if he did not give them up, I would resort to a remedy by which he would be required to surrender them, and he gave them back to me.

Soon after the arrival of the Presiding Elder I sought an interview and thus addressed him,—"Sir, I am informed you are required to reprimand me, and now I am ready to hear you." He laughingly said he had nothing to say, and gave me to understand that my action was endorsed by him. This occurred about the time the M.E. church was erected in Bloomington.

* * *

I continued improving my farm, collecting old outstanding debts etc. when not engaged with my legislative duties. . . . It was during this season that I consented to run for Congress. The leaders of the Whig party in the Legislature had obtained from me during my last session a sort of promise, that I would make the race for Congress instead of George J. Dunn who had twice been defeated. My friends urged me on all sides to make the race, but knowing that seven counties would have to be canvassed, thereby consuming more than three months of my time, and that it would cost me five hundred dollars in money, I hesitated. Dr. Davis, who had long represented the district in congress, and who was then the incumbent, was already in the field, as the Democratic candidate, and was backed by a comfortable majority variously estimated at from fifteen hundred to two thousand votes. I begged in vain to be excused from making the race, but I was assured by my friends that I could be elected, and urged to try it any how, especially when my party all over the district was calling for me to bear their standard through the campaign. At length I yielded and entered the field. My competitor Doctor Davis was quite popular. He was in the habit of treating his friends to whiskey, and was counted a jolly, good fellow.

As soon as I struck the trail of the Doctor I found he had been speaking slightingly of me, saying in many instances that George J. Dunn, the ablest man in the state, had failed to stand before him, and that I would not successfully meet him on the stump. This statement, and similar ones, were so often sounded in my ears as I passed around the district, that I determined to administer upon him severely, on the first approach of the first opportunity. Our first meeting occurred at Carlisle, in his own county, and at his home. The district was comprised of Sullivan, Monroe, Green, Lawrence, Davis, Knox and Clay counties. A large assembly had gathered at Carlisle from all parts of these counties, and my competitor was present at this, my first appointment in the county of Sullivan. When I got up to address the meeting I informed the people as to what my competitor had said concerning my abilities in his speeches throughout the district whither he had gone, and that in view of all these facts I did not think he had treated me as a gentleman would have done, to say nothing of what a Christian might be expected to do, and I hoped my audience would bear with me, while I paid him off for his badness, for he could not have known anything of neither my personality nor my abilities. I then declared that I was a better man in every possible way than my competitor, and that I would establish my proposition by proof.

Overhauling his record I demonstrated conclusively that he was a northern man with southern sympathies, sentiments and principles, and now scared him terribly for being a northern man with southern principles. I kept my opponent under my eye all the time, and I could not be mistaken as to the causes which painted his face with many different hues. My audience manifested their approval of my remarks by prolonged and repeated shouts and clapping of hands.

After I had pretty well exhausted myself upon him, I closed the speech by relating an anecdote of a personal nature. My competitor had lived a pretty fast life while in Washington, and the rumor was generally circulated that he had by his dissolute habits contracted a disgraceful disorder.

My story ran somewhat as follows: A certain young lady, a sister of a distinguished Democratic politician of my town, one day went out walking with her affianced. As the happy twain were slowly crossing "the commons" a certain black-and-white spotted hog crossed their path, a little way ahead of them, when the insipid young damsel turned to her beau with the solemn declaration, that for her part she could not see how that spotted hog lived.

"Why so?" inquired the attentive and now anxious young man.

"He has so many black spots on him," replied the coy maiden as she gave the word "so" a peculiar feminine emphasis, now looking sadly after the porcine brute.

"But he is in good order," said the unsuspecting youth, as he thoughtfully turned his eyes in the same direction, and his master, I have no doubt, feeds him well, so that he gets on famously, and is scarcely in need of your very active sympathies." "Don't you think so dear?" and he chucked her softly under her dimpled chin.

"But oh! Those horrid black spots," continued the lass as she demurely gazed into the love-blighted eyes of her adorer, "Why, Bennie, how can he live, for I have only one, and that nearly kills me!"

And then to hear the yelling that ensued.

Theophilus Adam Wylie captured this stump speech in the late 1830s in Bloomington, Indiana. Farmer ran for office in 1832, 1842, and 1845, likely creating scenes such as this in towns around south-central Indiana.

My competitor manifested the utmost consternation and humiliation, while the vulgar crowd fancying they could see some personal application for the story renewed the applause time after time, keeping up the applause for a long time. I applied the story rightly by referring to the black heart of my unscrupulous competitor. In this way I escaped many unjust suspicions.

When I had concluded, my opponent jumped up and said,—"You are a Methodist preacher, I believe."

"Yes," said I, "and I believe you are a blackslidden Methodist exhorter, and now if I could only succeed in converting you, why, then I will have saved the government I have no doubt from very [---] losses, pecuniary and otherwise."

Further my competitor said not, and I left the field with the odds in my favor.

Our next appointment was for the next day at the county seat, called Sullivan now; but "the Center" then. Fearing to meet me himself, my competitor got a powerfully built lawyer by the name of Wilson to answer my speech, but I made him speak first. Davis was present aiding and abetting his representative. Wilson began his speech by saying I was a smalty fellow, and I immediately interrupted him by calling to him to tell what I had said.

He refused, and I said, "Tell them what I said, sir."

He still declined and I said I would be ashamed to say what you have said, and persist in withholding what I said, so as to let the audience decide for themselves. I again besought him to tell it, but I could not get him to tell it by any sort of banter. When I came to reply to him I handled him pretty roughly, severely denouncing him by calling him an evil-minded fellow, wholly given up to obscene surmises, not forgetting Doctor Davis in my onslaught. I received many assurances by the audience that I had struck a popular chord.

On the next day we met at Merom the old county-seat on the Wabash. It was now my time to speak first. Davis was with me, but the lawyer had backed out. I again overhauled the Dr's congressional record and showed him to be a northern man with southern principles, and who was working for the interests of the people of the South, and came down on him heavily, and I soon saw that I was greatly damaging my opponent's course. After I had made my speech, I told the audience I would now make my opponent's speech, and forthwith I went over all his points, accurately, anticipating his entire speech, making it a stale affair before he got ready to rehearse it.

When his hour arrived he arose and asked to be excused from speaking. He became pretty discouraged, and about this time wrote to Grafton Croherly of Terre Haute that he was already whipped.

Our next appointment was at some prairie, the name of which I have forgotten. Davis having returned now sent out another lawyer to represent him in the discussion. This man's name was Allen. As my competitor was not present I said very little concerning him. After I had delivered my speech Allen got up to speak, and began a terrible tirade against my party. This opposition pleased me immensely, for I needed something of the kind to inspirit me. Allen had been accompanied from the county-seat by a large delegation of his friends who had felt desirous of witnessing the fight.

When he finished his speech I arose, and being greatly diverted, I laughingly told the audience that I lived in a town where we made "little gimbt lawyers," and that I had gotten leave of Judge McDonald (which was true) to eat up all these little fellows. "But," said I, "I will not eat him up at this time, as this is his first offence. But what shall I do with him," I cried, as I assumed, a deep contemplative attitude and look. Brightening up suddenly I said, "Well, my fellow citizens, I will tell you what I shall do with this fellow, — he is so green I am sure the ducks would like to eat him, let us then put a half bushel over him to keep the ducks from devouring him, and that if he ever repeated his conduct on a similar occasion, I would eat him up bodily, and then after a sufficient time had elapsed for my digestive organs to perform their proper functions, I would drop him upon some poor man's poorest spot of earth to reclaim it in some feeble manner from its barrenness and poverty."

This little bit of raillery so annoyed him, as repeated by his associates, that he left his business and moved over into Illinois, to get rid of his tormentors, and the character I had given him. He did not remain in the county a month after I analyzed him before a public audience.

I now traveled through the district successfully, meeting my competitor but once afterward during the campaign, and on that occasion he refused to hold a joint discussion with me. Davis became satisfied I was pressing him to the wall, and in his alarm, he fled to George J. Dunn, whom he implored "for God's sake come to my rescue, for if Farmer should defeat me it will be a disgrace to both of us." Mr. Dunn, quite as sensational as his confederate and democratic ally, now began sending out letters against me to many of the strongholds of the Whig party in the district. These letters were of such a damaging character, that I was thrown by them—Dr. Davis beating me by a few votes. Had these letters been withheld by Dunn, a leader of my own party too, I would easily have beaten my competitor.

As soon as I ascertained what Dunn was doing, (he did his work clandestinely, but did it well, nevertheless) I told him he was doing wrong, reminding him of the fact that I had always supported him by my votes and influence and begging him to at least remain neutral and let me alone.

He refused to do so, and took occasion to remind me of my action toward his kinsman General Howard, while I was a member of the Legislature. Of course I was then beaten, thereby loosing three month's time, and the amount of money expended in conducting a protracted canvass.

14

The Trip South, 1846

Eli Farmer never made it into the United States Congress. Following his failed campaign, he decided to go South anyway—not to the nation's capital, but to Natchez, Mississippi. Here he resumed his lifelong role of preacher, this time exhorting slaves from surrounding plantations. His story picks up onboard a steamboat at Louisville, Kentucky:

1846
After the election I concluded to spend the following winter down south, and accordingly I embarked for Natchez at Louisville, shortly after forming such a resolution.[1] The vessel on which I had shipped was heavily ladened, and carried about five hundred passengers.

Soon after our departure from port, I observed a gentleman who was very singularly clad. I myself was somewhat disguised, for prudential reasons, and I found myself considerably interested in my fellow passenger before mentioned, and I tried to divine his calling in life. Approaching him I asked him whether he was not a Catholic priest, and was answered affirmatively. He then, in answer to questions put by me, informed me that he lived at Lafayette, and had the watch care over the hands then constructing the Wabash and Erie Canal, about five hundred in number. Engaging him in a lengthy conversation, he told me how he was in the habit of managing the Irish element of his charge, especially at their [so] called "works." On one occasion he attended a place where his Irish parishioners proposed having a dance, and by obtaining permission to hold a little prayer meeting in advance of the dance, he succeeded in breaking up the spree.

This trip was made just before the Mexican war and I was very anxious to find out where his destination was, suspecting however, that he was on route to Mexico, but I saw I would have to approach him by slow approaches. We associated together intimately, for some four or five days, and I succeeded in sounding him as far as I wished to do so.

On the following Sabbath, a committee came to where the priest and I were talking, and one of their number said, "Father Clark, you are appointed to preach at eleven o'clock: and brother Farmer you will be expected to preach at 12 o'clock noon of today."[2]

My clerical friend was considerably startled when he heard me spoken of as a minister. After the committee withdrew I then addressed him, "Now, we have had a long, and to me, a pleasant interview and have gotten along well together. Tell me, if you please, what sort of friendship you have for other denominations?"

His reply, as near as I can now recall it, was, "O, none, they are heretics!"

He then asked me which denomination I was connected with, to which inquiry I returned a suitable answer after which I said, "Mr. Clark, you are to preach first today. You profess to be an honest man, and you may, or you may not, lay the foundation for strife here aboard this vessel."

It was arranged among us that we were to avoid stirring up strife, and to this end, it was also arranged that he was to preach upon the subject of the atonement, after which he was to retire while I was to preach a subject upon the divinity of the Scriptures. Seats were prepared for the congregation and after he had donned his clerical robes, girdles, etc., he preached a plain good sermon. At my hour I followed, speaking with great liberty. Upon the conclusion of my discourse, I announced I would preach at 3 o'clock on the lower deck, to a large body of men en route to Texas. I did this because I had been requested to preach there by some of the deck passengers with whom I was acquainted previously. After this announcement was made by me, the priest arose and said, "Tonight at early candle lighting I will preach again, in which sermon I will show the difference between the Protestant and the Catholic world," and then announced seven propositions he would discuss upon that occasion.

The first was the sacrament of the Lord's Supper, another was Holy Relics, another was Purgatory, another was the Prayers of the Virgin Mary. The others have gone out of my memory. With this the meeting was dismissed.

Before my second appointment arrived, many Baptists, Methodists, and Presbyterians made themselves known to me. I preached my second sermon at the appointed hour. Night came on and everything was made ready for Mr. Clark, whom we now knew to be no less a personage than a Catholic Bishop.[3]

Among the early strong declarations uttered by him was this, that when bread and wine were properly consecrated by a Bishop, they become literally the body and blood of Christ. As he went through his proposition, I took an occasional note for the purpose of aiding me to rightly state his positions. When he was about ready to dismiss the meeting I arose from my seat and addressed him [in] this manner, "Mr. Clark, have you any objections to answering a few questions which I wish to now propound for my own information."

"No, sir," said he, "we seek an investigation."

"Well," said I, "I understood you to say, substantially, that after the bread and wine were prepared properly for the Sacrament, they were literally the body and blood of Christ"?

"Yes, sir," he replied, "The Scripture is plain, "Except ye eat of my flesh and drink of my blood ye cannot be my disciples."

"Out of that grows a philosophical inquiry," said I, interrupting him. "If it be true," I continued, "that they so become literally the body and blood of Christ, what good will they do the soul, since they enter the stomach and there find the physical man, and thence pass off, as other food? I await your answer."

His voice faltered greatly as he mouthed over some unintelligible jargon, and after a painful and laborious attempt to extricate himself out of the pit he himself had digged, he at length sank down abruptly and retired in great confusion.

He was understood by others to stammer out that his declaration was a mere opinion of his own, whereat many of his auditors laughed derisively, and gave him to understand that they entertained but a poor opinion of his abilities as an instructor of the people.

Subsequently we had many a laugh at the expense of the poor misguided Bishop.[4]

Sectarians, Frontier Revivalists, and Roman Catholics

Any study of sectarians—individuals who belonged to one of the multiple sects and denominations in America—and the religious wars of the United States during the mid-nineteenth century must deal with the prejudices against Roman Catholics. The following observations relate to mid-nineteenth-century American Protestant prejudices against Roman Catholicism with reference to Farmer.

First, in spite of the sectarianism of the mid-1800s in Indiana, and in America generally, there was a growing sense of evangelical Protestant identity that transcended many sectarian differences. Farmer remarked that Methodists, Baptists, and Presbyterians made themselves known to him on the boat south. Baptists, Methodists, and Presbyterians could fuss among themselves but they were united in the presence of Catholics, as well as in relation to unorthodox Christian-related groups. This is part of the unique American religious experience that distinguished it from Christianity in Europe. Generally the various denominations recognized each other as part of the Christian family.

In the case of Farmer, Cumberlands, New Lights, Baptists, Presbyterians, and Quakers were affirmed, but not Unitarians, Universalists, or Shakers. Farmer did not mention encounters with Adventists (Millerites), Spiritualists, or Mormons, but he would probably not have included these either. This would be true for most Methodists of the period. The *Ladies' Home Repository*, one of Methodism's most popular magazines of the mid-1800s, frequently reported statistics about churches. In the May 1856 issue, an article on religion divided the churches of America into two classes, "evangelical" and "unevangelical." There were 4,056,000 evangelical church members in America and 236,000 unevangelical church members according to this report. But the Catholics were a special case. In the "unevangelical" column was a note indicating that Roman Catholic membership was not included, implying there was some question as to how Roman Catholics should be identified. The magazine added:

> The Roman Catholic Church, while its numerical strength has largely increased within the last century, has made but little native progress and its aggregate increase falls far short of the progress of other denominations. . . . It must be bourne in mind in this comparison that several most important abatements are to be made from this view of the Roman Catholic statistics,—first, that during this period the filibustering propensities of the American people had bought up, or fought into the original territory over two million of square miles, more than twice the original area of the country, and all that, save Oregon, perhaps Roman Catholics territory.

The article credited Roman Catholics with 2,200,000 adherents, Methodists with 6,000,000 adherents, and Baptists with 5,000,000.

The implication is that America was a Protestant, theologically orthodox, country. Roman Catholic growth was not through conversion but through immigration and territorial expansion. A great part of Farmer's support for the war with Mexico came from the conviction that if Texas was a part of Mexico it would be colonized by Catholics.

If point one is correct, then point two follows: Much of the mistrust of Roman Catholics stemmed from the perception that they brought to America what is basically a foreign, and not a "native," religion.

But for Farmer as well as other sectarians, there was a third and far more serious charge—this having to do with eschatology, or end times, and what was then the prevailing American populist sectarian understanding of the biblical Book of Revelation. For Christians with a more catholic understanding of the church, including Roman Catholics,

Orthodox Christians, Anglicans, Congregationalists, and some Presbyterians, there would be a return of Christ to the earth at the end of time. This was usually interpreted spiritually or metaphorically, and except for paintings of the last judgment, or for the intermittent times of fear and confusion that accompanied natural disasters such as earthquakes and plagues—often associated with end times—there was little preaching or speculation as to what this specifically would look like. In interpreting the Book of Revelation, these groups took the *preterist* view: the prophecies of Revelation were already fulfilled, or would not be fulfilled in time and space.

The *futurist* view of Revelation holds that it is to be understood more literally. Events symbolically described will take place in time and space in the near future and are associated with the second coming of Christ. This is the view of many modern fundamentalists. It became popular in the theological system called Dispensationalism, which was popularized in America after the Civil War. This view sees the course of history pessimistically. The world is getting worse and worse and can be redeemed only by Christ's direct intervention.

The *historicist* view of Revelation perceives that events described in the book are prophetic predictions being fulfilled in events taking place from the time of Christ until the present day. This view, which has fallen into disrepute currently, was popular in early America, especially among the revivalists. Many American frontier sectarians took it to new levels. It was this approach, for example, that enabled Millerites (Adventists) to predict the end of the world in 1844.[5] Events that were taking place at that time were prophesied in the Book of Revelation and were leading to a grand culmination, which could be either a physical return of Christ to set up an earthly kingdom (pre-millennialism—Christ comes before the millennium) or a gradual betterment of society in which the Kingdom will be established and then presented to Christ at his second coming (post-millennial—Christ comes after the millennium).

Post-millennial views that developed in England in various forms influenced many of the religious sectarians who came to America. The Puritans spoke of "a city set on a hill." William Penn talked about "a peaceable kingdom." These were related to the idea of American religious exceptionalism, that is, America is in God's plan for a future kingdom. In early America the established churches taught that the bettering of society associated with post-millennialism came about through civilization, education, and scientific progress. When the revivalists of the First Great Awakening came along, preachers such as Jonathan Edwards stated that the betterment of society would come through civilization growing out of religious awakening. The revivalist and reformer Charles Finney stood in this tradition.

For the frontier revivalists, however, the kingdom would come through conversions, or more specifically, through the generous outpouring of God's spirit. The success of the Second Great Awakening seemed a harbinger of this coming kingdom. Early revivalists interpreted the religious, emotional, and physical excitement generated by camp meetings as the "signs and wonders" that were to be associated with Christ's return. They differed from the Calvinist-inspired First Great Awakening revivalists in that they saw the millennium coming not primarily by civilization and refinement but by radical reform.[6] Slavery and intemperance were the evils that needed to be overcome. The Wesleyan Methodists, who broke from the Methodist Episcopal Church in 1844, were anti-slavery, pro-women's rights, anti-alcohol, anti-war, and post-millennial. The United Brethren Church was also anti-war and did not believe war was the process by which the kingdom would be realized. Persons such as Farmer believed war (the Mexican War and the Civil War) were part of God's plan to bring about world peace. Harriett Beecher Stowe was an anti-war Unitarian, but when she penned "Mine eyes have seen the coming of the glory of the Lord" it was understood as a post-millennial war cry.

However, the Book of Revelation speaks of obstacles: the anti-Christ, the great beast, the red dragon, and the great whore. It speaks of a religious ruler who would oppose God's people. For many of the Revelation historicists of Farmer's time, this could only refer to the pope and the Catholic Church. Placing Farmer among the historicists helps us to understand the background to the story of his encounter with the Catholic priest on his trip to the South and later to his ugly criticism of Roman Catholicism in the *Bloomington Religious Times* in 1853 to 1854 (chapter 16). He was working toward the second coming of Christ, and to do so, he had to fight the devil that he perceived Catholicism to be. And so Farmer vanquished a Catholic bishop while enroute to the South. Here his story continues:

On my arrival at Natchez, I met a son of an old friend of mine in Kentucky, whose name was Jones, and he was the stationed preacher for the M.E. Church in that city. His father owned the ground on which the campmeeting was held at which I was converted. At the request of my new friend I preached several sermons in the city of Natchez. While he and another minister who was appointed to preach for the colored people had me to assist him in holding a meeting among

Depiction of an African American revival meeting in the South in 1873

his people. During my preaching on Sabbath evening among the colored folks, many of my dusky auditors became shouting happy. Their pastor informed me it was not their custom to preach exciting sermons to the colored people, for they were afraid their strong animal natures would be too greatly effected by such preaching, and they would be injured in some way because of it.

A very wealthy planter who owned a large number of slaves prevailed upon me to go out some distance into the country to his plantation to preach to his bondsmen. I went out to the plantation with him and preached several days. The slaves for several miles around attended my meetings, and these meetings were eminently successful. The colored people would sing and pray, and by and by they would get happy and then begin to shout, and we would have truly refreshing times, so that the hours would fly by on rapid pinions.

Notwithstanding the patrols were ordered by all of their superior officers to cut to pieces any black man who might be caught strolling about after nine o'clock at night, many of my colored friends would let the hours go by unchecked. When they saw they had tarried so long at the meeting as to prevent their return home by the hour specified, such parties would then remain all night, singing, and praying and praising God. When the number was not too large, the planter with whom I was stopping would write a pass for each of the tardy slaves, so as they would not be troubled with the patrol.

Another wealthy planter showed me great attention and took me out to his plantation in his finest carriage to pray with his invalid wife, and to preach for his colored folks. I remained in this section nearly all winter, preaching, praying, and singing with the people, and enjoyed myself greatly, but the hours flew by apace, and the month of March came again, and I felt it my duty to return home.

Slavery and Revivalism before the Civil War

This study has noted that Methodists, along with Baptists, were the first in America to reach African Americans in any significant way with the Christian faith. The message of free grace (free will), an emphasis on Holy Spirit-related intense experiences, and the emphasis, at least in the early years, on the egalitarian nature of religion, resonated with African Americans, both slave and free. An additional point should be made that revival settings, especially camp meetings, gave blacks freedom to express some of their own religious understandings that dated back to Africa. Blacks were present at the Cane Ridge camp meeting that launched the Second Great Awakening in 1801. They flocked to early Methodist camp meetings, especially in Virginia, Delaware, and Maryland. Methodists were so successful in reaching blacks that by 1820 fully 20 percent of Methodist church members were African American, and this even after two splits, the African Methodist Episcopal Church and the African Methodist Episcopal Church Zion. In revival settings, and especially in camp meetings, blacks were known for their dancing and singing.

One recent study by William Courtland Johnson has examined the relationship between African primitive religion and early camp meetings.[7] Johnson argues that blacks were responsible for some significant features of camp meetings. Among these were ring circles, the handshake, shuffle-step dancing, the circle of prayer, the camp meeting procession, the reliance on visions and dreams, and probably even being "slain in the spirit." It has been noted elsewhere that black preachers such as Harry Hoosier were often more effective than whites in moving a crowd. The growing influence of blacks at camp meetings led to the tendency to "control" the emotionalism of African Americans, or at least to separate them from whites beginning in the 1820s.

While these early camp meetings were held wherever Methodism was present, the most intense areas of camp meetings before 1820 were concentrated along the mid-Atlantic seacoast and in Kentucky and Tennessee. As the population moved west, Indiana, Illinois, and Ohio became the centers of camp meeting fervor. However, while Farmer and others in Indiana presided over some wild camp meetings, camp meeting culture was already being tempered by the 1830s and 1840s.

In spite of the notable presence of blacks, it has been estimated that only about 5 percent of African American slaves were church members by the time of the Civil War. Part of this is because southern slave owners resisted the emotionalism of revivalism, fearing that it would lead to slave revolts. While southern Methodists supported slavery, they tended to do so while contending that Christian slaveholders had the obligation to be humane in relationships with slaves and to educate and Christianize blacks. Because of this the Methodist Episcopal Church South could count 245,500 black members by the time of the Civil War. After the Civil War the black members of the ME Church South formed a new denomination, the Colored Methodist Episcopal Church (CME, now called Christian Methodist Episcopal).

Although Farmer had been growing more and more disillusioned with the Methodist Church by 1846, his contacts in the South appear to have been with Methodists. Apparently, his winter preaching to southern slaves brought him much joy. Soon, though, it was time to journey home. As he relates below, this part of his excursion was also a happy time:

As we left the city in the beautiful steamer "White Cloud" on our return trip, seven other large steam boats pushed out into the stream, all upward bound. After we got under headway, all the boats commenced racing, keeping up the excitement incident to such reckless fun, during the next five succeeding days with varying success for each boat, the boat using the greatest amount of oil and beacon for fuel usually leading the others.

A boat called "Benjamin Franklin" came out ahead finally while our boat came in next after the victor, arriving at the mouth of the Ohio about a half a day behind the steamer. I desired to ascend the Mississippi to St. Louis, but after tarrying at fairs two days, was prevented from going up any further that river, by the ice in the stream, and so was compelled to go up the Ohio to Louisville.

Before returning home, I paid a visit to my friends in Kentucky among whom I tarried a couple of weeks. This trip was made in the year 1846.

15

Nonsectarian Sectarianism, 1840s to 1853

In the next part of his autobiography, Eli Farmer describes the beginnings of his Christian Union Church. Although some of his dates are off, the events he mentions took place in the 1840s and early 1850s.

After filling my senatorial term in the state Legislature, I gave out, one year in advance of the meeting to be held in my barn.[1] Having no railroad then, I took my wagon to Louisville, and there laid in a large supply of provisions for the occasion [in 1847].

To appease my union meeting the sectarian folks got up a campmeeting seven miles south of mine, so as to conflict with me and carry off my audience. Just before the time for their camp meeting, they became <u>afraid</u> their camp meeting would not be sufficiently attractive to take my audience from me, and so instead of holding a campmeeting they chose that time for dedicating their new church at Bloomington, and brought Doctor (now Bishop) [Matthew] Simpson to that place for that purpose. I went to them and tried to get them to put off their meeting, or to join them, as it was also a part of their program, to have Dr. Simpson to protract their meeting after the dedication services were over. They would not consent to this, and I then began praying to God to manifest His power among us, and convince the people we were right, and He did so. People attended our meetings from the country towns about us for many miles, and many were converted, and we were blessed with a memorable time.

During the year 1844 Mr. Morrow was the preacher in charge at Bloomington.[2] This man was very tyrannical, and objected to my preaching for people out in the back settlements. I told him I helped to pay him for preaching, and I thought I ought to be permitted to preach out there, because I charged nothing for it and found [it] myself.

He said I must work about home, as the people were complaining because I did not preach around home. Knowing he had the power to excommunicate me in case I disobeyed him, I did as he desired.[3] He told me I must assist at a two days meeting to be held in a short time at the cross-roads. Under his direction I preached at that meeting on Saturday and on Saturday night. Sabbath morning Morrow came riding out from town, accompanied by a great crowd of the <u>elite</u> from town. He required me to preach the Sabbath mornings also, and at its conclusion, he invited with great suavity of manner, his fashionable escort, to go with him to brother Neild's to dinner, saying nothing to any of the humble visitors present. There were a great many poor folks at this meeting who had no place to go to, to get dinner. I spoke to my wife, and she bade me invite all such to go with us, telling me she would go ahead in advance of us and prepare our dinners. I invited all of them to go home with me, and a great many friends accepted my hospitality.

Returning to the afternoon appointment, Morrow told me as I was doing so well he desired I should preach again. I felt so disgusted with his action toward the poor people, that I felt constrained to criticize such conduct in my sermon, and when I opened my mouth on that subject it had to come forth. I remember now that I told them, on that occasion, that if such conduct as that which I felt called upon to deprecate prevailed very largely among the brethren, that I then had no doubt the church at the cross-roads was on the way to hell. I felt that I had fully discharged my duty as I stepped out of the stand.

Shortly after returning home, Morrow and another brother came to my house, Morrow being in a high state of spite with me. "Brother Farmer," he exclaimed—"you have ruined all"!

I inquired to know the cause of this alarm, and was informed that I had insulted brother Neild. I replied that I had helped to elect brother Neild to be a member of the Board of county commissioners, and if he was the Methodist Church, I would "put on my spurs and ride him all over the country"—"but," said I, "you yourself, are the originator of this wickedness and God will damn you in the day of judgment if you do not repent." He and his escort immediately took their departure.

Some where near this period a very successful Methodist preacher by the name of Draper Chipman, urged me to leave the church with him, but I declined doing so, owning to the fact that at the time I was in the midst of a storm, and of course wanted to leave in an honorable manner. I requested him to accompany me to one of my appointments at Putnam's school house, and he did so and preached for me. In his sermon he literally denounced the tyranny of the M.E. Church, and severed his connection with that church declaring himself no longer a member of it, assigning at length his reasons for so doing.

At the conclusion of the sermon, I arose and sanctioned all that he had said, telling the people that I, of course, expected to be called to an account by the Methodist preachers for what I had there avowed, but I did not care how soon I was summoned to that account.

Some two weeks subsequent Morrow informed me I must attend the next Quarterly conference, being the Second Quarterly conference of that year, and I told him I had already decided to do so. I accordingly did so, and at the proper time my examination was gone into, the Presiding Elder asked me what I meant by my Christian Union meetings and church, I told him I meant a union of Christians, united in love, a union in Christ, a union in spirit and a union in the Scriptures. He then stated he knew of "no such church in our Discipline; and this now, is your first reproof —you must quit it."

I answered him, by informing him I found shelter under this clause of the Discipline, "Do good of every possible sort to all men."

He again admonished me I must quit it.

I now told him he was mistaken in his man, and I desired him to insert in the minutes of the Quarterly conference any complaints that had been lodged against me. I was then informed that the only charge against me, was the fact of my having endorsed Draper Chipman in his course in leaving the M.E church, and also for forming that church.

I said: "You allow me to form the Bible society, the Temperance society, Missionary and tract society. I may join any or all of these societies, and I commit no sin in doing so, but to form a religious society, I am told by you is a grievous transgression. Permit me now to suggest, brethren, that as the Methodist church is not my master, nor yet my confessor, I am not accountable to her for my action in this matter. I cannot possibly have any desire to fight her, but yet it would be well for you to allow me to go on as easily and as peaceably as you can. Your little gimlet big-headed parsons pursue me most mercilessly on every hand, and I intend now to give you potent thunder from this hour hence forth!"

"What," cried the astonished Presiding Elder, "you do not intend to leave the church?"

"But I do sir!" was the reply I made him.

He dismissed the meeting and took me home with him for dinner. As we sat at the table eating our dinner he asked: "Brother Farmer, you are not intending to leave us?"

"I am sir."

"I would rather part with any other member of conference than your self," said he with much feeling, "for you remember, you took my father and mother into the Methodist Church, and I used to wait on you when I was a little boy."

H[is] tears flowed freely as he begged me to remain. On the following morning (Sabbath morning) I occupied a back seat at the morning services, instead of going into the stand as usual. The Presiding Elder, (Mr. Robertson) seemed greatly embarrassed and preached with manifest difficulty.

Remaining quiet for a few weeks, I watched the current of public sentiment, after which I held a protracted meeting at Fairfax, and organized a church of seventeen members.[4] Draper Chipman assisting me in the meeting.

During the fall and winter I traveled about holding meetings and organizing churches. In the year 1848, we called a convention and organized a Conference, holding the convention at a point on Big Salt Creek, at which point my friends had formally established a campground for my former campmeeting.[5]

There were now only five preachers in our church, to wit: Draper Chipman, Wm Farley, Wm Smith, Jas East, and myself. We were assisted greatly in forming the conference by Dr. Whitted, a truly learned man of the New Light church.

After the formation of the Conference, we selected as the name for the new organization, the Christian Union, which greatly pleased Dr. Whitted who wondered why others had not chosen that name long before. We then fixed the appointments of our ministers, Chipman being stationed at Hettonsville, at which place our greatest strength numerically was then concentrated, and the other ministers being sent out to different fields of labor, while I traveled at large, preaching at such points where I was most likely to do good.

We labored with pretty good success during the year. Just after harvest was over, we held a big campmeeting at my old campgrounds, near the site of our first conference, which was largely attended. We called on Elijah Brown, who had come to us since our conference, to preach for us on Sabbath morning. Being an Old Whig, he took occasion to denounce the Mexican war.[6] This insulted several men in the congregation who had been connected with that war, and they opposed him. Draper Chipman helped him to escape by putting him in his (Chipman's) buggy, with Chipman's wife, and they rode off together and thus got away uninjured. This unfortunate event injured our meeting for a little while, but we finally got over the matter, and went on with the meeting.

In the summer of 1844 a convention was held near the state line between Ohio and Indiana, at which nine denominations were represented.[7] Immediately after the organization of th[e] constitution a resolution was passed by which a committee, composed of one from each denomination, was appointed to draft the rules necessary to unite us into one body. It was also agreed that each denomination, was to hand in to such committee their own creeds. During preliminaries, our ministers were out in adjoining neighborhoods to hold meetings.

As I was chairman of the committee referred to I did not hand in my creed till my fellow committee men had done so. I then extended to them as my creed—the Holy Bible. As each creed was handed in, such parts of the same as were urged to be suitable for adoption, were carefully and elaborately discussed, and then, in every instance, was voted down.

This was kept up two days and a half, of hard labor, too, and the committee was becoming discouraged. I now tried my plan, proposing the Bible as a guide in all matters whatsoever, urging my view, assuring the committee as God had manifested mercy, and goodness and wisdom in establishing a church, He could give, and had given laws for its government. We decided to accept the Bible as the only and sufficient rule of faith and practice for our organized Christian Union Church.

After settling this vexed question we decided that each church should, subject to the Bible, govern herself. This was done, also, upon my suggestion.

"What shall we call ourselves?" was the next inquiry.

"For what purpose have we come together?" I asked.

A brother answered by saying, "for Christian union."

"Well, then", I again asked, "Why will not that answer all purposes?"

And they all gladly received and adopted my suggestion and the name <u>was</u> adopted as <u>The Christian Union</u>. Our action was ratified by the Convention.

Christian Union Ideas

Any study of religious sectarianism in Indiana in the mid-nineteenth century would do well to study groups such as Farmer's Christian Union Church. It was not just one church, but several groups of churches that merged and divided and realigned themselves. At the same time that Farmer was testing out his Christian Union Plan, other like-minded persons throughout the Midwest were traveling somewhat similar paths. The Christian Union Church might be considered a movement rather than a denomination, since the individuals who were part of the movement preached against sectarianism.

One way the Christian Union Church worked against sectarianism was through its membership requirements. All that was needed was a conversion experience, one-on-one with God. Baptism and other rites were not necessary. It is also significant that the Christian Union Church took the bible as its only creed. A creed, usually understood as a *summary* of bible truth, is a sectarian marker. A rejection of such a summary, or statement of faith, shifts authority from collective wisdom to individual conscience. It is an example of egalitarianism carried to the extreme. This position was (and is) the position of the Christian Church.

There are several versions of how the Christian Union Church began. In his autobiography, Farmer includes a short history written by his wife. Here is Elizabeth Farmer's version of the story:

> The rise of the Christian Union in this section of Indiana central through the labors of Eli P Farmer, formally a member of the traveling connection of ministers of the M.E. Church, was occasioned by very natural but very powerful circumstances. He had joined that body of ministers as early as 1825, and had abundant opportunities of becoming acquainted with the Discipline governing the church, and also of ascertaining their strong sectarian prejudices and opinions. These objectionable features, of that denominational, he found to be insufferable, and he at length, after many years of forbearance, and dissatisfaction, occasioned by reason of them, decided to attempt the establishment of a church on more liberal principles. His dissatisfaction become greatly strengthened, as early [as] 1839, at which time, water Baptism was made a test of membership. Subsequent to his first formation of liberal views concerning religious subjects, he preached doctrine in harmony with the views now entertained

by the members of the Christian Union. This innovation upon the Methodist system, at a time when he was an active member of one of their conferences, caused many of their ministers to become jealous of, and hostile to him. To such an extent was their hostility carried by some of them, that one of his Presiding Elders, became insulting to him, and abusive, and refused often times to permit him to preach, notwithstanding hundreds of lay members of the church were every where desiring him [to] preach. His dissatisfaction at length became so overwhelmingly strong, that he was compelled to leave conference, and locate.

Subsequent to his location he returned to his home near Bloomington, where he awaited the opining of the path of duty by Providence. About a month after his return home, he was solicited by some Baptist people, living in an adjoining settlement, to hold meetings at stated intervals; a place called "Putnam's School House" in their vicinity and he made an appointment in compliance with the wishes of their committee. Shortly after this appointment, many others followed consecutively, of evenings, and the result was a great revival blessed that community, at which about one hundred persons professed religion, all of whom wished him to baptize them by immersion, and he did so.

As they then had no organized church he told them to join such church as best pleased them. They decided as they were doing well they would not join any sectarian church at all. He then proposed his plan of Christian union, calling his plan at that time "The Republican Church," being in opposition to tyranny. All of them united with

This photograph from the early twentieth century in Illinois shows a service of what Eli Farmer called "water baptism," or "believer's baptism," or baptism by immersion. Water baptism was a major issue between Methodists and "Campbellites" or Christian Churches. Farmer's acceptance of water baptism marked the end of his days as a Methodist. Immersion scenes in rivers were hardly known before the days of the Western Revival and growing sectarianism.

him, in organizing a church with a suitable number of Elders and Deacons. The members of the union were allowed to join or belong to other denominations. Some time after this church was organized, old father Putnam, who was an elder in the union, joined the Baptist church, with the understanding that he was to remain a member of the union.[8]

There is another account of the Christian Union Church in an encyclopedia of Kansas state history:

The churches forming the denomination called the Christian Union, trace their origin to the great revival which took place in the first half of the nineteenth century, which led to a larger liberty in religious thought, a greater freedom from ecclesiastical domination, and a closer affiliation of the people of different creeds. A number of organizations arose that had no connection, most important among them being the Evangelical Christian Union, which consisted of seven congregations in Monroe County, Ind. These were united in 1857 by Rev. Eli P. Farmer, who went into the army as a chaplain at the outbreak of the Civil war and as a result some of the congregations were broken up. During the war the intensity of the political strife became reflected in the services of the church to such an extent that many persons, both lay and clergy, withdrew from different denominations and joined the ranks of those who were impatient under the restrictions of ecclesiastical rule. Finally a call was issued for a convention to be held by all who favored "forming a new church organization" on broader lines than those of the existing denominations, free from both political bias and ecclesiastical domination.

    The convention met at Columbus, Ohio, Feb. 3, 1863, and adopted resolutions by which was formed a religious society under the name of Christian Union. In 1864 a general convention was held at Terre Haute, Ind., attended by delegates from several states, at which the action of the former convention was reaffirmed and a summary of principles was adopted as follows: The oneness of the Church of Christ; Christ the only head; the Bible the only rule of faith and practice; good fruits the only condition of fellowship; Christian Union without controversy; each local church self governing; political preaching discountenanced. From this time the movement spread rapidly, some of its best known leaders being J. F. Given, J. V. B. Flack, and Ira Norris. On his return from the army Eli Farmer joined the movement and remained in active service until his death in 1878.[9]

The inheritors of this movement are known today as Christian Union. The group reported 107 churches and 3,647 members in 2010.[10]

The early days of the union were difficult, though. Trouble arose from some Methodists in the group, as Farmer relates below:

Soon after its ratification, a couple of Methodist preachers who had pretended to be in harmony with us, managed to affect a reconsideration of the vote, and succeeded in stirring up considerable strife, and a diversity of opinions, and I saw that a division was imminent and I withdrew from the convention.

    Before adjourning, however, they decided to hold another convention in one year from that time, at the same place. They did so hold it but I did not attend it. These reverses did not cause me to despair. On the contrary, I kept up a correspondence with Mr. Hunt of Huntsville, Ind,

John Thomas of Jacksonville, Ohio, on the subject so near my heart, and they finally wrote me they had adopted my Christian union plan and were well pleased with it, and both of them urged me to come to their assistance.[11] My time was so employed I could not go.

Word came to me now, from these good brethren, that the work was spreading far and wide, in their respective regions, it had got in among the Quakers and was making inroads upon several societies of Friends, especially near Philadelphia, in the state of Ohio, my name being linked with this information.

I was again and again, urged by many Quakers, to go out into Ohio, to help them carry on the work. In the fall of this year, we effected a union with the old New Lights, at our next regular conference, calling the new conference "The central Christian Union Conference."

About this time our dearly love[d] brother Forbe went west, taking with him a letter of recommendation, and I have no doubt he did much toward spreading the reform out there. Chipman demanded higher wages, and a year's provision in advance, and required also that we should create a parsonage for him, else he would preach no more for us. Upon consultation, we left him without an appointment. He became insulted and leading off two or three of our preachers, he connected himself with the Campbellite church.

The Methodists, seeing our distracted condition, renewed hostilities upon us with greater power than ever before, and our cause was seriously injured. Many of our members emigrated to the west, while the rem[a]inder left behind, became widely scattered, or too much discouraged to attempt to do any thing, and went back to their former sectarian churches.

The Methodist preachers, supposing I was defeated now thought I would return to their Church. They determined at all events to break down this unionism, and for that purpose appointed their preachers about this time, who were especially charged with the duty of breaking us down. Both of these men were unscrupulous, and I succeeded in proving before public audiences that both of them had conducted the most palpable and wicked lies and slanders upon me, both of them knowing them to be such, one of the fellows being present in the courthouse in Bloomington when I did so.

I now began to hear dark hints about something which a Methodist preacher by the name of Mr. Morrow had done against me surrepti[ti]ously at a Quarterly conference, and I investigated the matter. He had inserted something in the Quarterly conference [minutes] derogatory to my character, after I had left the church, and I found out through squire James Robertson what it was. I proved Morrow to be another liar, by his own brethren, after which I established him as a liar in a great number of hand bills which I caused to be printed and distributed. Some of these hand bills, I caused to be pasted up in many conspicuous places in Jeffersonville during a session of the conference to which he belonged. This occasioned considerable excitement, and Morrow became so crippled, that he was transferred to the conference in California.

My means having sufficiently increased by the time the year 1853 arrived to enable me to do so, I bought a printing press, in order to be better prepared for my mission in warring against sectarianism. Of course, I was now assailed on every hand. At one time, three prominent editors, of religious papers, were fighting me fiercely, but I held my own with them. My paper was very extensively circulated in all parts of the United States, and our principles spread with great rapidity and power.

One of my ablest assistants during these years of toil, strife, and trouble was Brother Acton, whom I always found to be true and steadfast. I continued to remain with the Christian Union, until I met brother Bridges at Jeffersonville, some years since, when we united with each other and became one body.

16

The *Bloomington Religious Times*, 1853 to 1854

In 1853 Eli Farmer and two associates, Jesse Brandon and Harvey Murphy, started a newspaper, the *Bloomington Religious Times*. Brandon had newspaper experience and Murphy had a cause—temperance. Murphy also had an interest in phrenology, the study of the structure of the skull to determine mental capabilities and character. While the paper carried news and items of local interest, it was, at least editorially, a platform for Farmer to preach his convictions in a new venue. Farmer had successfully managed his salt mine and farm so that he had accumulated enough funds to launch the paper, which published its first issue on November 11, 1853. The paper ran until June 1854, and then Farmer and Brandon continued it another year under the name of the *Western Times*.[1]

Farmer had a number of convictions he wanted to write about. In fact, by this point in his life, Farmer's religious, moral, and political convictions were so intertwined that they represented one general philosophy. While he did not speak about manifest destiny as such, he believed strongly in America, its democratic institutions, and its future. As discussed elsewhere, he was a post-millennialist, believing that God's kingdom would be established on earth and that America somehow fit into that plan. Thus, he had supported the war with Mexico. With his opposition to slavery, he would soon support the Union cause in the Civil War. At this point, he was a Whig in politics, although he was often in conflict with leaders of the Whig Party. Farmer supported the cause of temperance and spoke out against the evils of alcohol.

Farmer and his developing convictions serve as an example of a broad, uncoordinated movement taking place primarily on the western frontier during the 1840s known as restorationism, the belief that Christianity should be restored to its original simplicity and purity. This was an effort to return Christianity to the way the apostles had taught and lived it. There were restorationist groups before in Europe, but these groups at best were minor sects. Restorationism thrived on the western frontier. Joseph Smith and the Mormons, William Miller and the Adventists, John Thomas and the Christadelphians, and Alexander Campbell and the Campbellites, as well as some Methodists and Baptists were working toward forms of restoration. It is also possible to mention secular utopian groups such as Indiana's New Harmony settlement as holding somewhat similar goals. Farmer certainly shared a belief in restorationism; it underlaid his dreams for a Christian Union Church.

In politics, restorationist groups tended to be republican with distrust of kings and parliaments and any form of concentrated power. Some restorationists withdrew from the world in gathered communities. Others, such as Farmer, were reformers. As a Methodist, even during his years of success as a Methodist preacher, he spoke disparagingly of "the authorities," which was a reference to traveling elders and conference leaders. Although he himself was a traveling elder, he identified with the local pastors. In the 1830s and 1840s he opposed the Internal Improvements Act because, among other things, it was associated with bankers and persons of influence. He opposed preachers who drew large salaries and shunned fashion and displays of wealth. In an article purportedly about temperance, Farmer argues for a return to simplicity and humbleness in all areas of life by railing against "leaders in both Church and State":

The subject of temperance is before us, and we must confess we dread the consequence seeing that temperance is of a threefold nature, and should be handled as such, without which great harm may be done.[2] All parties must say that the intemperance of the physical man is doing great harm; but we consider that intemperance either of the moral or intellectual man is more dangerous to the cause of the kingdom of Christ, and also [to] our liberties as a people, with all our free institutions. And we have no doubt that at this time both Church and State have lost the proper checks; and the leaders in both Church and State have become intoxicated with the love of money, of power, and worse than all, the pride of life, has so influenced them, that we fear the parties have turned the locomotives of Church and State to come in collis[i]on with each other, and must destroy or greatly injure the cause of Christianity as well as our free institutions; and if it was only them that would only suffer, that would do. But in this case those conductors and engineers will save themselves from being destroyed, and the class that bears the burden of the country will be the ones that must suffer, through the drunkenness of the leaders of Church and State.

We are afraid to risk all in the hands of those hirelings for they, almost to a man, are drones in the hives of nature and are consumers and not producers. Are they not the class that are doing the mischief? Let us take a few of them more closely. Go to every county seat and there you will find, sometimes one to six or seven preachers, of the different classes. All profess to be called of God to preach the gospel and to do unto all men as they would have others do to them: and sit down in their little station, and collect off of their poor laboring brother, and rouse to action all the powers of their burden bearing people to live right and pay their preachers well, and all will go well with them; and preach once or twice on Sabbath and spend all the rest of the week in preparing a little dry fancy sermon without soul or body to it instead of showing by their industry and humility the way to heaven. Their example leads to pride and laziness. They raise their families in the same way, and five or six such preachers is a curse to any county-seat, and will demoralize any place in the world. They will live more lazy than anyone else in town and live higher,—take more authority than any other people; wear more fine clothes, get more money than almost all the rest of the drones. So their example will ruin the young people,—for they will follow their example and be drunk with pride and sin.

Restorationism was but one reason for Farmer to start a newspaper of religious opinion. By 1853 he had identified with a new cause: the Republican United Brethren Church. The Church of the United Brethren in Christ grew out of the Methodist revival in Pennsylvania in the early 1800s. The United Brethren preached Methodist doctrine, held revivals and camp meetings, and were episcopal (used bishops) in church polity.

KIRWAN'S LETTERS.
LETTER III.

MY DEAR SIR,—In my last letter I commenced a statement to you of the causes which, in early life, caused my misgivings and distrust as to yours being a true church, and as to its holding the true faith. I referred to some incidents connected with the claims of your priests to miraculous power, with the doctrine of purgatory, and with praying to the saints. I shall now proceed with a statement of some more of those causes.

The doctrine of confession, is one of the primary doctrines of your church. It requires every good papist to confess his sins to a priest, at least, once a year. If any sins are concealed, none are forgiven. This doctrine makes the bosom of the priest the repository of all the sins of all the sinners, of his parish, who make a conscience of Confession.— And this is one of the scourges of the fearful power which your priests have over your people. And with this doctrine of Confession, is connected the power of the Father Confessor to grant Absolution to the confessing penitent. It is sometimes affirmed, and then denied, to suit circumstances, that the priest claims such power. But Dr. Challoner, in his "Catholic Christian Instructed," Chap. 9th, asserts this power, and on what he deems Scriptural authority. And I never knew an individual who came from Confession, with the privilege of partaking of the Communion, who did not feel and believe that his sins were forgiven him. And if they were not immediately forgiven, they would be, on the performance of the prescribed penances. You, sir, will not say, that I either mistate or misrepresent the doctrine.

Now for some of my early impressions upon this subject. Father M. held frequently his confessions at our house. He sat in a dark room up stairs, with one or more candles on a table before him. Those going to Confession followed each other on their knees, from the front door, through the hall, up the stairs, and to the door of the room. When one came out of the confessing room, another entered. My turn came—I entered the room, from which the light of day was excluded, and bowed myself before the priest. He made over me the sign of the cross, and after saying something in Latin, he ordered me to commence the detail of my sins. Such was my right that my memory soon failed in bringing up past delinquencies. He would prompt me, and ask, did you do this thing, or that thing? I would answer yes, or no. And when I could say no more, he would wave his hand over me, and again utter some words in Latin, and dismiss me. Through this process I often went, and never without feeling that my sins were forgiven. Sins that burdened me before, were now disregarded. The load of guilt was gone. And I often felt, when prompted to sin, that I could commit it with impunity, as I could soon confess it, and secure its pardon. And this, sir, is the fearful and fatal effect of your doctrine of Confession and Absolution upon millions of minds.

The questions however often came up—Why does the priest go into a dark room in the daytime? Why not speak to me in English, and not in Latin? How can he forgive sin?— What, if my sins, after all, are not forgiven? And I always found that I could play my pranks better after confession than before, for I could go at them with a lighter heart. Very early in life, my confidence in this doctrine of Confession was shaken, and at a later period I came to the conclusion that it was a priestly device to ensnare the conscience, and to enslave men.

(CONTINUED.)

RELIGIOUS TIMES.
ELI P. FARMER EDITOR.
BLOOMINGTON JANUARY 20, 1854.

FIRE WATER.

Few persons have suffered more from the evils of this all-destroying element of Fire-Water, which has been instrumental in the hands of sin and Satan, of the destruction of millions of the best of our race, ruined them, and families of the best stock in the world, who have been ruined for both worlds, than ourselves.

She entered the battle fields with our fore-fathers, in the struggle of the Revolution of '76;—gave a false stimulant in the work, in the hour of adversity, warming their hearts in all their social parties and festivals, and was found by their sides on the bloody field of battle;—cheering them in all their struggles, and when victory came to our relief, she failed not to cheer the weary, bleeding soldiers and officers, wisely winning their affections, blinding their judgments, leading their appetites and passions, to bow at the altar of Bacchus, where she sacrifices thousands annually.

There has been a war of extermination of this great evil declared, which will, and ought to, call forth, all the energies of the physical, moral and intellectual man. But is it right to make it a political test in our elections? Let us think.

Our father being of the stock of '76, in early life, was taken by her charms. Some years after the contest of '76, as I understand, by tradition, he descended the Ohio river, and with old Anthony Wayne, in Kentucky, fighting and guarding the Colonies of that wide spread wilderness for two years; then accompanied by one of his companions in arms penetrated the wilderness of Indiana, and an unbroken forest, of five hundred miles, to the State of Virginia, the land that gave him birth. Our father married Sarah Price, the daughter of John Price, then descended the Ohio river, the second time, with a boat load of ammunition and arms, for the benefit of the army. This Fire-Water a common beverage, wherever they found her, still cheering their weary bodies and minds, and yet no evils appeared unto them. For as yet the light of science and religion had not illuminated their benighted land. Our father still vigorous, and accumulating property fast; his property, twice destroyed by the Indians; the third time by fraud, and the fourth time by fire, he, getting in years and a weighty family, drove him to the altar of Bacchus, there to find relief with the old soldiers, in similar situations, who would spend their time and money in telling over their battles and sufferings.

In the fall of 1811, my mother, having a small legacy coming to her, we moved to Virginia. The weight the family fell upon my brother and myself.

In the spring of '20, my brother and myself concluded to return to Kentucky, with a boat load of grindstones. Mother being unwilling we should leave the family behind, we settled all the debts of our father, but one small one of thirty two or three dollars, which was mostly a *Whiskey* debt, for we were unwilling to pay a man to destroy our own father. We passed means into the hands of mother and a brother, under age, so that they might build a small family boat, and move themselves, that we might not be accountable for the whiskey debt. They, to whom the debt was coming, came on down fifteen miles, where we were loading our boat, and levied on our boat and stopped us, we were still unwilling to pay the debt The man to whom it was coming, agreed that if my brother and myself would go security for our father he would let us move. Seeing that the river would soon fall, and that we might not get off that spring, if we missed that water, we agreed to go security for our father; understanding that we would fight it off at some other time, and we have that debt to meet yet. Our father died in a few days after. We brought the family back to Kentucky, set them up to housekeeping again, and paid for the schooling of the children, gave our mother a cow and a horse, and in the spring of '22, we came to this place, at twenty eigth years of age, where we have resided almost thirty two years. As the old settlers of this county well know, have fought the stagger juice, with a steady hand almost alone for many years. We have had our lives threatened. We have spent hundreds of dollars, to fight down the evil of ardent sprits, in the pulpit and on the stump, before any came to our relief. And now if we will hold a steady hand we will succeed, but we ought to act with propriety.

We think it imprudent to make it a test in the political field, or in the Legislative halls. 1st, Because the candidate wishes to be on the strong side of the political question, and to make sure his election, he will be found fighting against the Temperance cause, unless he be a man that is willing to sacrifice himself for the benefit of the cause. Few men are willing to spend time and money to sacrifice themselves, for the good of the cause. The candidates on the Temperance side will be unnerved, when fighting without a prospect of success. And if elected he is sworn to support the Constitution of the State, and of the United States. So he may be bound to violate his oath or word, to the people. It does appear alarming to the Republican part of our citizens to see the Ministers standing at the head of church and State, with a political and religious scourge in hand, threatening political and religious death if not obeyed. This seems much like blending church and state together.

We have no objection to see a Minister when not employed by his church, to run for office—when standing on a level with their fellow-citizens. We also think it deleterious to our free institutions, for Ministers to stand at the head of our Legislators direct them as sworn officers how to legislate.

We would be pleased to see the Ministers stand in their own place. All past experience has proved to us, that when Ministers have the power they are the most dangerous persons in the world, to the rights and liberties of the people. It savors too much of Popery and Romanism.

We will be found side by side with Ministers of every denomination, to carry light and reformation into every part of our country; that legislation may follow the light, and reformation Then legislation will grow out of the light of reformed minds, and pure motives. Under the present plan, we may succeed in getting a law passed to put down the evil, but in the next Legislature—the people having the power will elect members to destroy that system, and loose again the tiger of Intemperance; hoisting the flood gates of misery;—sweeping off the cause of temperance and kingdom of Christ; and destroy the redemption of men.

If ministers would leave their homes and salaried stations, and take the world for their diocese, like Christ and the Apostles: we would soon moralize and spiritualize the world. Then Temperance would spring up in every heart, family, kingdom and country. Brethren, if religion can not bear this, we had better give it a pinch of *Maccaboy Snuff* and let it sneeze itself to death.

The above was written before the Temperance Convention, was held at Indianapolis recently, and is not to be considered as opposed to the Temperance cause, but we are of the opinion, that the duty of the ministers is to take the broad commission of Christ, "Go ye into all the world and preach the Gospel, to every creature." We think that gospel reformation should follow temperance reformation, and the power of gospel reformation will give strength to accomplish and carry out the temperance reform is the harbinger of the religion.

In this article by Eli Farmer, he again takes temperance as his subject, this time using it to tell woeful stories from the American Revolution to the death of his father before making observations concerning preachers and legislators.

They organized separately from the Methodists, not because of any doctrinal or polity differences but in order to reach German-speaking people, particularly in Pennsylvania, Ohio, and Indiana. The United Brethren were also pacifists and when one of their number in Indiana, P. C. Parker, volunteered for the army before the Mexican War in the 1840s he was expelled from the church for "immorality" (going to war). Those who supported Parker, basically over the issue of pacifism, organized to form a new denomination, the Republican United Brethren Church.

In a time of sectarianism, when splintering and forming and reforming was taking place for the slightest of reasons, tracing this group and the groups it had affinity with present a challenge. Several groups in Ohio were also splintering from the United Brethren Church.[3] These Ohio groups would play an important role in Farmer's future life. They would meet together with Farmer at a gathering in Ohio in 1864 that would result in the formation of a viable Christian Union Church.

In the mid-1850s Farmer never mentioned the Ohio Republican United Brethren. His cause was that of the Indiana Republican United Brethren. He had believed strongly in and supported the Mexican War. He felt that Parker had been wrongly expelled, as he had acted out of conscience. Furthermore, Parker's conscience had been in service to a righteous cause, and more than that, a civil cause. For Farmer the expulsion was another example of the misuse of episcopal power. Farmer's word for this, consistent with his republican convictions, was "tyranny," a word that appeared frequently in the newspaper and then later in his autobiography.

The *Religious Times* presented itself as the official organ of the Republican United Brethren. The first issue carried the church constitution and bylaws and statements of faith. It is symptomatic of the sectarianism of the age that Farmer, at the very time he was editing the official paper of the Republican United Brethren, was himself trying to pull together his own denomination, the Christian Union. Eventually they would find common cause, but that was not apparent in 1853. Farmer was also trying to keep a relationship with the Methodists. This would go badly after the paper was started because the Methodists understood that an attack on United Brethren "tyranny" was also an attack on Methodist "tyranny" and the criticism did not sit well. Even worse was when Farmer directly called out the Methodists as in the following passage:

Brother Dew has done well in joining the M.E. Church, for it is an animal church, where the animals are collected together; where the Bishop is the herdsman, and drives them about like stock.[4]

At the time Farmer co-owned a newspaper, Methodists were becoming more established as a traditional denomination. As such they were cooperating and finding common ground with Baptists, Presbyterians, Quakers, and Episcopalians. Even with their growing respectability, however, they had problems with Universalists, Roman Catholics, and Campbellites. By 1853 Farmer had shown himself to be in concert with Campbellites on many points, including restorationism. This can be seen by comparing his rhetoric and actions with articles written by William Phillips in the *Western Christian Advocate* in 1835 to 1836 (later published in book form).[5] Phillips showed that Campbellites differed with Methodists on four important issues: baptism (Farmer had been willing to use immersive baptism as the Campbellites did since the late 1830s); creeds (with his Christian Union denomination, Farmer had dispensed with any creed other than the Bible itself, similar to Campbellites); tradition (Farmer's Christian Union Church accepted all orthodox traditions, that is all traditions that tended toward evangelicalism); and church government (Farmer spoke out against church authority, from itinerant preachers to bishops, which agreed with the lack of hierarchy in the Campbellite church).

To the Methodists, when Farmer identified with the Campbellites he had not only abandoned Methodism but worse, he had identified with the enemy. There were repercussions. Farmer reports on at least one instance when the Methodists in Brown County disputed even the Republican United Brethren Church because Farmer was a preacher for it in a meeting house built for use by multiple Protestant denominations:

We wish to pursue the bloody footsteps of this episcopal dog, which shows to all discerning minds, that destruction and misery are in all his ways; either in mind, body, or the rights of the mass. . . .[6]

Some days since, we were called upon by the republican united brethren, to assist in holding a big meeting in the town of Nashville, where all classes of people contributed to assist in building a meeting house for the benefit of the town and people; and when not occupied by the Methodists, that all others might use it for preaching. The brethren with ourself, met at the place of worship and commenced service. We were called upon by the brethren on Saturday night to close by singing and praying. As soon as we arose and commenced singing, the most of the Methodist women as we supposed in great haste, followed; showing that they loved darkness rather than light because their deeds were evil, as the Scriptures say. The congregation was very much annoyed indeed, on account of the great confusion. After song and prayer, one of them came to us and informed us that we were not allowed to preach in the meeting house, we asked the reason why. The answer was we are determined to put you and your paper down. This is the substance of the words of the messenger, as well as we can recollect.

Now we make an appeal to all thinking persons, to judge between us and them. We agree that we have said some hard things against the episcopal government, which is the quintessence of all tyranny. We think all true Republicans will go against that one man power, the Bishop.— the disturbances made by the Methodists was a violation of law, and we think, if the officers of the county will do their duty, they will make them pay for it. If any of the wicked were to do as they have done, they would put the law in force against them, and punish them well; but they have said by their joining the church, that we can do what we please, and escape the punishment of the law. They are like that man who stole his neighbors hay. We stealing he said, "LORD, know odds what the hands do, so the heart is right." The name of honesty, or religion, goes a great way with some folks. The name is all there is of it; but let us look into the design, or principle, of their conduct. It means that, 1st We will make a scapegoat of Farmer to bear off all our sins; and we can whip the United Brethren over Farmer's shoulders and inure the progress of the meeting. 2nd we will teach the United Brethren that if they do not cho[o]se just such creatures as we may like, they shall not preach here:—we will let them know that they must bow to the image of the beast, or they cannot.— unless they have the mark in the forehead or hand they cannot deal with us. Is not this the very spirit of Popery, proven as plain as can be?

At the end of this last passage, Farmer shows his anti-Catholic sentiments, referring to images from the biblical Book of Revelation and asking if the image of the beast is not

RELIGIOUS TIMES.

"If the foundations be destroyed, what can the righteous do?"

VOL. I. BLOOMINGTON, IND., FEBRUARY 17, 1854. **NO 10.**

PROSPECTUS OF THE RELIGIOUS TIMES.

The object of this Paper is the dissemination of Religious, Scientific, Literary, Agricultural, Political, and other useful knowledge. It is issued weekly, (on Friday,) in Bloomington, Indiana.

One-half of it, edited by Eli P. Farmer, is devoted exclusively to Religion, its principle object being to excite the Christian world to a sense of their duty, and induce them to do away with Sectarianism, and unite in a single body.

The other half, edited by Harvey Murphy and J. Brandon, is devoted to General and Political News, Science, Literature, Agriculture, and whatever other useful Intelligence may suggest itself from time to time.

Each Number of the Paper will contain a Mathematical Problem, the Solution of which will be given in the succeeding Number. Sometimes several methods of solving the same Problem will be given. Some difficult ones will be given for the amusement of the learned, while others will be of simple, the Solution being designed to illustrate some principle in Mathematics.

TERMS.—One dollar and twenty-five cents, in advance; one dollar and fifty cents, due in four months after the reception of the first Number; or two dollars, if not paid till the expiration of twelve months.

☞ To any person sending us the names of five subscribers, accompanied by six dollars, we will send the sixth copy free of charge.

N. B.—The money sent at our risk, provided the Post Master's receipt be taken for the same.

All Communications, and letters on business relating to the Paper, to be directed (pre-paid) to the Religious Times, Bloomington, Monroe county, Indiana.

Advertisements inserted at the usual (moderate) prices.

RELIGIOUS DEPARTMENT:
ELI P. FARMER Editor.

GOVERN THE CHILDREN.

The youth of the country are soon to hold its destiny in their hands. And as they are now governed will they hereafter govern. Neibuhr says in his letters, "freedom is quite impossible when the youth of a country are devoid of reverence and modesty." We confess we have sometimes feared for the future of our land, when we consider the the character of the rising population.

Young America is so fast, has so little reverence for the past, and such unfailing faith in progress of the aggressive order, that his hands seem unsafe receptacles of so great a trust. Our Puritan forefathers were strict disciplinarians, and New England owes its power and glory to this fact. Parental control is now very much relaxed. This is a bad state of things, and should be changed. Boys need control as much as bread and butter. Niebuhr, whom we must again quote, says;

"I would warn every one, whose child shows a bad disposition, to hold him in while he is young, for there is not much fear of breaking his spirits. His innate impudence will keep him from this, and I feel, by myself, that our faults cannot be torn up with too much violence in childhood, before they have taken too deep a root. —*Portland Transcript.*

CORRESPONDENCE.

Brother Farmer:—If you think the following worthy, please give it a place in the Times;

Not long since, I traveled in company with b . Hamblin, through the counties of decatur, Ripley, and Franklin, delivering lectures on the reasons assigned for a separation in the church of the United Brethren in Christ, and the establishing of a new organization, bearing the name, Republican United Brethren. The reader is referred to the first and second numbers of the Religious Times, in which will be found the reasons, (or the principle ones of them,) set forth at length. But I believe the Resolution on War, as set forth in the Discipline of the old Church, has not yet been published in any of our Proceedings, nor the amendment that was offered by br. Markwood; hence, thinking it not unimportant to the majority of your readers, I proceed to give it verbatim:

"The spirit which leads men to voluntarily engage in national warfare, is wholly anti-Christian, and ought not to be tolerated by us."

I will now give the amendment as offered by br. Markwood, in General Conference, which may be found in the Minutes of said Conference:

"The spirit which leads men to voluntarily engage in national warfare, without there appears to be just grounds for such warfare, is wholly anti-Christian, and ought not be tolerated by us."

This amendment was lost by the following vote: Yeas 5, Nays 38.

The reader will bear in mind that, according to the above vote, even if there should be "just grounds for such warfare," he is unholy if he engage in it.

I will now give a brief synopsis of the arguments I used against the above Resolution:

In the first place I spoke of the injustice done to br. P. C. Parker by the Annual Conference, but more particularly of the principles involved in the proceedings with him, a full account of which may be seen by reference to the first number of the Religious Times. I then took the ground that the Resolution conflicted with the Constitutional provisions of our Civil Government; that it was anti-republican; and that it was not sustained by the Word of God.

1st. That it conflicts with the Constitution will be evident to any who will take the trouble to examine the 3d Article of the Confederation, which solemnly binds every State in the Union to defend each other.

2d. It is anti-republican, because it forbids the only means of maintaining a Republican Government. Where, I ask, exists the spirit of volunteering in behalf of one's own and his neighbor's good?—in a Monarchy? No; if it does, it is not allowed to develop itself. Where, then, does it exist? Answer, it exists in the heart of every true patriot—every friend of liberty—every opposer of tyranny; for it is the free-will offering of our own lives for the liberty of our neighbors—our brothers.

That it is contrary to Scripture is evident from the following passages, which I hope the reader will carefully examine, bearing in mind that wherever the word "centurion" occurs it means a military officer, and that "devout" means pious, or religious: Neh. 4:18; Rom. 17:1 to 29; Luke 7th; Acts 10:1 to 7, and 19 and 20.

On a certain occasion, after the conclusion of my lecture, br. Hamblin arose to offer church privileges, if any were present that desired them. At this time we were informed that brs. Chittenden, Rily, and Stearnes, were present, (three elders from the old church,) and desired to speak. Br. Hamblin remarked that if they were present and desired to speak, they could have the privilege. [Note. We were credibly informed the next day that br. Stearnes asked Father O. if he was acquainted with the man that was to deliver the lecture, and that he said he was not; that br. S. returned, "I am going down to hear myself, and I must not go in till dark —for if they see ME, they will not open their mouths." I suppose that br. Stearnes placed a full estimate upon himself.] Br. Chittenden arose, with book and paper in hand, and came forward. He then proceeded to remark that br. Parker was expelled for leaving his circuit without permission and refusing to make acknowledgments to the Conference. He remarked, further, that the Resolution on War, as it stood in their discipline, did not mean to prohibit the members from defending their natural rights, either individual or national, if there were just grounds for it. Suppose, said he, a preacher was traveling along the road, and a fillibuster was to meet him with a drawn sword, and make war upon him, then the preacher would be justifiable in defending himself. The Resolution, he continued, has reference only to national warfare, when there is no call for the services of the church. He then referred to the Revelation of St. John, in which he saw three unclean spirits like frogs come out of the mouth of the dragon, and out of the mouth of the beast and of the false prophets; for they were the spirits of devils, which went forth to the kings of the whole world to gather them together to the battle of the Great Day of God Almighty— and also to the declaration that the swords should be beaten into ploughshares, and spears into pruning hooks —and that the nations should learn war no more.

This was about the drift of his argument—but it is obvious to the reflecting mind that he never touched a single point in question. I informed the brother that he was a poor marksman, for he had shot at me, and missed the wall. I then asked br. Chittenden to inform the congregation what circuit br. Parker left. After studying a moment, he remarked that he did not know. I then told him that as he had made the assertion, I demanded of him the name of the circuit he left. He then said he believed that it was Franklin and Morgantown circuit. I told him that I lived on that circuit when br. Parker left home, and that br. Hanway traveled on that circuit then, and that br. Parker had no circuit that year. He then stated that he believed that br. Parker was only to fill a portion of the time for some other brother, or that he was so informed.

I know not what the brother's information on the subject was, but the truth is:—brother Parker had no work assigned to him at that time— and I do hope that the misrepresentation of that subject will hereafter cease to circulate.

I then offered them what I considered a fair chance. I told them to set the time and place, and that we would meet them and test our principles by the standard of truth, before an impartial tribunal—but they refused.

In conclusion let me ask—Is it not a great pity that ministers of the gospel (without informing themselves, for they certainly would not if they were informed) will take a stand against the Constitution of their country, which, if carried into effect, would destroy the Government which protects their lives, their property, their wives, their little ones—gives them the right of suffrage, and above all, protects their religion, and guards them while they worship. O that the Lord would open the eyes of the blind, unstop the ears of the deaf, and burst the bands of tyranny, is my prayer. WILLIAM TAGGART.

PIGEON ROOST.

In Franklin county, Indiana, north of the town of Brookville, the pigeons congregate now-a-nights in prodigious numbers. The woods, over a space of ten miles in length, by five in breadth, are nigtly filled by countless multitudes of these birds, that light upon the braches and pile upon each other in such enormous masses, that the stoutest limbs give way, killing in their fall, thousands of their destroyers. Mornings and evenings the air is darkened by swarms of myriads of myriads of pigeons. The flocks are miles in extent, and sweep over the heavens like thunder clouds. The roar of the innumerable wings during the hours of arrival and departure is tremendous. Hundreds of hogs are engaged in devouring the birds that are killed by various causalities. The people in that vicinity are tired of shooting among the ærial hosts.

Any person who desires to kill a few thousand in the course of a night, takes gun and ammunition, enters the roost, sits down and fires as often as he can load, directly upward, and his game tumbles down around him. It has been remarked, facceiously perhaps, that some sportsmen have been overwhelmed and nearly crushed by the fall of birds following a shot.

A genuine sportsman would not enjoy such murderous operations as these, but men who are fond of shedding blood, even if it be that of birds, should snatch their guns, take the stage, and away to the roost. —*Cin. Com.*

the very spirit of "popery," that is, the Pope, and by association the Catholic Church and its adherents. This was a strain that appeared in many of Farmer's articles.

Nevertheless, not all that Farmer opined in the *Religious Times* was critical or angry. He also could reflect on positive spiritual and uplifting moments. Note that in the following article he references "the millennium," which for post-millennialists such as himself was the expected day of peace and harmony over all the earth:

We have just returned from the Brown County quarterly meeting, held by the Republican United Brethren at which we had the inexpressible pleasure of seeing and conversing with many of the friends of the cause of Christ and almost everyone was speaking encouragingly about the progress of religion in his own and adjoining neighborhoods.[7] At the meeting referred to we had the pleasure of witnessing a great many royal genuinely old fashioned conversions. May the work of the Lord continue to spread and may it gather strength and velocity till it shall fill the whole earth—until the glorious millennium shall be announced at hand by the guileless Nazarene.

On Monday morning we left. . . . We soon reached the old Pilgrim Inn established by Judge Talbert [Taggart?] at the time of the first settling of Bartholomew.[8] But the old veteran of the cross has since fallen asleep leaving his inn to his warm hearted son Wm Taggert. It still remains the home of the brave and an asylum for the poor, a place where the weary pilgrim finds all his wants supplied without money and without price[.] The inn is located on a beautiful eminence over looking a rich fertile valley and ornamented with a beautiful little rivlet which pours its sparkling beverage into the house to quench the thirst of the weary pilgrims. The surrounding scenery together with the kindness and affection of the inmates renders it almost a little Heaven on earth. Notwithstanding all of this the time at length arrived when we must depart. And when we gave the parting hand to the members of the family and the preachers and brethren that resorted thither for refreshment, for rest, and for the sake of conversation, their smiling countenances spoke love in their hearts with a language that hypocrisy can never imitate.

In the next section of Farmer's article, he expresses nostalgia for the life he lived in Indiana when it was a frontier. He fondly lists Methodist preachers who have passed away. And then he gives a defense of his religion, stating that it is the same religion he carried to camp meetings and fledgling towns thirty years before. He has not changed, but Methodism has.

We mounted our faithful beast and made our ways up the tributaries of the Big Salt until we passed over the divide on Bean where the heavens grew black and rain began to pour[,] fell down to pour down on each side in torrents.

The rain fell on each side behind and before and all around us which together with the mud that was thrown from the hoofs of the big-footed horse rendered us very uncomfortable to say nothing about beauty. We thought of the time when our pilgrimage on earth shall number three score and considering the short space between that and death and anticipating which the joy of heaven which we hope to share—the direction of our thoughts were changed.

Opposite: Besides showing the masthead for the Bloomington Religious Times *and Eli Farmer as religious editor, this front page of the newspaper for February 17, 1854, gives Farmer's reason for printing the paper: "to excite the Christian world to a sense of their duty, and induce them to do away with Sectarianism, and unite in a single body."*

We thought of The villages[,] towns and churches which had been founded near us in the past thirty-two years while we had been engaged mostly in the ministry; of the magnificent dwellings which had been erected where Indian wigwams had formerly stood and the beautiful farms where hunters were want to roam and the railroads were naught but by-passes once were known. We then turned our attention to the old gospel battleground and saw there two-edged swords in hand James Scott, James Haven, Calvin Rutter, Armstrong, and Wiley all of whom were valiant soldiers and co-workers in the cause of Christ. Fiery dart has slain most of them. They have gone to reap their reward at the right hand of him who died to save sinners. . . .

We now wish to say to the religious part of the members of the ME church[:] that ground we now occupy is the same as we have always carried and preached and we intend to carry out as long as we shall live. Those preachers . . . who pass for Methodist preachers but who were like whitened sepulchers and wickedness we have succeeded in exposing them to the public as this we consider one of the principle duties of devoted Christians. Among the preachers br. Crary was the first one we labored with, who acted the part of a Christian. We then hoped that the matter was at rest when they were informed that our standing in the church was good. Shortly after that we went to the quarterly meeting at which the elder showed us all the kindness that a man of God could. We felt much pleased and took part in the worship and often preached among them and had happy times. . . .

We have the same cartridge box, the same ammunition, the same revolver, the same two-edged sword that we carried in forming the ME church in this country. With these weapons (furnished us by the creator) we have fought our way through thick and thin and when establishing the ME church here we had to swim waters, climb mountains, suffer with cold and heat almost without clothes. Then we carried needle and thread to mend our own clothes and at least once had to sell the last cow leaving our children without milk. That year my wife wove cloth to pay for shoe leather being unwilling that we should stop traveling. We continued to travel and preach until we brought into the fold over 5,000 persons. We paid out money to help build the best meeting houses in the state. Now we think it hard that we cannot have the privilege of preaching to them occasionally when nothing immoral can be laid to our charge. But some of our Methodist brethren use hard language being "hard case" at best. But we wish to inform them that it was considered all right when it was used in their favor for their cause. Now they pronounce it low and vulgar.

Now In conclusion we stand firmly upon this Scripture which is represented in the General Rules of the Methodist Discipline by Father Wesley which we consider Methodism as we have labored 32 years in endeavoring to establish true Methodism. We therefore expect to hold a steady hand in doing all the good we can of every possible sort to all men and when attack[ed] by those little gimblet preachers who are usurpters in the kingdom of Christ we shall pay them in a gospel way as we may think fit. But all ministers we expect to meet as brethren.

The Closing of the *Religious Times*

Farmer's newspaper had a short publishing life. Although it gave him as much or more notoriety than anything else he did, it was not one of his greatest achievements. For much of the paper's existence he was involved in controversy. And no wonder—Farmer's prose was rambling, sarcastic, full of opaque references, inflammatory, and excessive. He quickly attracted critics, and when attacked Farmer attacked back, railing against injustice. It is not always clear whom he was attacking, since he often identified individuals only by name and not by affiliation or roles. It is interesting that Farmer gives only passing mention in his autobiography about his time as editor and does not even mention the paper's name. While the paper was launched to be an organ of a new denomination, Farmer's autobiography never mentions the Republican United Brethren Church, nor his involvement with the group, which eventually faded as a separate denomination.

As the *Religious Times* was closing, Farmer was looking to the future. As usual, he was attacking the way established churches operated while hoping to bring the various sects together with his Christian Union philosophy. But, he was choosing a divisive issue, that of water baptism, to try and unite them:

Sept. 2, 1854
We wish to inform our friends, and patrons in general, that we intend to have printed a monthly pamphlet that we think will be adaptable to the wants and wishes of the religious world. For we often find ourselves praying thy kingdom come thy will be done on earth as it is in heaven; and still carry out our sectarian views: We mean by this, pray for one thing and practice another and show great inconsistency. This work will aim at pointing out what should be the test of membership[:] fellowship and communion. In the first place we wish to embody all the editorials of the past year. And 2nd, on law. 3rd Water baptism as the great source of so many divisions in the Christian Church; and if possible be the means of bringing all the different branches of the Christian Church together that consistency may appear in all the true Christians that may be brought into the unity of the spirit of Christ and bonds of peace.

17

Methodists Up-and-Coming without Farmer, 1850s

As Eli Farmer was moving past his days as an editor of the *Bloomington Religious Times* and continuing to work toward a Christian Union Church, the Methodists were taking off. In 1856 the quadrennial General Conference of the Methodist Episcopal Church was held in Indianapolis, Indiana. Besides being a railroad center for what was still commonly called "the West," Indianapolis had become a thriving center of industry and business. Community leaders believed their city compared favorably with many eastern cities and were pleased to be able to showcase its finer points to the Methodist national meeting attendees. One of those showplaces was the newly built Union Station, one of the finest of its kind in the nation. The city greeted the delegates warmly. The sessions of the conference were held at the statehouse. Leading citizens hosted the 205 delegates (all male and all clergy), along with other guests, in their homes.

Methodists in Indianapolis and throughout the state were also eager to show their brethren from the East and from the rest of the country how well the church had been thriving in Indiana. It was an accomplishment to have the conference in the Hoosier State, as the Methodist Episcopal Church had not until this time ventured so far west. The Indianapolis Methodists had much to show. Fewer than forty years before there had not been any Methodist Church in Indianapolis. The first Methodist building was a hewn-log house purchased in 1824. By 1829 the log church had been replaced by a brick edifice. Eventually it would be known as the Meridian Street United Methodist Church.

Across the state Methodism's membership was approaching 97,000. In 1852, because of church growth, the state had divided into four annual conferences. Since the population of Indiana at that time was around one million, about one out of every ten Indiana residents was a member of a Methodist church. Methodist Sunday schools enrolled many more. Indiana could count nearly 650 Methodist churches, more than all the Presbyterian, Baptist, Congregationalist, and Roman Catholic churches combined. Indiana Methodism could also claim two very fine colleges, Indiana Asbury (now DePauw University) and Fort Wayne Female College (now Taylor University).[1]

Several of Indiana's favorite Methodist sons had gained recognition. Four years before, the general conference in Boston had elected two Indiana men, Matthew Simpson and Edward R. Ames, to the episcopacy. Simpson, the first president of Indiana Asbury, was at the time a leading editor of the denomination. In addition to Simpson and Ames, other Methodist pioneer preachers had been honored in the first of a number of histories and biographies that would soon be written about Indiana Methodists. In 1853 F. C. Holliday had published a biography of Allen Wiley.[2] Wiley had been converted at one of the first camp meetings in the state, "about five miles above the town of Harrison" in 1808, and had gone on to be one of a number of Indiana's Methodist heroes. Included in the book are some of Wiley's writings on the encouragement and instruction of young preachers. Like other reports, Holliday's book gives a glowing description of the advance of Methodism in Indiana.

All of the reports and stories that were part of the general conference also impressed one special conference guest. Frederick J. Jobson was an official visitor to the conference from the Methodist Church in England. Jobson came not only to bring fraternal greetings to the Americans but to report to the mother church in England how Methodism in America was faring. Because of his importance he was chosen to be hosted in the home of Indiana governor Joseph A. Wright.

In a series of letters to England and then in a book, Jobson was profuse in his praise for America, for Methodism, and for Indianapolis.[3] Whatever others had heard about Methodism in the West, Jobson explained that what he saw was prosperity and progress. Had the word gotten out that Methodists disdained education? Jobson spoke of fourteen Methodist universities, where the sons of the more wealthy American Methodists were being trained for useful and honorable service in State and Church. In addition the Methodists had established "two seminaries, seventy academies, and many common day

In 1856 the General Conference of the Methodist Episcopal Church met in the Indiana Statehouse in Indianapolis, pictured here twenty years later.

schools." He mentioned eleven different denominational periodicals with 285,461 subscribers. Jobson added, in a remark not without significance, that he had been invited to preach at a Methodist camp meeting but declined, thinking the outdoor preaching might affect his health.

About the same time that Jobson wrote in 1857, R. M. Eddy published an article in the *Methodist Quarterly Review* titled "Influence of Methodism upon the Civilization and Education of the West." Eddy spoke of Methodism's influence on the betterment of society. He quoted a justice of the Indiana Supreme Court: "But for the Methodist Church and the Methodist ministry, this country would have sunk into barbarism."[4] The end result of revivals and camp meetings, according to the article, was to advance knowledge, tame the frontier, and promote civilization: "Villages and neighborhoods not a few, which were in a state of almost semi-barbarism, under the Divine blessing, Methodism has elevated, refined and placed on the upward grade."

Not all Methodists of that era would have been pleased if they had read Jobson's report or Eddy's article. A group of Methodists, especially including the circuit preachers, had also been impressed by Methodism's rapid growth in Indiana. But, similar to Farmer, they were not so sure that growth was the same as progress. There were already complaints that Methodism was becoming too much like the other denominations, seeking wealth and fashion and influence rather than the things of the Spirit.

One of the concerned circuit preachers was the venerable Peter Cartwright. About the time of the general conference in Indianapolis, Cartwright published his autobiography.[5] At least by Methodist standards, it was a best seller, in part because Cartwright was a good storyteller and also because Cartwright defended old-fashioned Methodism. Cartwright had preached in Indiana in 1804 when his circuit in Kentucky crossed the Ohio River into Clark's Grant (in today's Clark County and surrounding counties). He recounted those early years when Methodism was poor and simple, but faithful. In those days, he wrote:

> [The Methodists] could, nearly every one of them, sing our hymns and spiritual songs. They religiously kept the Sabbath day; many of them abstained from dram-drinking, not because the temperance reformation was ever heard of in that day, but because it was inedicted in the General rules of our Discipline. The Methodists of that day stood up and faced their preacher when they sung; they kneeled down in the public congregation as well as elsewhere, when the preacher said, "Let us pray."
>
> There was no standing among the members in time of prayer, especially the abominable practice of sitting down during that exercise was unknown among early Methodists. Parents did not allow their children to go to balls or plays; they did not send them to dancing-school; they generally fasted once a week, and almost universally on the Friday before each quarter meeting. If the Methodists had dressed in the same "superfluity of naughtiness" then as they do now, there were very few even out of the Church that would have any confidence in their religion. But O, how have things changed for the worse in this educational age of the world![6]

At the age of ten Cartwright had attended Cane Ridge, the granddaddy of all camp meetings. He had preached for fifty-five years and had been a delegate to eleven general conferences. He claimed that two to three months every year he lived in the "tented grove." Because of this Cartwright was probably known by sight to more Methodists than any other leader, including bishops. He slept under trees, he outwitted infidels, and he debated Calvinists. He had run for Congress in Illinois against Abraham Lincoln. Jobson mentions meeting Cartwright in his book.

Part of the tension in the church was over education, particularly education that was presented as an alternative to revivalism.[7] Cartwright had this to say on the education of Methodist preachers:

> I do not wish to undervalue education, but really I have seen so many of these educated preachers who forcibly reminded me of lettuce growing under the shade of a peach-tree, or like a gosling that had got the straddles by waddling in the dew, that I turn away sick and faint. Now, this educated ministry and the theological training are no longer an experiment. Other denominations have tried them, and they have proved a perfect failure; and is it not strange that Methodist preachers will try to gather up these antiquate[d] systems, when enlightened Presbyterians and Congregationalists have acknowledged that the Methodist plan is the best in this world, and try to improve, as they say, our system, alleging that our educational institutions have created a necessity for theological institutes? Verily, we have fallen on evil times.[8]

While many of the Methodist ministers who had moved to cities and larger towns saw new opportunities to reach persons of influence and means for the gospel, with a greater opportunity to bring good to the nation, others believed the Methodist mission was to win souls for Christ, especially among those neglected by society—as did Farmer. The Methodist movement in England was really launched when John Wesley began field preaching to miners. The image of Wesley preaching to miners still drove many of the early circuit riders. When Allen Wiley gave his advice to young ministers he reminded them:

> But if the (man of God) were to indulge his feelings, he would gladly go to certain congregations which are partial to him, and which are his favorites; but his duty requires him to go to those who need him most. Which are the congregations and families that stand most in need of the particular attention of a minister? Not the most intelligent, wealthy, and accomplished, that would be to him the most agreeable; but the ignorant, the poor, the uncouth, whose minds are an unclosed and uncultivated waste, and will so remain, unless the humble, faithful orthodox preacher attend to their case; for infidelity, for all of its boasted good-will; Unitarianism, with all of its pretended superior illumination; Socinianism, with its vainglorying; Arianism, with all of its caviling at orthodoxy; and Universalism, with its pretended philanthropy, will never hunt up the outcasts of men and better their condition.[9]

In spite of all the glowing reports at the Indianapolis general conference and the projections of Methodism's growing influence and bright future, Methodism in the 1850s was still very much a religion of and for the common people. Methodism is the story of a religion on the edges of society making its way into the mainstream, but in 1856 it was not exactly accurate to say that it had arrived. One telling statistic was the value of church properties. If social standing and wealth are reflected in the value of church buildings, Methodists nationally were on the bottom of the scale. According to the 1850 federal census, which reported church membership, number of churches, and value of church properties, the ranking of denominations by local church property values was as follows:

> Unitarian, $18,449
> Dutch Reformed, $12,644
> Jewish synagogues, $11,987
> Presbyterian, $3,135
> Baptist, $1,244
> Methodist, $1,174

To those on the ground at the time, though, it seemed that Methodism had come a long way from its humble beginnings. There was pride on one side, and disdain on the other. Some, such as Farmer, had already left the Methodist fold because of the changes from frontier Methodism to established Methodism. Thus, Farmer was not a part of this chapter of Methodism—when the general conference came to Indianapolis. He had already explained why in an editorial in the *Bloomington Religious Times* on March 24, 1854:

Peter Cartwright, one of the most popular of the group known as the "old time" Methodists. His autobiography contains one of the best-known accounts of frontier Methodism.

> We wish again to lay before a generous public the reasons why we became a Methodist, and why we continued so long among them, and then left them; and why we now so strenuously oppose them.
>
> When we first became acquainted with that body of people, they were an humble people,—plain, kind, and persevering. In those days, you might tell a Methodist wherever you went. Their plainness and humility, gave them a stand above all others,—they stood as a beacon-light that marked the road to heaven; and this gave them favor in the eyes of the world, and they increased very fast. The preachers carried zeal and religion wherever they went, and they sought out every settlement, and spread through all the different parts of the world, and bore much persecution, their zeal still increasing, until they became very numerous. Then pride and popularity began to find its way into the ranks of the Methodists. We well remember when these things began to grow. The old preachers began to guard against the evils; but when the old veterans began to fall, others that joined for the spoils, filled the ranks. The old ministers had kept the salaries low, in order to keep out the money-hunters; but

as the old stock fell off, by death, the young set began to fill the ranks, both in the ministry and in the General Conference. About this time the Episcopal power began to show, as these tyrants began to get power, and they began to exercise the same to the great injury of the church. The old ministers that were yet living, still tried to preach and uphold the original doctrines and usages of the church; but in a short time the money hunters got the ascendancy, and began to rule with a rod of iron. Then the storm began, and it has grown worse and worse every day since.

We saw the power had fallen into bad hands. We saw that they were tyrants, and would show no quarters when too late to change. We saw that we had spent our youthful strength to make a nest for a class that was making a bad use of it. The power now lay entirely in the hands of a class that were doing harm, and no chance to check their onward march in evils.— in the fall of '39, being well-nigh worn out, we located, that we might be out of their reach, as we thought. But the episcopal power, still growing stronger, they still pursued us, to make use of us to collect money for them to revel on in the house of God. We were unwilling to help carry on the devilment. They still grew more vicious and hard, so after a long time, when there appeared no chance to live in peace, in seeing that we were now in years, and had a great many friends in the Methodist church, we hated to leave. We had taken about five thousand into the church.

The locality generally began to suffer; and now they will hardly license a man that they cannot use in any shape they may wish. They will kill off the local preachers in a short time. They are at it as fast as they can or dare to, without hurting their general arrangement. And now, right among them, there is a great portion of members that are trying to get lay delegation in the church; and have been petitioning the general conference for a change in that matter, but we have no idea that there will ever be any change in the government; and at their next general conference, which will be at Indianapolis, there will be, we think, a great split in the church, if these tyrants do not bend; and we think they will not, because they come in for money and power, and they have got it and will keep it. And we think they are aiming to grasp after the power of Church and State, by means of the temperance cause, and the excitement break down the split, and they still will gain money and power. And if they fail, they will hold all the funds of money and property, which is very great in the United States and then that part will go to the Catholics with all that will bend. And they may change the government on both sides some, in order to hold together, and afterwards slide back into the old plan by legislation, as the people can bear it. Then the line will be drawn on the Protestant Christian and great s'aughtering will take place.

18

The Civil War, 1861 to 1865

The next major event in Eli Farmer's life after closing down the *Bloomington Religious Times* newspaper was the Civil War. This section of his autobiography is full of the action of the war, concern and pride for his sons, many of whom served in the war, and information about the part he played in this major conflict. Here again, he is writing from memory and emotion, and so, he mixes up dates somewhat, moving back and forth in the four years of the war. What we know for sure is that two of his sons, Joel and William, served in the Eighty-Second Indiana Volunteer Infantry. Both mustered in on August 30, 1862. He states that five of his sons served in the Union Army. We know that one other, James E., served and died in Memphis, Tennessee, in December 1865.

Eli Farmer also served in various capacities according to his account below. At the Battle of Perryville, Kentucky, where his sons were stationed, he helped the army surgeon, Doctor William H. Lemon, tend to wounded and sick soldiers. Here and elsewhere, he prayed for and with the Union soldiers. It is interesting to note that early during the war, when he was helping to recruit soldiers, he turned down an offer to be a chaplain only after he was assured that the young Methodist preacher who wanted the job was in agreement with his Christian Union plan. Late in the war, about twenty miles from Chattanooga, Tennessee, where part of the Union Army was encamped, he preached with a Baptist preacher in the Christian Union manner, "getting up quite a revival" and converting many souls.

While the Civil War disrupted Farmer's progress toward developing a Christian Union Church, the connections he made with soldiers and officers—particularly from Ohio—may have helped his cause. For it would be fellow seekers from Ohio who would merge with his Indiana Church after the war and finally start a Christian Union denomination that would take root and grow from that time forward. But before those seeds were planted, Farmer tells the tale of his boys and him in the Civil War:

It is not at all surprising that when the slaveholder's Great Rebellion broke out that the military fever raging in the veins of union men everywhere throughout the country should visit each one of my boys and fill their hearts with patriotic emotions.[1]

The reader need not now be astonished at the statement, when I assure him, that five of my boys were soldiers in the union army.[2] *The husbands of both my daughters were also among the first patriots to rush to the defense of the Flag of our country.*[3] *More than that, two young* men in my employment, young men whom I raised from early infancy, also joined the ranks of the "Boy in Blue," and fought through the war. We felt in common with every other friend of the union, that it was our duty to save the country.

I at once began making union speeches and beating up for volunteers in every section where I could do any good. After which I concluded I must go myself, as so many of my boys had already gone. I organized a company of cavalry and the boys wanted to elect me captain of the battalion, but I refused to accept, telling them I preferred to go as a private, and that that position with the privilege of preaching for them, would be quite as exalted a position as I could aspire to.

I succeeded in getting them to elect John Wylie in my place.[4] When we came to be examined I was not accepted owing to my advanced age. I now assisted in forming another company, a company in which five of my boys enlisted, and the boys urged me to secure the appointment of chaplain for myself. With some such designs I accompanied this company to Madison, Ind, at which place their regiment was organized. At this rendezvous I found a young Methodist preacher by the name of McNaughter, who was very anxious to be chosen chaplain of the regiment, and after many interviews with him I became fully satisfied that he had become converted to the Christian union plans and, upon his promise to carry out our wishes, I succeeded in securing a commission for him as chaplain.[5]

Telling my boys I would meet with them again, as soon as possible, I returned home knowing they had received orders to go to Louisville. When the Regiment arrived in that city, one of my boys wrote to me to come at once, as they [had] gotten marching orders again. The rebel army was then clearly surrounding that city, and our army was already having many a bout with their enemies down there.

When I arrived in Louisville, I found that the regiment was several days ahead of me, and the army was drawing the rebels before them. Fortunately for me, a nephew of mine, and who was named in my honor, Eli P. Farmer, was the commander of the barracks in and about the city, and by his assistance I was able to ascertain the whereabouts of [the] regiment. . . .

Getting aboard the cars I went to Shepherdsville, Ky, and there left the cars, as the rebels had so damaged the railroad track as to render further travel by rail on that road impossible. I got off the train late in the afternoon, and at once tried to hire a man to take me to the army, but I was told the journey was too hazardous at that time, owing to the fact that guerrillas were infesting all that region. I said I would go through some way or die trying, and started out afoot.

I shortly overtook a squad of soldiers. They were all well armed. We traveled on some distance together, and arrived at Bardstown about midnight, which place was filled with soldiers. As I entered the inner line of pickets, I was told to keep quiet as the army was momentarily expecting a general engagement. After much trouble, I at length succeeded in getting a good bed that night in a hotel where I slept soundly till breakfast time next morning.

When I laid down I felt very sore and tired, having walked further that day than I had done in the same length of time, during a period of thirty years.

After eating my breakfast, I started out afoot on the Springfield road. Although footsore and wearied, I yet journeyed on rapidly, reaching Springfield about two hours by sun, in the afternoon. Here I tried to get something to eat, but the two armies seemed to have literally eaten everything as they went along. I was ravenously hungry and tried to get something to eat at every house I came to but failed. I at length found an old man who told me he had laid by a few viands, and he would divide with me.

I accompanied him to his house and his wife set out a humble repast before us. After finishing our little meal, he informed me he thought a battle was impending, as the officers had sent their wives back to this place for safety. This made me more anxious than ever to get up with the boys, and I started on towards Perrysville. I traveled on rapidly, and late at night overtook some army wagons.

As I tried to pass them, one young man asked me where I was going; I told him.

He then inquired where I was from, and when I mentioned the name of "Bloomington," he sprang off of his horse and ran to me, crying out enthusiastically, "I know you, I know you."

He was a son of an old time friend of mine, by the name of Hoover of that city and was an aid-de-camp of General [Don C.] Buel, charged with the duty of bringing up the army wagons.[6] The poor fellow who was as warm hearted and brave a man as I met in the army, afterward fell in battle. He died where an American citizen would most desire to die, in defense of his country, with his last fading glances turned to the victorious flag of his "free hearts hope, and home."

As I rode along he asked many questions about our town and our mutual friends, and I gave him all the information I could. In order to rest me he had walked about four miles while I rode his horse. He was compelled to go into camp with his command for the night, and after bidding him farewell, I journeyed on in pursuit of our main army.

After losing considerable time in taking a wrong road at a crossing, I at length reached a high bridge spanning the Salt River. The armies had had a little battle at this point, and there were many dead bodies of horses, yet to be seen scattered about, pretty thickly along the road side. Crossing over, I found some straggling soldiers on the other side who had stopped to rest. One of their number begged me to tarry all night with him, saying he would go on with me early next day, and I laid down to take a nap. After a time I opened my eyes, and the stars were shining mildly upon me, and thinking of the oncoming battle, I sprung to my feet and awakened my companion, telling him to hasten, as I wished to reach the army before the battle began.

He failed to keep up with me, although a stout young man, and I went on ahead. Hurrying on about five miles further I overtook my Regiment, and the first man I met of my company was my son Joel. When he saw me he cried out loud, yet none of the less a hearty welcome, and then the boys whom General [Morton C.] Hunter was forming in line of battle in order to go and drive the enemy from a certain large spring, nearby, called me to them, and bombarded me verbally with a great multitude of questions.[7]

After sending the boys off for the purpose indicated, Gen'l Hunter escorted me to this Head Quarters, where we found breakfast about ready to be spread. Addressing myself to Col [M. B. Walker], at Head Quarters, I said, "Col I came here to do all the good I possibly can, and I am now ready for service, ready to go where I can do most for the cause."[8]

Dr [William H.] Lemon suggested that I help look after the Hospitals, and immediately fastened a strip of red flannel around my left arm, as an evidence of my connection with that department.[9]

The cook announced breakfast and we sat down in our little mess, to partake of our little meal, just at sun rise. We had scarcely attacked the viands before us, when the battle was opened. We sprang to our feet, and got ready for the work in hand. Col Walker prepared the regiment for the fight and we now awaited the call of the commanding General. The battle began far off to our right, but it was now drawing rapidly toward us. With great anxiety I closely inspected the faces and actions of our boys, to see if I might be able to discover any thing that would presage the soldierly qualities of the company and regiment. I could not look upon so many familiar faces, faces of boys whom I had known from their earliest infancy, without thinking of their kindred far away, so that they all seemed equally endeared to me, and I walked backward and forward down the line giving them the best advice I could suggest, telling them over and over, to be careful and not aim too low.

They manifested no excitement. They acted more like they were going out to roll logs than going out to be targets for rebel bullets and rebel shot and shell. Pretty soon Captain Wylie *came running to me and begged me to take charge of a large amount of money which he had just drawn for the company, and also his fine gold watch.*

I unthoughtedly did so, and then many of the boys ran to me and deposited their valuables with me. Several of the company also wished to deposit money with me, but having time now, for a moment's reflection, I declined accepting it, telling them I proposed to go into the fight myself, with them.

The battle went on, on our right wing till our army whipped the enemy, and captured, if I rightly recollect, about seven hundred prisoners. The battle was kept up without an intermission all day and about half an hour after night fall. We had taken up a position early in the day, on the left, under General Reasean.[10] Frequently during the day Genl Reasean rode up and down the line encouraging the men, and waiving his sword, to give additional emphasis to his commands. I could never conjecture how he escaped being perforated through and through by the leaden hail showered all around him through all those dreadful hours of carnage.

I rendered all the services I could, carrying off the wounded and assisting in ministering unto them. My son Joel had charge of an ambulance. The losses were heavy on both sides. I am confident I saw as many as one thousand wounded men on a space of ground not exceeding an acre square. We succeeded at last in whipping our enemies and they fell back before us, but we paid for our victory.

To show how dearly it was purchased, here is one instance. While going about in discharge of my duties, I met captain Rovenscraft, of Bloomington, whom I asked as to the number of men he had. He told me he entered the fight with thirty-three men, but come out of it with only fifteen. This battle was fought about four miles west of Perrysville [Perryville, Kentucky].

We drove the enemy beyond the town where we stopped all night. The weather now turned quite cold, and wet, and bad every way. We were without tents and many of our boys suffered a great deal. Our chaplain was entreated to give up his tent for the benefit of some sick and wounded soldiers, but he cruelly and brutally refused to do so. This act of immorality, of course, made him many enemies.

We pursued the enemy until we arrived at Dick Robinson's camp ground, where they made a brief halt, but we soon dislodged them. I now became fully satisfied that the enemy would not stop to fight us again, and I told my boys I would return home and look after some business requiring my attention.

I remained at home some time, but after settling up my business affairs, I returned to the army again. While traveling over the Louisville and Nashville railroad, on my return to the army, and when our train had about reached the state line, between Kentucky and Tennessee, we were attacked by a large band of guerillas. They threw our train off the track, by placing a number of cross-ties in a cow pit at a suitable place for their murderous business. They began firing into the train before the cars were entirely thrown from the track. Their chief object was robbery, and it did not require a great deal of time to attend to that business. Rushing into the cars, they thrust the muzzles of their guns into our faces, and demanded our money and other valuables.

A party of union soldiers, a mile or so behind us, hearing the firing, came to our rescue, and drove off these mouraders. We formed in the pursuit, and chased them about two miles, and succeed in recapturing several horses which they had stolen from us. We captured about twenty of their guns. We also killed and wounded several of their number, and captured a few prisoners.

We remained there until about midnight, when another train, in charge of a Bloomington man by the name of John Armfield came to our relief. On the following morning the new train took us into Nashville. At this city I found a train of army wagons about ready to relieve for the main army out at Tryune. The train was provided with a large escort, as our road was everywhere infested with guerillas.

Returning to the army at Tryune, I found the chaplain absent, and at once commenced discharging his duties by request of the regiment. I was several times offered a commission as chaplain but I refused it. Our camp at this place occupied a very high hill,—and was a beautiful place, the ground being shaded with a dense growth of large Blue Ash trees.

After remaining here a long time, I began to think of returning home again, but I deferred doing so for a little while in order to escort the wife of the Quarter Master, and also the wife of captain [William W.] Browning, of Nashville, Ind, to their homes in Indiana.[11] By the assistance of a fellow by the name of Samuel Moore, of my town, I succeeded in getting our passports out of the camp. Young Moore accomplished this for us, and also got a pass for himself to Nashville Tenn, as I afterward learned, by a pretty free use of what was called a fair article of brandy among the high officials.

Captain Browning accompanied us as far as Nashville Tenn. Both of the women in my charge had several children, and it kept me busy to look after the entire party. North of Nashville some distance, the rebels had torn up the track for a mile or so. I was compelled to carry our trunks, valises, children, etc, across this breach in the road, and I found it anything else than a light task. Helping them all change cars, etc., I brought Mrs Browning and children to Bedford, Ind, and her companion and family [to] Bloomington, at which place she had relatives, who assisted her in getting home from this place.

Remaining at home a short time, I again went back to the army. I was summoned thither this time, by the intelligence that my son William, and Col Tilscum had recently been wounded, and were lying in a critical condition.[12] I should have had a great deal of trouble in getting out of Louisville on my return this time, had it not been for the kindness of Capt Mr Ward, who at this time was charged with the duty of issuing passes to such persons as were allowed to go in and out of the city. I had known this gentleman long and intimately, aforetime, at Bloomington, and

Artist Henry Mosler's rendition of the Battle of Perryville, in which at least two of Eli Farmer's sons fought.

he helped me to get away on a south bound train. Captain Ward gave me an introduction to the conductor of our train, whom I afterward found to be a clever gentleman. He seated me in the rear car among a number of wealthy ladies, many of whom were accompanied by their children, all bound for Nashville. These Ladies were well supplied with provisions, and all of them urged me to dine with them.

I found Genl Hunter of Bloomington, at Nashville, engaged on a court martial. This excellent gentleman and brave and accomplished officer, helped me in getting a conveyance to the army, sending by me a lot of choice wines and other delicacies, to our sick and wounded soldiers.

Our train from Nashville out en route to the army, was delayed at one point about 24 hours, by reason of the train in advance of ours colliding with another train, and we remained in the cars all night. As we were crowded we had to maintain a sitting posture through all those wary hours of waiting and anxious suspense.

On the following day we arrived in Chattanooga, and I went around among the hospitals in search of my wounded boy. After a great deal of time had been consumed, and after much trouble, I at length sought him out. He was sorely wounded, and I found him suffering considerably. His shoulder bone had been badly damaged by a ball, and a part of the bone taken out. The army surgeons wanted to amputate his arm at the shoulder but he was unwilling. He had a high fever upon him, and was very much debilitated. I stayed at his bedside day by day waiting on him.

As soon as he improved sufficiently so not to require constant watching, I would frequently preach to the people, as I wished to be as useful as possible. By and by the fever left him, and he then improved rapidly. The army was now stationed at Bingold, some twenty miles from Chattanooga.

As soon as my boy's afflictions would allow I joined the main army at Bingold, where I attended to the duties of chaplain again. I succeeded in getting up quite a revival here. Many souls were converted, and many professions of religion made, and I found the Christian union plan worked admirable even here in the army. A Baptist minister aided me largely in this good work.

Remaining with the army at this point, I again went down to Chattanooga to look after my son, and to make myself useful generally, in the hospital at that place. While at this place I availed myself of frequent opportunities of admiring the beautiful and sublime scenery everywhere spread out before us, and also of looking over the several battle-fields in the vicinity, picking up several relics here and there, some of which I now have at my home.

I labored zealously among our sick and wounded boys in the various hospitals in and about Chattanooga. One of the hospital stewards said to me one day, something like this, "Mr Farmer, you work too hard. If you do not take some rest you will kill yourself."

I told him I had to work to save my life, for I needed exercise. I began now to make arrangements for bringing my boy home. As soon as I got consent of the surgeon in charge of the Hospitals, I found many other sick and wounded boys very anxious to accompany me home. Poor fellows, how they longed for the pleasures and comforts of their distant homes. By persistent entreaties I finally got consent also to gratify their wishes. Most of these were Ohio volunteers.

When we come to get aboard the Hospital train, I found the number of applicants far greater than I could well look after, but I could not find it in my heart to disappoint one of their number. Every car was densely crowded. I almost exhausted myself attending to their every wants, fixing their bandages, dressing their wounds and the like. I was compelled to set up all night in the cars during the first night after our departure. While bathing my face next morning, I was accosted by one of the chief surgeons, who inquired whether I had slept any during the night, and when I assured him I had not, he urged me to go to his quarters and take a good nap. I told him I was afraid to do so, lest my services might be required by my boys. He bade me go to his quarters with him, telling me he had some vinegar which would help me. I went with him and was greatly strengthened and refreshed by partaking of a small portion of his vinegar. This vinegar tasted strangely enough, very much like a pretty palatable article of spirits.

We were compelled to leave one poor fellow at Nashville Tenn. He had been shot through the lungs, but was in a fair way for a happy recovery.

At Louisville we found ample arrangements had been made for our accommodations. Immediately after my arrival at Louisville, I went out in search of conveyances with which to transfer the Ohio men to a steamboat bound for Cincinnati. It seemed to me that everybody wished to extortion on the poor boys, as nearly every teamster and driver, demanded double prices for their assistance. I experienced great difficulty in transferring them to the boat.

After getting rid of this large party, I turned my attention to the remainder of my party. Getting them into street cars I managed by dint of great labor to convey them over to New Albany, where we took the cars for our several homes in Indiana.

When I got home I was immediately attacked with sickness, and was so protracted thereby, that I never went back to the army.

My boy grew worse for a while after our return home and did not get any better until his wound broke and let a piece of cloth out which had been shot out of his coat and had been embedded deeply in the wound, by the bullet inflicting the injury. When the cloth was removed he improved rapidly.

Thinking he had recovered he again returned to the army, joining it at Atlanta where he tried to enter his old company, but was refused. They gave him his discharge and sent him back home. My son Joel so pleased his superior officers by his manner of handling beasts of burden, that he attracted the attention of General [William T.] Sherman, and was put in charge of his carriages and war ambulances, and so crossed over with that distinguished officer, in the memorable march "from Atlanta to the sea."

But I shall not weary my readers, with any details connected with the late war, else I should again repeat the wonderful story connected with that unparalleled tramp through Georgia, and my thoughts like birds would again cluster around the equally memorable capture of whole armies in Virginia, subsequently, and also the final grand _____ in the National Capitol.

These events connected with the losing labors of our surviving glory-crowned heroes, are yet living in the minds of millions of American citizens, which memories will only freshen in eternal bloom as the advancing years bear us out into the future. It affords me infinite satisfaction, when I remember how well our beloved Indiana sustained her military powers, all through these dreadful years of strife, and how her women, and maidens rejoiced, with more than Spartan pride and patriotism, when, with <u>victory</u>, emblazoned upon his proud and free banner, "Johnny came marching home."

My heart is tender and mine eyes are filled with tears, when I now think of those who came not back, and with a deep, though subdued sorrow—I fain would weep over the far off graves where the unconfined bodies of our blessed dead lie buried. Though many of them like my poor boy, who died at his post at Memphis, turned their eyes homeward in the hour of their final dissolution, and died that their country might live to bless the generations yet to come; yet they are not forgotten.[13]

My boy even the week before his death wrote to his mother the cheering intelligence he hoped to be at home in a short time. A week later a fellow officer of his company, brought home his inanimate body, and deposited it at our door, ere we knew, misfortune had befallen him.

Immolating himself on the sacred alter of his country, he dared to die for his country, and he is now at rest.

Eli P. Farmer.

If the world was made up of such men as Eli P. Farmer, it would be high time for honest men to leave it in a hurry.—*Decatur Local Press*

What has Eli P. Farmer done to set the whole whig press yelping at him? and what does the editor of this little dog fennel Gazette know about Eli P. Farmer? Mr. Farmer is a Methodist minister of good standing in his church. Stands high in the masonic fraternity—was at one time Grand Chaplain of the Grand Lodge of Indiana—served with credit in the Senate of this State for three years. A Whig unyielding in his principles, never wavering in sunshine or in shadow. He is now a candidate for Congress. It may be wrong for him to have taken this step. We certainly have no desire to see him elected, and would greatly prefer the election of either Mr. Carr or Col. Gorman, but it is unjust to charge him with being a dishonest man.

Although this brief article was published while Eli Farmer was running for the state senate decades before his death, it talks about the type of man Farmer was and mentions many of his activities, such as his being grand chaplain of the Grand Masonic Lodge of Indiana.

Conclusion

Christian Union at Last, 1863 to 1881

The Civil War disrupted life everywhere throughout the United States. Many families lost sons, fathers, brothers, and others in the war. Eli and Elizabeth Farmer may have counted themselves lucky to have lost just one son, as many families lost many more. The country would soon be struggling to reconstruct a society whose economy had been built on a system of slavery. Many African Americans would flee north, along with the Union soldiers. Many Americans would head west to settle in new states and territories. Back at home in Indiana, the landscape of people was forever changed. Farmer talks about this as his story resumes:

When I began looking up my little flocks, after my return from the army, I, of course found them greatly scattered. A great many of our churches were entirely broken down by the war. The first thing I did, however, was to organize a little church in my own neighborhood which was composed for the most part of my own family. Others of our churches went back to those with which they had formally been connected.[1]

I found most of my people among the Christian Union which arose in Ohio, under the labors of Given, Bowman, Shaw and others, during the year 1863—these men, stripping themselves of sectism, and uniting on the Bible. I attended one of the their councils, and became fully satisfied that our systems were the same, and I at once united with them, and it gives me pleasure to say I have been laboring with them continuously since that period. It also affords me happiness to be able to state that the church is developing itself and growing rapidly. We have District, Annual and General Councils.

* * *

Time flies by a pace, and I come now to conclude this book.

I am now about eighty years old. I am closing up my affairs, so as to be ready when the long deferred summons comes, to pass over the dark rolling river. I look across with pleasant emotions and fond anticipations. The brightness of the heavenly world is soon to break in upon my now dimmed vision. As I turn one last look back, scanning the innumerable unwritten events connected and blended with the scenes referred to herein, I am astonished that a kind providence has been so merciful to me—even me. As I thus look, I can say with old David,—"I have been young, and now am old; yet have I not seen the righteous forsaken, nor his seed begging bread."

I have succeeded in rearing a large family, all of whom among those who are living, are professors of religion, are bravely bearing all their classes, and are doing their duty, so far as I know. Although my lines have by no means always fallen in pleasant places, I, yet, do thank God for that His kind providences have always encompassed me around about, and my life has been lengthened out far beyond the time allotted to my fellow men. When I shall be called upon to leave this world, I want to leave my family well provided for in every proper way, till the family shall be reunited in the celestial city where separation will no more sadden the heart of friends and kindred.

I now ask all men and all women, to forgive me for any and every wrong, whether imaginary or real, which such person, or persons, may think I have done at any time. Let me die in peace. I linger, and yet I linger, a little loath to speak the sad word—"fare-well," for I fain would yet again invite all to try to meet me in the better world, to which I believe I am now going. There, up there, our fortunes will be forever secured, and our youth immortal be.

I say, again, for the last time, I would be afraid to go back, could I have the power to do so, and live my life over with the view to improving it, were I to be circumscribed by the same narrow limits, so far as educational advantages are concerned, so that I think I can partially say, in the terse, strong language of undaunted, heroic, little Paul,—"I have fought a good fight, I have kept the faith—I am now ready to be offered."

> I am
> "Only waiting till the shadows
> Are a little longer grown;
> Only waiting till the glimmer
> Of the days last beam is flown;
> There, from out the gathered darkness,
> Holy, deathless stars shall rise,
> By whose light my soul shall gladly
> Tread its pathway to the skies."

Eli Farmer—Reflections

Eli Farmer finished his autobiography in 1874 and lived another seven years, dying at the age of eighty-eight in 1881. A postscript with the Farmer manuscript, written by William Farmer, Eli's son, tells of his father traveling to Nebraska at the age of eighty-seven.

Farmer's early life reads like a Western adventure novel. It includes accounts of Indians, wild animals, frontier lawlessness, bravery, hard work, entrepreneurship, and vicious fights. His camp meeting religious conversion, his call to preach, and his revival exploits personify the Second Great Awakening. His ability to improvise and pragmatically adapt the Christian message to the western frontier helped to create the American generic religious culture. His quest for a union of Christian churches—based on the conversion experience alone—transcended sects and helped to develop the American evangelical religious ethos. His story offers insight as to how Methodism was able to dominate frontier religion and how that Methodism underwent change and left some, such as Farmer, who did not change, in its wake.[2] The religious controversies in which Farmer was involved reflected and contributed to the egalitarian and sectarian subculture that is still very much alive and perhaps even dominates twenty-first century America, and, by extension, worldwide Protestant Christianity. A number of para-church ministries and the independent church movement are in that lineage. There are not too many steps between Farmer and modern Pentecostalism.

Nor are there many steps between Farmer and the strand of American culture that stands firmly for independence, self-reliance, and freedom from government interference, be it from Church or from State. For his story is more than just an account of religion. It offers insight into day-to-day life on the frontier, including the building of early settlements, military service from the War of 1812 through the Civil War, antebellum politics,

Rev. Eli P. Farmer,

Died at his residence near Bloomington, Sunday morning, February 6th, in his 88th year. Deceased was born in Virginia in 1794, and emigrated to this State soon after its admision into the Union. His life has been closely identified with the material and religious development of the State for nearly three-score years and ten.

His profession was that of the ministry, but his means of temporal subsistence were derived from the farm. In his ministerial career he introduced the novel practice of giving the people a free gospel, and in all his experience, extending over a long life, he was never known to ask any congregation or church for a contribution in his own behalf. He was a chaplain in the late rebellion, and notwithstanding the hardships and privations to which he was subjected (which he could have escaped by remaining at home, as he was nearly seventy years old at the breaking out of the war), he uniformly refused to receive any compensation from the government, and so all through the long and bitter struggle the old man followed up the army in all the labors and hardships encountered, endeavoring to strengthen the arms and encourage the hearts of the brave boys who were fighting for the Union, by dispensing the everlasting gospel.

Thousands of people all over this State who, thirty, forty and even fifty years ago, waited upon his ministry, delight to-day in recounting incidents of his life, camp-meeting scenes, etc., all of which indicate that he was a revivalist of marvelous power. It is said that in the olden time quite frequently the camp meetings of that period were little better than failures, but invariably the arrival of Mr. Farmer, which generally was announced by his mounting the stand with a song, electrified the audience, a result intensified when he began speaking in his inimitable style. He was a powerful man physically as well as religiously; in fact, he has been regarded as the strongest and most active man in the State. This fact made him feared by a class of bullies that always infested camp-meetings, and several times he was compelled to leave the sacred desk and soundly chastise those who were disturbing his meeting, and always with success.

A portion of a long tribute to Eli P. Farmer, apparently published soon after his death in February 1881, in an unknown newspaper. This clipping, kept in the church archives of the First United Methodist Church in Bloomington, Indiana, states, among other things: "Invariably the arrival of Mr. Farmer [at a camp meeting], which generally was announced by his mounting the stand with a song, electrified the audience, a result intensified when he began speaking in his inimitable style."

businesses of the nineteenth century, and the movement from a seemingly lawless frontier to a civilized state. Farmer was brash, opinionated, and unbridled, but his fierce love of God, morality, family, friends, and country—as well as Christianity—are qualities that helped make America what it is today.

Notes

Introduction: Religion in Post-Revolutionary America

1. Eli P. Farmer, Autobiography, 2, Farmer Manuscripts, 1818–1874, Lilly Library, Indiana University, Bloomington. The material presented in this book is abridged from Farmer's more lengthy story.

2. Charles Blanchard, *Counties of Morgan, Monroe, and Brown: Indiana* (Chicago: F. A. Battey and Co., 1884), 397–98; Rebecca A. Shepherd, Charles W. Calhoun, et al., eds., *A Biographical Directory of the Indiana General Assembly, 1816–1899*, 2 vols. (Indianapolis: Select Committee on the Centennial History of the Indiana General Assembly and Indiana Historical Bureau, 1980), 1:123.

3. The first serious history on Indiana Methodism came out in 1853: Fernandez C. Holliday, *Life and Times of Rev. Allen Wiley, A. M., Containing Sketches of Early Methodist Preachers in Indiana . . . also including his original letters, entitled "A help to the performance of ministerial duties"* (Cincinnati: L. Swormstedt and A. Poe, 1853). This was followed by: William C. Smith, *Indiana Miscellany: Consisting of Sketches of Indian Life, the Early Settlement . . . together with biographical notices of the pioneer Methodist preachers of the state* (Cincinnati: Poe and Hitchcock, 1867); Stephen R. Beggs, *Pages from the Early History of the West and North-West: Embracing Reminiscences and Incidents of Settlement and Growth, and sketches of the material and religious progress of the States of Ohio, Indiana, Illinois, and Missouri, with especial reference to the history of Methodism* (Cincinnati: Methodist Book Concern, 1868); Fernandez C. Holliday, *Indiana Methodism: Being an Account of the Introduction, Progress, and Present Position of Methodism in the State . . . with sketches of the principle Methodist educators in the state down to 1873* (Cincinnati: Hitchcock and Walden, 1873); J. C. Smith, *Reminiscences on Early Methodism in Indiana, including sketches of various prominent ministers, together with narratives of women eminent for piety, poetry, and song . . . with an appendix containing essays on various theological subjects of practical interests* (Indianapolis: J. M. Olcott, 1879); and John L. Smith, *Indiana Methodism* (Valparaiso, IN: John L. Smith, 1892). A series of conference histories were written throughout the 1900s. Some of the more notable ones were William Warren Sweet, *Circuit Rider Days in Indiana* (Indianapolis: W. L. Stewart, 1916); Sweet and H. N. Herick, *A History of the North Indiana Conference of the Methodist Episcopal Church, from its organization in 1844 to the present* (Indianapolis: W. K. Stewart, 1917); Augustus Cleland Wilmore, *History of the White River Conference of the Church of the United Brethren in Christ* (Dayton, OH: United Brethren Publishing House, 1925); S. H. Baumgartner, *Historical Sketches and Historical Data for the Indiana Conference of the Evangelical Association, 1835–1915*, 2 vols. (Cleveland: Publishing House of the Evangelical Association, 1915–24); Adam Byron Condo, *History of the Indiana Conference of the Church of the United Brethren in Christ* (N.p.: Indiana Conference, 1926); Jack J. Detzler, *The History of the Northwest Indiana Conference of the Methodist Church, 1852–1951* (Nashville, TN: Parthenon Press, 1953); Frederick Norwood, *History of the North Indiana Conference, 1917–1956: North Indiana Methodism in the Twentieth Century*, vol. 2 (Winona Lake, IN: North Indiana Conference Historical Society, 1957). All of these are basically denominational family histories written for the faithful and emphasize growth, progress, and success with emphasis on buildings, budgets, and biographies. Camp meetings and revivals, even in the earlier works, are treated as passing expressions of frontier faith that served a purpose at the time but beyond which the Methodist Church had advanced.

The Indiana Methodist histories were following the example of the denominational histories. There are a number of Methodist histories written in the nineteenth century that in many ways are informative and helpful. With the possible exception of Jesse Lee, *A Short History of the Methodists in the United States of America, beginning in 1766, and continued till 1809; to which is prefixed a brief account of their rise in England, in the year 1729* (Baltimore: Magill and Clime, 1810), however, most seem intent on presenting Methodism as a church with humble beginnings that was coming or had come of age. Almost all are East Coast oriented. One of the best known of these, Abel Stevens, *History of the Methodist Episcopal Church in the United States*, 4 vols. (New York: Carlton and Porter, 1864–84), covers Methodism to 1820 and runs to nearly two thousand pages. The index lists Indiana for three pages. Camp meetings garner seven pages with one page given to "extravagances."

One of the first historians to do serious analysis of Methodism in the twentieth century was Sweet, who taught at DePauw University for a number of years (and thus had Indiana connections). He was credited for making American religious history a specialized field of academic study. He wrote twenty-seven books, including the two on Indiana Methodism mentioned above. Sweet's work is invaluable, but Sweet (and many of his students) operated with a viewpoint that reflected the thought of historians in the early twentieth century. He tended to see American Protestantism in general, and Methodism in particular, as part of a great civilizing force—a march toward progress helping to make America great. It is in this vein that one understands Elizabeth K. Nottingham, *Methodism and the Frontier: Indiana Proving Ground* (New York: Columbia University Press, 1941). Nottingham deals with camp meetings, revivals, and sectarianism, but tends to interpret these as psychological and sociological early steps on the way to civilization and maturity.

4. Nathan O. Hatch, *The Democratization of American Christianity* (New Haven: Yale University Press, 1989), 1.

5. A. H. Redford, *Western Cavaliers: Embracing the History of the Methodist Episcopal Church in Kentucky from 1832 to 1844* (Nashville, TN: Southern Methodist Publishing House, 1876).

6. Nathan O. Hatch, "The Puzzle of American Methodism," *Church History* 63, no. 2 (June 1994): 175–89.

7. As quoted in James R. Rogers, *The Cane Ridge Meeting-House* (Cincinnati: Standard Publishing, 1910), 54.

8. James B. Finley, *Autobiography of Rev. James B. Finley; or, Pioneer Life in the West*, edited by W. P. Strickland (Cincinnati: Cranston and Curtis, 1853), 165.

9. Peter Cartwright, *Autobiography of Peter Cartwright: The Backwoods Preacher*, edited by W. P. Strickland (New York, Carlton and Porter, 1856), 46. While it is sometimes stated that other denominations besides Methodists held camp meetings, such claims are difficult to verify. In four Indiana denominational histories there is not the first mention of camp meetings: I. George Blake, *Finding a Way through the Wilderness: Tracing Baptist History in Indiana* (Indianapolis: Central Publishing, 1983); Henry K. Shaw, *Hoosier Disciples* ([Saint Louis]: Bethany Press, 1966); L. C. Rudolph, *Hoosier Zion* (New Haven: Yale University Press, 1963) regarding Presbyterians; and Otho Winger, *History of the Church of the Brethren in Indiana* (Elgin, IL: Brethren Publishing House, 1917).

10. Nathan Bangs, *A History of the Methodist Episcopal Church*, vol. 2 (New York: T. Mason and G. Lane, 1839), 141.

11. J. B. Wakeley, *The Patriarch of One Hundred Years: Being Reminiscences, Historical and Biographical of Rev. Henry Boehm* (New York: Nelson and Phillips, 1875; reprint of Henry Boehm, *Reminiscences of Rev. Henry Boehm*), 128.

12. Lee, *Short History of the Methodists in the United States of America*, 311.

13. Charles A. Johnson, *The Frontier Camp Meeting: Religion's Harvest Time* (Dallas: Southern Methodist University Press, 1955), 63.

14. Nathan Bangs, *A History of the Methodist Episcopal Church*, 4 vols. (New York: Phillips and Hunt, 1880). Bangs traces the spread of camp meetings from their "western" beginnings but sees them mostly as special meetings that contributed to the growth of Methodism but then fell into disfavor. See also Stevens, *History of the Methodist Episcopal Church in the United States*.

15. William Warren Sweet, *The Story of Religions in America* (Chicago: Harper and Brothers Publishers, 1930), 8. Sweet's books *Methodism in Indiana: The Rise of Methodism in the West, Being the Journal of the Western Conference, 1800–1811* (Nashville, TN: Smith and Lamar, 1920) and *Circuit Rider Days in Indiana*, emphasize the history of Methodism in Indiana mostly by telling the story of leading Methodist figures, the decisions and reports of the annual conferences, and the establishment of institutions.

16. Annie Grace Wardle, *History of the Sunday School Movement in the Methodist Episcopal Church* (New York: Methodist Book Concern, 1918), 127–29; Riley B. Case, *Evangelical and Methodist: A Popular History* (Nashville, TN: Abingdon Press, 2004), 49–51.

17. On the Holiness Movement as a precursor to Pentecostalism, see Jay Riley Case, *An Unpredictable Gospel* (New York: Oxford University Press, 2012), 3–6. This book estimates that by the year 2000, Pentecostalism claimed 425 million adherents worldwide (p. 5). On the spread of Pentecostalism, see Gary B. McGee, "To the Regions Beyond: The Global Expansion of Pentecostalism," in *The Century of the Holy Spirit: 100 Years of Pentecostal and Charismatic Renewal*, edited by Vinson Synan (Nashville, TN: Thomas Nelson, 2001), 68–96.

Chapter 1: Eli Farmer's Family and Childhood, 1788 to 1813

1. As used in the eighteenth and nineteenth century the word "enthusiasm" referred to uncontrolled emotionalism. It was a word almost always used pejoratively.

2. H. H. Moore, *The Republic to Methodism* (Cincinnati: Cranston and Stowe, 1891), 98.

3. Church and Methodist membership is discussed in Elijah Embree Hoss, *William McKendree: A Biographical Study* (Nashville, TN: Cokesbury Press, 1914), 88–98.

4. As quoted in D. A. Hayes, "Why America Should be Missionary," *Northwestern Christian Advocate*, August 18, 1897.

5. Postmillennialism is a view of end time that holds that Christ's kingdom will so spread across the earth that the "millennium," the thousand years of peace, will be established. At that time, after the millennium, Christ will come to rule on earth. This belief factored into Eli Farmer's prejudice against Catholics (See Chapter 14).

6. "Scriptural holiness" is a phrase repeated in early Methodist *Disciplines*. The first of these was Thomas Coke and Francis Asbury, *A Form of Discipline for the Ministers, Preachers, and Members of the Methodist Episcopal Church in America* (New York: W. Ross, 1787). For examples of early writing on scriptural holiness, see the first few unnumbered pages in Coke and Asbury, *The Doctrines and Discipline of the Methodist Episcopal Church in America* (Philadelphia: Henry Tuckniss, 1798), http://www.enterhisrest.org/ichabod/methodism_coke.pdf.

7. Methodist preachers were "sent," not "called," as in other denominations. Before Methodism became established the "appointments" were not to settled religious communities but to territories. They intended not to minister to believers but to make believers. Jesse Lee, *A Short History of the Methodists in the United States of America: Beginning in 1766 and Continued Till 1809, to which is prefixed, a brief account of their rise in England in the year 1729* (Baltimore, 1810), 162.

8. Ellen Eslinger, *Citizens of Zion: The Social Origin of Camp Meeting Revivalism* (Knoxville: University of Tennessee Press, 1999), 162–84.

9. As quoted in Harlow Lindley, *Indiana As Seen by Early Travelers* (Indianapolis: Indiana Historical Commission, 1916), 464.

10. Eli P. Farmer, Autobiography, 1–89, Farmer Manuscripts, 1818–1874, Lilly Library, Indiana University, Bloomington.

Chapter 2: The Formative Years, 1814 to 1818

1. Eli P. Farmer, Autobiography, 24–71, Farmer Manuscripts, 1818–1874, Lilly Library, Indiana University, Bloomington (hereafter cited as Farmer Autobiography).

2. This portion of Farmer's story picks up on page 41 of the Farmer Autobiography. From 1813 to 1816 Farmer spent six months in the army and had several different jobs in Virginia.

3. William Faux, "Memorable Days in America; Being a Journal of a Tour to the United States," in *Indiana as Seen by Early Travelers*, edited by Harlow Lindley (Indianapolis: Indiana Historical Commission, 1918), 301.

4. The reference is to the miners in England who were among the first in England to respond to John Wesley's revival message.

5. Elizabeth K. Nottingham, *Methodism and the Frontier: Indiana Proving Ground* (New York: Columbia University Press, 1941), 177–78. Nottingham compares the frontier revival with Wesley's revival in England in the 1740s. The reference to Kingswood and Chowden are references to places where Wesley preached to miners.

Chapter 3: Spiritual Searching and Conviction, 1817 to 1820

1. Eli P. Farmer, Autobiography, 61–73, Farmer Manuscripts, 1818–1874, Lilly Library, Indiana University, Bloomington.

2. "The General Rules of the Methodist Church," in *The Book of Discipline of the United Methodist Church, 2016* (Nashville, TN: United Methodist Publishing House, 2016), 77–80.

3. Thomas Coke and Francis Asbury, *The Doctrines and Discipline of the Methodist Episcopal Church in America* (Philadelphia: H. Tuckniss, 1798), 159.

4. Peter Cartwright, *Autobiography of Peter Cartwright: The Backwoods Preacher*, edited by W. P. Strickland (New York: Carlton and Porter, 1857), 62.

5. Puritan Calvinism was not easily flexible. Jonathan Edwards (1703–1758), perhaps colonial America's greatest theologian, wrote an entire book, *Freedom of the Will* (Boston: S. Kneeland, 1754), to make it work intellectually. The original title indicates how difficult it was to reconcile free will with Calvinism: Jonathan

Edwards, *A Careful and Strict Enquiry into the Modern Prevailing Notions of that Freedom of Will, which Is Supposed to Be Essential to Moral Agency, Vertue and Vice, Reward and Punishment, Praise and Blame* (1754; repr., London: Thomas Field, [1762]).

6. To complicate matters, the Anglican thirty-nine articles were written by Thomas Cramner, who was himself strongly influenced by Calvinism, in *The First Prayer Book* (1549), the book that was a precursor to Great Britain's *Book of Common Prayer*.

7. One of Calvinism's doctrinal points was the affirmation of "limited atonement," the understanding that Christ's death was for the elect. But if for the elect only, did God not care for the rest of creation? Unlimited atonement was the belief in universal love.

8. Unlimited atonement would default to free will, but it is important to understand how it got to free will. If salvation is by grace, it is not by works; personal choice can be considered a work. Wesley believed in total depravity (with the Calvinists) but believed that persons were given a special gift of grace that would enable them to respond to God's love (prevenient grace or free grace). Persons have what can be considered free will but it is the result of free grace.

9. Timothy L. Smith, *Revivalism and Social Reform in Mid-Nineteenth-Century America* (New York: Abingdon Press, 1957).

10. Postmillennialism and restorationism will be mentioned several times in this study. Postmillennialism is the view that the world will become increasingly Christianized until Christ's kingdom is established and Christ returns to rule over the earth. This was a common view during the First Great Awakening in New England and New Jersey. Jonathan Edwards, a Calvinist, was a millennialist. The difference is that the Calvinists who espoused postmillennialism believed Christ's kingdom would come by the gradual Christian civilizing of society. The Methodists believed it would come by revival. Either view meshes well with a belief in American exceptionalism.

11. The relationship of the Campbellites (the followers of Alexander Campbell) and the Methodists will be discussed later. Its importance for this study is that when Farmer left Methodism it was in part because he was drawn to the Campbellite doctrines.

12. Henry K. Shaw, *Hoosier Disciples: A Comprehensive History of the Christian Churches (Disciples of Christ) in Indiana* (Saint Louis: Bethany Press, 1966), 31.

13. L. C. Rudolph, *Hoosier Zion: The Presbyterians in Early Indiana* (New Haven: Yale University Press, 1963), 34–35. The quote is taken from Sidney E. Mead, "Denominationalism: The Shape of Protestantism in America," *Church History* 23 (December 1954): 301.

Chapter 4: Reclaimed, 1820 to 1822

1. Eli P. Farmer, Autobiography, 74–84, Farmer Manuscripts, 1818–1874, Lilly Library, Indiana University, Bloomington.

2. Ernst Troeltsch, quoted in Richard Niebuhr, *The Social Sources of Denominationalism* (New York: Meridian, 1922), 29.

3. In an otherwise excellent article, by Angela Tarángo ("From Pueblos to Pentecostals," *Christian History* 102 [2012]: 4–12), in a section titled, "Sinners' Bench and Altar Call," she credits Charles Finney with introducing the "sinner's bench" and the "altar call" to American religious culture. It is incorrect to make this claim. Finney had not even begun to preach when the altar call was a staple in Methodist camp meetings in the early 1800s. The revivalism of Finney is an important part of the Second Great Awakening but it is associated with a different locale (primarily New York) and at a different time (primarily from 1825 to 1835) than the earliest Methodist camp meetings. Inasmuch as Charles G. Finney used an altar call (although there are no references to the altar call in Finney's book, *Lectures on Revival* [New York: Leavitt, Lord and Co., 1835]), he borrowed it from the Methodists, not the other way around.

4. J. B. Wakeley, *The Patriarch of One Hundred Years, Being Reminiscences, Historical and Biographical of Rev. Henry Boehm* (New York: Nelson and Phillips, 1875), 134–35. Boehm (1775–1875) is a key figure in United Methodist history. He supervised the translation of the Methodist *Discipline* into German in 1807 and helped start the Evangelical Association, a Methodist-type church that eventually merged into the United Methodist Church.

5. "I appeal to you therefore, brethren, by the mercies of God, to present your bodies as a living sacrifice, holy and acceptable to God." (Romans 12:2)

6. It is worth noting that Phoebe Palmer followed the implications of her teaching to advance the cause of women speaking in the church. In her book *Promise of the Father, or, a Neglected Spirituality of the Last Days* (Boston: H. V. Degen, 1859), she makes the argument that in the New Testament the Holy Spirit, promised by the Father, would fall on both men and women.

7. In the process of writing this book the author attended a Pentecostal revival meeting in Howard County, Indiana. The service lasted three hours and twenty minutes. During that time there was shouting, clapping, dancing up and down the aisles, an invitation from a church attender to be annointed, and movement to and from the altar railing. There was exuberant singing and prayers for healing. The preacher at one point stood on a chair. Several persons were "slain in the spirit," that is, they fainted under the intensity of the religious experience and fell flat on the floor (and soon after recovered). Sometime in the mid-1970s, one of the editors of this book had a similar experience at a Pentecostal meeting in downtown Indianapolis, Indiana (although the preacher did not stand on a chair).

8. Ellen Eslinger, *Citizens of Zion: The Social Origins of Camp Meeting Revivalism* (Knoxville: University of Tennessee Press, 1999).

9. William Cronon, George Miles, and Jay Gitlin, eds., *Under an Open Sky: Rethinking America's Western Past* (New York: W. W. Norton, 1992). Cronon comments that "Little if anything that happened in this great revival was new." This book about Farmer proposes that a great deal about camp meetings and the Western Revival *was* new, and the influences are being felt even today.

Chapter 5: "God Has Given Me This Place," 1822 to 1826

1. Eli P. Farmer, Autobiography, 84–113, Farmer Manuscripts, 1818–1874, Lilly Library, Indiana University, Bloomington.

2. One very good study on the subject of American Methodism and sanctification is John L. Peters, *Christian Perfection and American Methodism: The Wesleyan Doctrine—Its Development and Deviations* (New York: Abingdon Press, 1956). For more information see Charles Edwin Jones, *A Guide to the Study of the Holiness Movement* (Metuchen, NJ: Scarecrow Press and American Theological Library Association, 1974).

3. A quarterly conference was a meeting with the presiding elder in charge of a circuit. Among other things, it was a business meeting. At quarterly conferences pastors were recommended for ministry and, when appropriate, given licenses. A quarterly conference was held for all the churches on the circuit, which meant there would be a huge crowd. Because some had come from a distance, a conference sometimes lasted overnight and involved camping. Thus it was ideal for a camp meeting. It was one of the features that worked in the Methodists' favor. Conferences will be referenced later in the chapter.

4. The fact that Farmer was given credentials as a first step in his preaching career is significant and should not be overlooked. Farmer was unsure whether or not he should be a Methodist. The quarterly conference voted to give him credentials to preach. Usually, a license to "exhort" was a first step toward credentialing for preaching. Being credentialed immediately obviously took Farmer by surprise. He indicated that he realized almost at once that it was a call from God to which he was disobedient and which brought him grief.

5. The sense of a calling for Farmer and many other early preachers was so strong that not to be acting on the call was associated with disobedience and backsliding.

6. The Methodist Church would scarcely ever place a person on trial from the early twentieth century on. However, it was not uncommon during the frontier days.

7. It is worth noting that Farmer was not invited to preach by any people in Bloomfield, nor was he sent by the presiding elder of the Methodist conference. He just went, and with no lack of confidence. He would claim the community. He evidently held at least some of his meetings in the Greene County Courthouse.

8. N. E. Lamb, comp., *The Autobiography of Abraham Snethen: The Barefoot Preacher* (Dayton, OH: Christian Publishing Association 1909), 14.

9. Jack Barber, *The Early History of Greene County, Indiana* (Worthington: N. B Millson, 1875), 65; *History of Greene and Sullivan Counties, State of Indiana* (Chicago: Goodspeed Brothers and Co., 1884), 325. The county histories are uneven in how accurately they reported early county history. For the most part, they were not written by trained historians. These two histories, however, mention Farmer and several of the persons whose

names are in Farmer's account. There is also a mention of Farmer's campground and the "First old pioneer Methodist camp-meeting held in the oak woods just north of Fairplay," Indiana. Farmer mentions an appointment in Fairplay later in this chapter.

10. A "noted infidel" in Farmer's eyes did not necessarily mean a bad person, but one who was not yet a believer. The accusation against Farmer was that he was advancing himself financially through his preaching. The truth is that Farmer had no financial support at this time.

11. A protracted meeting in modern terms would be called a revival, which would include a series of scheduled services. It would be an indoor meeting compared to a camp meeting, which would be an outdoor meeting where people would come from a great enough distance that they would need to camp. Farmer evidently intended to bring in additional preachers for this revival.

12. "Attending another appointment" is the same as saying continuing to another preaching point on the circuit. It is quite likely by this time that Farmer had several preaching points.

13. The common practice among circuit riders was to schedule a service or a meeting on the spot. The congregation assembled on the spot also by having persons go door-to-door and announce the services. If there was some response, as there was in this case, the house was added to the circuit for regular preaching.

14. This particular story about the Quaker couple is included because it relates to a discussion later in the study on Farmer's ideas of Christian Union (and sectarianism). While on the one hand, Farmer's story shows that he was open to all Christian expressions, on the other hand, his story will come to illustrate frontier sectarianism.

Chapter 6: Officially Methodist, 1825 to 1826

1. Eli P. Farmer, Autobiography, 117–20, Farmer Manuscripts, 1818–1874, Lilly Library, Indiana University, Bloomington.

2. Peter Cartwright was probably the best known of the early western frontier revivalist preachers. Eventually he rode a preaching circuit in Illinois where he served in the Illinois General Assembly and ran against Abraham Lincoln for Congress. He is quoted several times in this study.

3. Farmer makes a curious and interesting reference to "old sisters" in this passage. Does it refer to old age or old in terms of revival experience? Camp meetings should have been a new phenomenon in Greene County. Except for the Cumberland Presbyterians, the Methodists were the only religious group there and they had been there only a year. It should be noted: 1) Farmer is fully in charge in the first year of his first appointment; 2) the place of women as a key revival component is already established; 3) the altar, referred to already, is central in this camp meeting account. A skeptic might remark that Farmer is manipulating the meeting. It is likely that Farmer suspects the old sisters will "get happy" and that will change the tone and course of the meeting.

4. Alan Heimert and Perry Miller, eds., *The Great Awakening: Documents Illustrating the Crisis and Its Consequences* (Indianapolis: Bobbs–Merrill, 1967), 340–53.

5. Walter Brownlow Posey, *Frontier Mission: A History of Religion West of the Southern Appalachians to 1861* (Lexington: University of Kentucky Press, 1966), 25–26.

Chapter 7: Good in Prayer and Singing, 1826 to 1827

1. Eli P. Farmer, Autobiography, 120–41, Farmer Manuscripts, 1818–1874, Lilly Library, Indiana University, Bloomington.

2. Despite the fact that the Methodist system was highly organized there were frequent problems. In Farmer's case the people of his new appointment had not known of his coming. It was also not unusual for pastors to miss appointments, perhaps because of weather or sickness or missed communication, or because of getting lost. Sometimes pastors got discouraged and simply abandoned the field. Methodists needed to be adaptable and flexible.

3. This was only Farmer's second official year as a traveling preacher, but as the appointed preacher of a circuit he had freedom and authority to choose and appoint his "helpers" even, in this case, if the helper was a seventeen-year-old boy without a license or any preaching experience. Farmer used this authority to send the young man to an uncharted "field," "somewhere around Attica," Indiana.

4. Big Pine Creek flows into the Wabash River just northwest of Attica, which is in Fountain County, Indiana.

5. "Serpent Handling," *Dictionary of Pentecostal and Charismatic Movements* (Grand Rapids, MI: Regency, 1988) 777–78.

6. See Deborah Vansau McCauley, *Appalachian Mountain Religion: A History* (Urbana: University of Illinois Press, 1995). McCauley defines Appalachia more narrowly than some studies and does not include southern Indiana as part of her definition. However, it can be argued that most of what she observes about "mountain religion" would also apply to southern Ohio and Indiana. It is an indigenous form of American Protestantism developed quite apart from outside influences featuring, at least in the early years, Methodists and Baptists and developing into Holiness and Pentecostal expressions.

7. Universalists believed that all souls would be saved eventually. Universalists later merged with Unitarians. Apparently, universalism stood outside the pale of what Farmer thought constituted a Christian body. Farmer believed that only those who worked toward salvation and were accepted by God would be saved. All souls *could* be saved, but all would not necessarily be saved. Thus, his calling was to save as many souls as possible for God's kingdom.

8. "Open the doors of the church" is a phrase meaning to offer an invitation to be a church member.

9. One excellent study is Ellen Jane Lorenz, *Glory Hallelujah! The Story of the Camp Meeting Spiritual* (Nashville, TN: Abingdon, 1980). Lorenz is the granddaughter of E. S. Lorenz, United Brethren denominational music editor. His collection of earliest camp meeting songbooks can be found at United Theological Seminary, Dayton, Ohio.

10. B. St. James Fry, "The Early Camp-Meeting Song Writers," *Methodist Quarterly Review* 41 (July 1859): 407.

11. Theophilus Arminius, "Account of the Rise and Progress of the Work of God in the Western Country," *Methodist Magazine* 16, no. 8 (1819): 304.

12. *The Journal and Letters of Francis Asbury*, vol. 3 (Nashville, TN: Abingdon Press, 1958), 398.

13. Lorenz, *Glory Hallelujah*, 134.

14. Ibid., 78–86. Lorenz traces the camp-meeting spiritual's development under these headings: 1) Sunday school songs; 2) Gospel songs and choruses; 3) Influence on twentieth-century hymnals; and 4) Serious compositions quoting camp meeting spirituals. See also Riley B. Case, "From Spiritual to Gospel," in *Understanding Our New United Methodist Hymnal* (Bristol Books, 1989), 50–61.

Chapter 8: Taking on Lafayette, 1827 to 1828

1. Eli P. Farmer, Autobiography, 143–63, Farmer Manuscripts, 1818–1874, Lilly Library, Indiana University, Bloomington.

2. Eli P. Farmer married Elizabeth W. McClung on January 15, 1828, in Montgomery County, Indiana, "Indiana Compiled Marriages, 1802–1892," Family History Library, Salt Lake City, UT.

3. Arthur B. Wang, "History of Trinity United Methodist Church, Lafayette, Indiana, 1825–1971," unpublished manuscript (copy in author's possession), 1. This account reveals the troubles Reverend H. Buell endured because of the "grog shop," yelling, and gunfire. It speaks of Farmer who followed Buell and although injured in the scuffles later performed healings at a camp meeting. Farmer's account does not mention the injury or the healing. The church history, however, does not give Farmer credit for the founding of the church, attributing that to Buell and the previous pastor.

4. Lorenzo Dow, *History of Cosmopolite, or, the Four Volumes of Lorenzo Dow's Journal Concentrated in One . . . to which is added the "Journey of Life"* (Wheeling, VA: Joshua Martin, 1848), 599–601.

5. Nathan O. Hatch, *The Democratization of American Christianity* (New Haven: Yale University Press, 1989), 36.

6. Ibid.

Chapter 9: Sickness, Location, and Washington Circuit, 1828 to 1830

1. Eli P. Farmer, Autobiography, 159–65, Farmer Manuscripts, 1818–1874, Lilly Library, Indiana University, Bloomington.

2. The best discussion of the Cumberland Presbyterian Church in Indiana can be found in L. C. Rudolph, *Hoosier Faiths: A History of Indiana's Churches and Religious Groups* (Bloomington: Indiana University Press, 1995), 117–22. The church grew out of the Cane Ridge camp meeting and the Kentucky revival of 1800 and was the least Calvinistic of all the Presbyterian bodies.

3. Farmer lists the order of his children incorrectly or is referring only to the first two children he had with his second wife, Elizabeth. His first child, John Farmer, was born to his first wife, Matilda, ca. 1824 (see Chapter 5). In 1828 Eli and Elizabeth had their first child, James, and a year later their son Melville was born. For James, see "James E. Farmer," https://www.findagrave.com/memorial/28858341/james-e.-farmer. For Melville Farmer see 1850 U.S. Census for Eli P. Farmer in Richland, Monroe County, Indiana, roll: M432_161, p. 242B, image 53, Ancestry.com.

4. According to conference records, in 1830 Alfred Arrington was appointed to Lawrenceburg in southeastern Indiana—which is an indication of how large an area the circuits covered. See Indiana Methodist, United Brethren, and Evangelical Ministers' Appointments, 1800–1900, in Indiana United Methodism Collections, Archives and Special Collections, Depauw University, http://palni.contentdm.oclc.org/cdm/ref/collection/methodist/id/2872.

5. Elmo A. Robinson, "Universalism in Indiana," *Indiana Magazine of History* 13 (March 1917). There will be more discussion about statistics on the Indiana frontier later in the book. The U.S. census reports that there were only two Universalist churches in Indiana in 1850.

Chapter 10: Harvest Time, 1830 to 1832

1. Eli P. Farmer, Autobiography, 173–83, Farmer Manuscripts, 1818–1874, Lilly Library, Indiana University, Bloomington.

2. Brother Wallace was probably David Wallace (1799–1859), who was a member of the Indiana House of Representatives from 1828 to 1831. He was governor of Indiana from 1837 to 1840.

3. Josiah Strange, like James Armstrong, was a highly respected leader in early Indiana Methodism. Note that Farmer calls almost everyone associated with the church "brother" or "sister." This is another indication of the egalitarian nature of early frontier churches, especially the populist churches such as Methodist and Baptist.

4. Berry R. Sulgrove, *History of Indianapolis and Marion County, Indiana* (Philadelphia: L. H. Everts and Co., 1884), 581.

5. Abel Stevens, *A Compendious History of American Methodism* (New York: Hunt and Eaton, 1867), 425. Stevens observed that in the years from 1790 to 1865, the increase of the U.S. population averaged 35.8 percent for every ten years, compared to Methodist growth of 56.7 percent. This is not counting Methodist breakaway groups.

6. L. C. Rudolph, *Hoosier Faiths: A History of Indiana's Churches and Religious Groups* (Bloomington: Indiana University Press, 1996), 14.

7. Almost all histories of American Methodism cover the division of 1844 between the Methodist Episcopal Church and the Methodist Episcopal Church South. One succinct account is found in Wade Crawford Barclay, *History of Methodist Missions*, vol. 1, *Early American Methodism, 1769–1844* (New York: Board of Missions and Church Extension of the Methodist Church, 1949), 357. The two Methodist Episcopal Churches plus the Methodist Protestant Church were reunited in 1939 to form the Methodist Church. See John M. Moore, *The Long Road to Methodist Union* (Nashville, TN: Abingdon–Cokesbury Press, 1943).

8. Holland N. McTyeire, *A History of Methodism: Comprising a View of the Rise of this Revival of Spiritual Religion in the First Half of the Eighteenth Century . . . and the means and manner of its extension down to A.D. 1884* (Nashville, TN: Southern Methodist Publishing House, 1888), 3. McTyeire can make his claim only if he defines "South" as Kentucky, Tennessee, Virginia, Delaware, and Maryland. Even Christine Leigh Heyrman in *Southern Cross: The Beginnings of the Bible Belt* (New York: Alfred A. Knopf, 1997), notes that while the evangelical approach to faith eventually came to characterize southern religious culture, it did not dominate religious culture in the early 1800s.

9. The Wesleyan Methodist story and the Free Methodist story are perhaps best explained by members of the individual groups. For the Wesleyan Methodists see Orange Scott, *The Grounds of Secession from the M. E. Church* (New York: C. Prindle, 1848). For the Free Methodists the classic work is Leslie Ray Marston, *From Age*

to Age a Living Witness: A Historical Interpretation of Free Methodism's First Century* (Winona Lake, IN: Light and Life Press, 1960).

10. Russell E. Richey, "The Formation of American Methodism: The Chesapeake Refraction of Wesleyanism," in *Methodism and the Shaping of American Culture*, edited by Nathan O. Hatch and John H. Wigger (Nashville, TN: Kingswood Books, 2001), 197.

11. Charles A. Johnson, *The Frontier Camp Meeting: Religion's Harvest Time* (Dallas: Southern Methodist University Press, 1955).

12. William Courtland Johnson, "To Dance in the Ring of All Creation: Camp Meeting Revivalism and the Color Line, 1799–1825" (PhD diss., University of California, Riverside, 1997). Early criticism of camp meetings linked "barbarous" practices with the presence of blacks. These criticisms relate to the theory that the word "Hoosier" was a term of derision linked with the black evangelist Harry Hoosier, some of whose converts migrated to Indiana.

13. The "Delmarva Peninsula is . . . occupied by the entire State of Delaware, and portions of Maryland, and Virginia." It is "bordered by the Chesapeake Bay on the west, and the Delaware River, Delaware Bay, and Atlantic Ocean on the east." WorldAtlas.com (last modified September 29, 2015), https://www.worldatlas.com/webimage/countrys/namerica/usstates/lgcolor/delmarva.htm.

14. William H. Williams, "The Attraction of Methodism: The Delmarva Peninsula as a Case Study, 1769–1820," in *Perspectives on American Methodism*, edited by Russell E. Richey, Kenneth E. Rowe, and Jean Miller Schmidt (Nashville, TN: Kingswood Books, 1993), 31. Curiously, while Williams analyzed a number of ethnic, demographic, and sociological factors contributing to Methodism's growth, he makes almost no mention of camp meetings.

15. Abel Stevens, "Methodism: Suggestions Appropriate to Its Present Condition," *Methodist Quarterly Review* 42 (1860): 122.

16. Leaders in the Methodist Church and denominational historians do not like to dwell on regional and social tensions, but these tensions have characterized the church throughout the years. The relationship between the camp meeting and the development of the "spiritual" or gospel hymn has already been discussed. Almost all of the Methodist-related gospel hymnals were published in Cincinnati or Chicago. A much more traditional and European hymnal was associated with the more sophisticated East. Official hymnal committees were dominated by easterners. The influence of New York can be seen in the Methodist Episcopal Church hymnal of 1878. It includes no camp-meeting spirituals or gospel hymns. Of its 1,178 hymns, only 7 were associated with anyone west of Rochester, New York, or south of Washington, DC. Of 307 authors in the hymnal, 66 were Anglican or Episcopal, 22 were Congregational, 20 were Presbyterian, 14 were Unitarian, 13 were Lutheran, 13 Roman Catholic, and only 10 were from the Methodist Episcopal Church. In 1905 when the Methodist Episcopal Church and the Methodist Episcopal Church South cooperated to issue an official "Methodist" hymnal, it is significant that out of 748 hymns, fewer than 10 were associated with anyone west of Rochester, New York, or south of Washington, DC. See, Riley B. Case, *Understanding Our New United Methodist Hymnal* (Wilmore, KY: Bristol Books, 1989), 58.

17. Abel Stevens, *History of the Methodist Episcopal Church of the United States of America*, vol. 4 (New York: Phillips and Hunt, 1884).

Chapter 11: Greencastle, Location, and Brown County, 1833 to 1838

1. There appears to be a change in tone at this point in the Eli Farmer Autobiography (Farmer Manuscripts, 1818–1874, Lilly Library, Indiana University, Bloomington). There is a partial manuscript that covers the earlier years of his life. It is possible that Farmer recorded this section at some earlier date and then added the later material when he finished his manuscript in 1874. The earlier part of the story is affirming of Methodism, whereas the later material is critical of Methodism. In addition there is some confusion as to the sequence of events in the last half of the manuscript when these events are checked from other sources. What we know for sure is that Farmer was appointed to Greencastle in 1832, then stayed home for three years and began to develop a circuit in Brown County. He was appointed to Brown County circuit in 1837 and then to Danville in 1838. Farmer then withdrew from the Methodist preaching conference in 1839. During the 1840s he preached for the Methodists and also without denominational attachment, and pursued his Christian Union plan. He also went into politics, losing some campaigns, but serving in the Indiana State Senate from

1842 to 1845. He took a trip to the South in 1846. In 1853–54 Farmer edited the *Bloomington Religious Times*. He and his five sons served in the Union army during the Civil War. See the biographical sketches for him that were published in Bloomington, Indiana, newspapers, in the Farmer Papers, Lilly Library, Indiana University, Bloomington. For his preaching record see *Minutes of the Annual Conferences of the Methodist Episcopal Church for the Years 1773–1828*, 2 vols. (New York: T. Mason and G. Lane, 1840) and *Minutes of the Annual Conferences of the Methodist Episcopal Church for the Years 1829–1839*, vol. 2 (New York: T. Mason and G. Lane, 1840).

2. Eli P. Farmer, Second Manuscript, 183–96, 232, Farmer Manuscripts, 1818–1874, Indiana University, Bloomington (see note 1 above).

3. There is one reference to Farmer in the history of the Greencastle church: "In 1832 the Indianapolis District was brought under the jurisdiction of the newly established Indiana Conference. Assigned that year [sic] to the Greencastle Circuit was Eli P. Farmer, a veteran of the War of 1812 who was reported to be an earnest and ready talker, but a rough, uncultivated man." See Clifton J. Phillips, ed., *From Frontier Circuit to Urban Church: A History of Greencastle Methodism* (Greencastle, IN: Gobin Memorial United Methodist Church, 1989), 10.

4. Farmer is mistaken about the age of his son. His oldest son, John, would have been no more than eleven at this point, having been born no earlier than 1823. See note 3, Chapter 9.

5. These were probably the early salt mills of Monroe County in Salt Creek Township. See *History of Lawrence and Monroe Counties, Indiana, their People, Industries, and Institutions* (Indianapolis: B. F. Bowen and Co., 1914), 220, 229, 427.

6. This may have been the period of Farmer's first entry into Brown County, which would figure prominently in his life the next few years. He is evidently preaching without appointment and operating his business at the same time.

Chapter 12: Danville, Christian Union, and Sectarianism, 1838 to 1842

1. Eli P. Farmer, Autobiography, 241–45, 250, 253, Farmer Manuscripts, 1818–1874, Lilly Library, Indiana University, Bloomington.

2. When the Methodists were accused of sectarianism it was often because they taught, or appeared to teach, that persons who belonged to other denominations had probably not had a conversion experience and were therefore not "redeemed." Thus, when Baptists or Presbyterians attended Methodist camp meetings and were "converted," they were urged to join the Methodist Church. This was called "sheep stealing." This incident reported by Farmer may have convinced him there was some truth to the charge because he soon offered his Christian Union Plan.

3. This is the first mention of Farmer's Christian Union Plan, which will figure prominently in his views of sectarianism and his decision to leave Methodism and start a new denomination. A point will be made that the impetus behind the plan—that a conversion experience is the basis for a unity that transcends all sectarianism—is the key in the development of a common evangelical religious ethos in America.

4. The sectarian understanding of the church will be discussed later, but it is worth noting here that Christian Union Baptists and Presbyterians were following the Methodist practice of receiving members on the basis of their testimony of conversion without reference to baptism or any kind of instruction.

5. Matthew Simpson was one of the best-known Methodist bishops of the nineteenth century. He was a friend of Abraham Lincoln and preached Lincoln's funeral message. However, at this point he was a young man in his twenties (not yet a bishop) and the newly appointed president of Indiana Asbury. See George R. Crooks, *The Life of Bishop Matthew Simpson of the Methodist Episcopal Church* (New York: Harper and Brothers, 1891).

6. There will be three reasons why Farmer separated himself from the Methodists: 1) Methodists had become fashionable and were in the process of departing from primitive Methodism; 2) Methodists were too sectarian. Sectarianism will be discussed further; 3) Farmer becomes accepting of the doctrine of believers' baptism by immersion.

7. Simpson was dating the beginning of Methodism to John Wesley's gathering of believers into classes after his conversion experience in England in 1739.

8. It appears that, at least in Farmer's mind, there is a two-tier class system among Methodist preachers. The traveling elders, who were the full members of the conference, and the local preachers and lay pastors, who were less important.

9. This is the first time Farmer connects the word "sectarianism" with the Methodists.

10. The nomenclature and reference is significant. Phillip May was appointed to the Bloomington "station" for the year 1840–41. By 1840 Methodists in Indiana claimed 52,000 members distributed in four conferences and ten districts. Appointment of preachers was in one of four categories: 1) a "mission," meaning it was a new work subsidized by other churches; 2) a "special" appointment, such as serving as a presiding elder, or, in the case of Indiana, serving at Indiana Asbury College; 3) a "circuit," meaning the preacher or preachers were responsible for anywhere from two to thirty different churches; or 4) a "station," meaning a single church was strong enough to support a preacher by itself. In 1840 there were two mission appointments, fifteen special appointments, 129 circuit appointments to ninety different circuits, and seven station appointments. These do not count hundreds of "local" preachers who did not itinerate. The station churches were desired and prestigious appointments, implying standing. Stations in 1840 included Bloomington, Crawfordsville, Indianapolis, Jeffersonville, Madison, South Bend, and Terre Haute. Thus May, at least in Farmer's eyes, was a Methodist "authority" and a person of influence. See Indiana Methodist, United Brethren, and Evangelical Ministers' Appointments, 1800–1900, in Indiana United Methodism Collections, Archives, and Special Collections, Depauw University, http://palni.contentdm.oclc.org/cdm/ref/collection/methodist/id/2872.

11. Farmer's loyalties are in transition. He shows his attraction to Campbellism by his comment that they won the debate. He is still hoping, however, to be a peacemaker and reconcile Campbellites (the Christian Church) and the Methodists with his Christian Union Plan.

12. A "water revival" would be anathema to Methodists. In a "water revival" believers would be baptized by immersion to signify their conversion. The implication was that Methodists previously baptized by sprinkling were not truly Christians. All of this was part of the sectarian wars taking place at this time between Methodists and Campbellites.

13. The various terms and phrases that Farmer used about the religious controversies of that time offer insight into the issues. The term "public square religion" is another way of speaking of his Christian Union plan. It implies a common public religious position that transcends sectarianism.

14. Methodist preachers at this time were appointed for one year. The conference year was not the same as the calendar year. Isaac Owen's appointment was two years after Phillip May's, in 1842 to 1843. Owen evidently respected Farmer enough that he wanted his help in building the new church. It would be interesting to know how Owen might have interpreted these events.

15. R. Carlyle Buley, *The Old Northwest Pioneer Period, 1815–1840*, vol. 2 (Indianapolis: Indiana Historical Society, 1950), 417–18.

16. The religious sociological understanding of the differences between "sect" and "church" can be traced through such writers as Ernst Troeltsch, *The Social Teachings of the Christian Churches*, 2 vols. (London: Allen and Unwin, 1931); Richard Niebuhr, *The Social Sources of Denominationalism* (New York: Henry Holt, 1929) and *Christ and Culture* (New York: Harper and Row, 1951); and Roger Finke and Rodney Stark, *The Churching of America, 1776–1990* (New Brunswick, NJ: Rutgers University Press, 1992).

17. The last two hundred years of Methodism in America would serve as a good example of the process a sectarian group undergoes to become mainstream.

18. Charles Blanchard, ed., *Counties of Morgan, Monroe, and Brown, Indiana: Historical and Biographical* (Chicago: F. A. Battey and Co., 1884), 480.

19. One of the best observers of these groups is the Mennonite historian J. C. Wenger, *The Mennonites in Indiana and Michigan* (Scottdale, PA: Herald Press, 1961).

20. Ministers in Massachusetts argued in 1743 for the right to forbid itinerant preachers from entering their parishes. In 1744 a public statement was issued against George Whitefield, titled *The Testimony of the President, Professors, Tutors, and Hebrew Instructor of Harvard College in Cambridge, against the Reverent Mr. George Whitefield and His Conduct* (Boston: T. Fleet, 1744). See also Alan Heimert and Perry Miller, eds., *The Great Awakening: Documents Illustrating the Crisis and Its Consequences* (Indianapolis: Bobbs-Merrill, 1967), 340–53.

21. Nathan Hatch, "The Puzzle of American Methodism," in *Methodism and the Shaping of American Culture*, edited by Nathan O. Hatch and John H. Wigger (Nashville, TN: Kingswood Books, 2001), 35.

22. Edwin Scott Gaustad, *Historical Atlas of Religion in America* (New York: Harper and Row, 1962); *A Compendium of the Ninth Census* (Washington, DC: Government Printing Office, 1872), 514–25.

23. Gayle Williams, "Andrew Wylie and Religion at Indiana University, 1824–1851: Nonsectarianism and Democracy," *Indiana Magazine of History* 99 (March 2003): 17. The article is an excellent account of the sectarian–nonsectarian controversies surrounding Indiana University.

24. Ibid., 2–24.

25. Ibid., 24.

26. Quoted in Crooks, *Life of Bishop Matthew Simpson*, 504–5.

Chapter 13: Politics, 1830s to 1845

1. Eli P. Farmer, Autobiography, 197, 200–2, 210–20, Farmer Manuscripts, 1818–1874, Indiana University, Bloomington.

2. Samuel Bigger (not "Bigler") was governor of Indiana from 1840 to 1843. It appears that Farmer refers to Bigger as governor even though the events Farmer is narrating here take place in the 1830s. However, in his reference to "snowing Bigler under," Farmer is referring to the 1842 campaign.

3. Farmer calls Paris Dunning "governor" but Farmer is writing from the perspective of the 1870s. Dunning was Indiana governor from December 1848 to December 1849. The events of this part of the chapter took place earlier, when both Farmer and Dunning were candidates for the state legislature. The internal improvements program went bankrupt between 1839 and 1841.

4. Farmer is mistaken about Hensley's name. He was probably speaking of Thomas Jefferson Henley, who was a member of the Indiana General Assembly from 1832 to 1842 and Speaker in 1840. Henley went on to serve in the U.S. Congress from 1843 to 1849. Thereafter he moved to California.

5. The distinguished representative may have been Charles Butler, a financier from New York who was involved with the bonds the state of Indiana was using to finance its internal improvements program. Butler advised and consulted with Indiana's General Assembly after the state went bankrupt between 1839 and 1841. He was influential in the creation of "An Act to Provide for the Funded Debt of the State of Indiana, and for the Completion of the Wabash and Erie Canal to Evansville, 1846" also known as the Butler Bill (*Journal of the House of Representatives of the State of Indiana, During the Thirty-First Session of the General Assembly* [Indianapolis: J. P. Chapman, 1846], 720). See Lee Newcomer, "A History of the Indiana Internal Improvement Bonds," *Indiana Magazine of History* 32 (June 1936): 106–15; and Governor James Whitcomb, *Mr. Butler's Letter to the Legislature of Indiana, and Other Documents in Relation to the Public Debt* (Indianapolis: Morrison and Spann, 1845).

6. Despite Farmer's unhappiness with the Methodists, at this time he still had standing in the Methodist Church as a local preacher relating to the Bloomington church, but without appointment.

Chapter 14: The Trip South, 1846

1. Eli P. Farmer, Autobiography, 222–27, 376, Farmer Manuscripts, 1818–1874, Indiana University, Bloomington.

2. Father Michael J. Clark was the first Catholic resident pastor in Lafayette, Indiana, serving from 1843 to 1857. See Herman Joseph Alerding, *The Diocese of Fort Wayne, 1857–September 1907: A Book of Historical Reference, 1669–1907* (Fort Wayne, IN: Archer Printing, 1907), 218.

3. Farmer was mistaken in the supposition that Father Clark was a bishop.

4. Farmer expressed strong anti-Catholic views when he was editor of the *Bloomington Religious Times*. In his writing for the *Times* he makes reference to the events of this encounter on the steamboat. In his autobiography his only references to Catholicism are in this present chapter. It is possible that his views mellowed later in life.

5. It is worth noting that William Miller was originally Methodist and came out of a similar revivalist milieu as Farmer.

6. See for example Timothy L. Smith, *Revivalism and Social Reform in Mid-Nineteenth-Century America* (Nashville, TN: Abingdon Press, 1957).

7. William Courtland Johnson, "To Dance in the Ring of All Creation: Camp Meeting Revivalism and the Color Line, 1799–1825" (PhD diss., University of California, Riverside, 1997).

Chapter 15: Nonsectarian Sectarianism, 1840s to 1853

1. Eli P. Farmer, Autobiography, 253, 260–63, Farmer Manuscripts, 1818–1874, Indiana University, Bloomington (hereafter cited as Farmer Autobiography).

2. Farmer is incorrect about the year of William Morrow's appointment to Bloomington. Morrow was appointed in 1845 and then reappointed for a second year in 1846. The second year appointment is an indication that the Methodists were moving away from their tradition of one-year appointments only. Preachers in "station" churches such as Bloomington preferred to stay longer since these were prestigious appointments. See Indiana Methodist, United Brethren, and Evangelical Ministers' Appointments, 1800–1900, in Indiana United Methodism Collections, Archives, and Special Collections, Depauw University, http://palni.contentdm.oclc.org/cdm/ref/collection/methodist/id/2872.

3. "Excommunication" was not a Methodist word. One could be dropped from the roll of approved pastors but it had to be done by action of the annual conference. At this point Farmer was still considered a Methodist preacher. The only authority Morrow had was through his influence. This story reveals Farmer's unhappiness with what he perceived was Morrow's and the Methodist Church's growing identification with "the elite."

4. This would probably be a church that would relate not to the Methodists but to the Christian Union.

5. The Methodists at this time had not yet begun to establish camp-meeting sites, preferring to hold these at different places for the convenience of the circuits. Here is mention of a "campground," which will serve as a home base for the fledgling Christian Union denomination.

6. Political statements on national issues are sometimes involved in church controversies. Not all of Farmer's friends held the same political views as him. For instance, Farmer supported the Mexican War, while many western Americans did not. This will be discussed in the next chapter on his editorship with the *Bloomington Religious Times*.

7. The year was probably 1847. In 1844 Farmer was still a state senator. The mention of nine denominations opens the door to questions as to how many different groups were operating with Christian Union ideas during the 1830s, 1840s, and 1850s. The republican and egalitarian sentiments brought about by the U.S. Constitution fed revivalism, individualism, and frontier independence. While these forces contributed to the proliferation of groups known as sectarianism, it also led to a strong reaction against sectarianism, which as they used the word, suggested denominationalism. It may be impossible to sort out all the various groups. One of the best studies that attempts to do this sorting is L. C. Rudolph, *Hoosier Faiths: A History of Indiana Churches and Religious Groups* (Bloomington: Indiana University Press, 1995), 60–111, which deals with developments in the larger movement of Disciples, Church of Christ, Christian Union, and numerous other similar groups especially as they developed on the western frontier. Indiana and Ohio were at the center of much of this activity.

8. Farmer Autobiography, 248–49.

9. Frank W. Blackmar, ed., *Kansas: A Cyclopedia of State History, Embracing Events, Institutions, Industries, Counties, Cities, Towns, Prominent Persons, Etc.*, vol. 1 (Chicago: Standard Publishing, 1912), 343–44.

10. Eileen W. Lindner, ed., *Yearbook of American and Canadian Churches, 2010: The New Immigrant Church* (Nashville, TN: Abingdon Press, 2010), 363.

11. William Hunt (1789–1875) was a colorful, rebellious Methodist circuit rider whose life in many ways paralleled that of Farmer. He was an early settler in Randolph County, Indiana, and became so well known that the village of Huntsville was named after him. Hunt was an ardent revivalist but unlike many revivalists was anti-abolitionist. He was in and out of favor with the Methodist authorities. He was expelled, tried, and restored on at least two different occasions from the Methodist conference. In 1844, about the same time Farmer was having troubles with the Methodists, Hunt seceded from the church and founded a new denomination called the Republican Methodist Church. The group wrote a *Discipline* that stated, among other things, that "local ministers and preachers are equal to the traveling ministers and preachers." All members voted on church issues and there was no provision for bishops or presiding elders. Hunt's story is told in an unpublished manuscript by Gregory P. Hinshaw, "Old Billy Hunt: Methodist Circuit Rider, Indiana Pioneer, and Anti-abolitionist" (2010). Copies of the manuscript can be found at the William Henry Smith Memorial Library, Indiana Historical Society, Indianapolis; Indiana United Methodism Collection, Archives, and Special Collections, DePauw Libraries, Greencastle, IN; and the Randolph County Historical Society, Winchester, IN.

Chapter 16: The *Bloomington Religious Times*, 1853 to 1854

1. "Indiana Newspapers Available at Indiana University, Bloomington," in "Microform Guide: Newspapers: Indiana," IU Libraries, https://libraries.indiana.edu/; "About *Religious Times* (Bloomington, Ind.) 1853–1854," Chronicling America: Historic American Newspapers, National Endowment for the Humanities, Library of Congress, https://chroniclingamerica.loc.gov/.

2. *Bloomington Religious Times*, May 26, 1854.

3. There is a rather extensive account of this splintering in J. L. Luttrell, *History of the Auglaize Annual Conference of the United Brethren Church, from 1853 to 1891* (Dayton: United Brethren Publishing House, 1892), 92–105.

4. *Bloomington Religious Times*, April 21, 1854.

5. William Phillips, *Campbellism Exposed, or, Strictures on the Peculiar Tenets of Alexander Campbell* (Cincinnati: J. F. Wright and Swormstedt, 1837).

6. *Bloomington Religious Times*, April 21, 1854. The idea of sharing a community building for various churches sounds good but does not always work. As a sidebar to this discussion in 1883 in Ligonier, Indiana, a case was brought to the civil court in Noble County to settle a matter between Methodists and the Christian Church (Campbellites). In 1836 in the Hawpatch area of Lagrange and Noble Counties land was given for a burial ground and for a building to serve as a school, a church, and for other public gatherings. A building was erected by the Protestant Methodists in 1849 and was used by Baptists, Presbyterians, Methodist Episcopalians, and Protestant Methodists for worship. In 1877 a new building was erected, again to serve the community but under the following restriction: "Said house shall be free to all orthodox denominations when not in use by the said Protestant Methodist church." When the Christian Church began to use the building, dissension arose over whether the Christian Church qualified as an "orthodox denomination." It is one of the very few cases in which a civil court had to decide on a matter of Christian doctrine, namely, what constitutes an "orthodox denomination." The trial was lengthy and bitter with the decision finally in favor of the Christian Church. A book was written which, among other things, records the verbatim report of the testimony of the two sides: J. H. Edwards, et al., eds., *Orthodoxy in the Civil Courts* (Cincinnati: Standard Publishing, 1891).

7. *Bloomington Religious Times*, March 3, 1854.

8. Brown County was formed partially from part of Bartholomew County. Judge Talbert may be Judge James Taggart, one of the first settlers in Bartholomew County. This judge had a son named William Taggart, who was a preacher. Both are buried in Taggart Cemetery in Brown County, Indiana. See "James Taggart," https://www.findagrave.com/memorial/21316703/james-taggart; "William Taggart," https://www.findagrave.com/memorial/21316878/william-taggart.

Chapter 17: Methodists Up-and-Coming without Farmer, 1850s

1. Fernandez C. Holliday, *Indiana Methodism, Being an Account of the Introduction, Progress, and Present Position of Methodism in the State, and also a History of the Literary Institutions Under the Care of the Church, with Sketches of the Principle Methodist Educators in the State* (Cincinnati: Hitchcock and Walden, 1873), 127–47. For number of churches in Indiana see "Table XL: Churches, in the United States, 1870-1860-1850," "Table XLI: Churches of All Denominations, by States and Territories, 1870-1860-1850," and "Table XLII: Churches, Fifteen Selected Denominations, by States and Territories, 1870" in Francis A. Walker, *A Compendium of the Ninth Census (June 1, 1870) Compiled Pursuant to a Concurrent Resolution of Congress and Under the Direction of the Secretary of the Interior* (Washington, DC: Government Printing Office, 1872), pp. 514–29.

2. Fernandez C. Holliday, *Life and Times of Rev. Allen Wiley. A. M., Containing Sketches of Early Methodist Preachers in Indiana . . . also including His Original Letters, entitled "A Help to the Performance of Ministerial Duties"* (Cincinnati: L. Swormstedt and A. Poe, 1873).

3. Frederick J. Jobson, *America and American Methodism* (New York: Virtue, Emmins and Co., 1857).

4. T. M. Eddy, "Influence of Methodism upon the Civilization and Education of the West," *Methodist Quarterly Review* 39 (April 1857): 284.

5. Peter Cartwright, *Autobiography of Peter Cartwright: The Backwoods Preacher* (New York: Carlton and Porter, 1857).

6. Ibid., 71–72.

7. When Indiana Asbury was founded, assurances were made that the primary purpose of the school was to prepare students for service in the world. It was not to be seen as a school to train preachers.

8. Cartwright, *Autobiography*, 207.

9. As quoted in Holliday, *Life and Times of Rev. Allen Wiley*, 80. Wiley had written many articles for the *Western Christian Advocate* (a Methodist weekly, published from 1834 to 1929), which Holliday used for his book. In the quote here, Wiley refers to Socinianism. Believers in this religious strain, dating from the 1620s, believed in God and the Christian scriptures but did not believe in the divinity of Christ or in the Trinity.

Chapter 18: The Civil War, 1861 to 1865

1. Eli P. Farmer, Autobiography, 265–78, Farmer Manuscripts, 1818–1874, Lilly Library, Indiana University, Bloomington.

2. Farmer's sons included John A. Farmer, born ca. 1824, whose mother was Matilda (Allison) Farmer, and the following sons born to Eli and Elizabeth (McClung) Farmer: James E., (ca. 1828–1865); Melville, born ca. 1829; Joel, born ca. 1839; William, born ca. 1841/42; Eli, born ca. 1843; Burton, born ca. 1845/46; and Asberry, born ca. 1847. For John, see Chapter 5. For James, see Chapter 9, and "James E. Farmer," https://www.findagrave.com/memorial/28858341/james-e.-farmer. For Melville, Joel, William, Burton, and Asberry Farmer see 1850 U.S. Census, Richland, Monroe, Indiana, roll: M432_161, p.242B, image 53, Ancestry.com. For William, Eli R., Burton, and Asberry, see 1860 U.S. Census, Richland, Monroe County, Indiana, roll: M653_282, p. 544, Family History Library Film *803282,* Ancestry.com. The roster of enlisted men for Company F, Eighty-Second Indiana Volunteer Infantry, in Alf[red] G. Hunter, *History of the Eighty-Second Indiana Volunteer Infantry: Its Organization, Campaigns, and Battles* (Indianapolis: Wm. B. Burford, 1893), 224, lists Joel A. Farmer and William M. Farmer, both of Bloomington, Indiana, who mustered in on August 30, 1862. William was discharged November 11, 1864, due to wounds. Joel mustered out on June 9, 1865. The whereabouts of Farmer's other sons is uncertain as no definitive records have been found to date. However, Farmer states that one of his sons died in Memphis, Tennessee, after battle, and FindAGrave.com has a listing for James E. Farmer, whose tombstone lists Eli and Elizabeth as his parents, and his death date as December 26, 1865. It states that he was 32 years old.

3. Eli and Elizabeth Farmer had three daughters: Matilda, born ca. 1832; Sarah, born ca. 1836; and Harriet, born ca. 1851. For Matilda and Sarah, see the 1850 U.S. census for Eli P. Farmer, roll: M432_161, p. 242B, image 53; for Harriet see the 1860 U.S. census for Eli P. Farmer, roll: M653_282, p. 544, Family History Library Film 803282.

4. The Richland Rangers were organized in Monroe County, Indiana, during the summer of 1863, with Captain John Wylie commanding. See Charles Blanchard, ed., *Counties of Morgan, Monroe, and Brown, Indiana: Historical and Biographical* (Chicago: F. A. Battey and Co., 1884), 420.

5. At least two of Farmer's sons, Joel and William, joined the Eighty-Second Indiana Volunteer Infantry in August 1862 (see note 2). One of the chaplains for this regiment was Samuel McNaughton, who received his commission on September 2, 1862, according to the roster of officers for this regiment in Hunter, *History of the Eighty-Second Indiana Volunteer Infantry*, 178.

6. Major General Don Carlos Buell was commanding officer of the Army of the Ohio (Union), under which at least two of Eli Farmer's sons served in the Eighty-Second Indiana Volunteer Infantry during the Battle of Perryville, Kentucky, on October 8, 1862.

7. Colonel Morton C. Hunter was commanding officer of the Eighty-Second Indiana Volunteer Infantry and was later promoted to general. Hunter, *History of the Eighty-Second Indiana Volunteer Infantry*, 177.

8. According to Brett Schulte, "862[n]d: Union Army of the Ohio, 8 October 1862," TOCWOC—A Civil War Blog, May 31, 2010, http://www.brettschulte.net/CWBlog/2010/05/31/862gd-union-army-of-the-ohio-8-october-1862/, M. B. Walker was colonel of the first brigade of the first division of the Third Army Corps in the Army of the Ohio. The Eighty-Second Indiana Volunteer Infantry served under Walker's command.

9. Doctor William H. Lemon of Bloomington, Indiana, mustered into the Eighty-Second Indiana Volunteer Infantry in September 1862 and was commissioned as surgeon of the regiment in May 1863 (Hunter, *History of the Eighty-Second Indiana Volunteer Infantry*, 179).

10. This may have been General Lovell H. Rousseau from Kentucky, who was promoted to major general for his bravery at the Battle of Perryville. See Schulte, "862[n]d: Union Army of the Ohio, 8 October 1862" and "Lovell H. Rousseau," https://www.findagrave.com/memorial/8246628/lovell-h.-rousseau.

11. Captain William W. Browning of Nashville mustered into the Eighty-Second Indiana Volunteer Infantry in August 1862 and was honorably discharged in December 1864. Hunter, *History of the Eighty-Second Indiana Volunteer Infantry*, 181. See also Weston A. Goodspeed, "Military History of Brown County [Indiana]," Genealogy Trails, http://genealogytrails.com/ind/brown/military-history.html.

12. William M. Farmer's entry in the Indiana Digital Archives, https://secure.in.gov/apps/iara/search/Home/Detail?rId=1210552, states that he was discharged on November 11, 1864, at Kingston, Georgia.

13. According to his entry in FindaGrave.com, James E. Farmer died on December 26, 1865. (See note 2.)

Conclusion: Christian Union at Last, 1863 to 1881

1. Eli P. Farmer, Autobiography, 280–83, Farmer Manuscripts, 1818–1874, Lilly Library, Indiana University, Bloomington.

2. For all of his unhappiness with the Methodist church in later years, it appears that Farmer could never completely divorce himself from his Methodist roots. If the entire manuscript was written late in life, it is telling that he remarks then that preaching on the Franklin circuit was the best year of his life (1831–32). And despite his unhappiness with the Bloomington Methodist Episcopal Church it is believed that he attended there in later life. Church records include a tribute to his life. His obituary records that his funeral was held in the Bloomington Methodist Episcopal Church.

Index

Acton, _____, 167
Adventists (Millerites), 137, 155, 156, 169
African Americans, 4, 78, 158–59, 110, 193, 205n12; revival meeting (illus.), 157
Alabama, 111, 114
Aldersgate (London), 7
Allen, _____, 151
Allison, John (Eli's father-in-law), 58
Allison, Matilda. See Farmer, Matilda Allison
Allsup family, 58, 59
Altar, 14, 15, 43–47, 49, 110, 127, 200n3; (illus.), 46
American Colonization Society, 36
Americanization of Christianity, 111
Ames, Edward R., 179
Anabaptists, 45, 136
Anglicans, 8, 37, 40, 42, 68, 111, 134, 136, 156, 205n16
Appalachian Mountains, 9, 74
Arianism, 182
Armfield, John, 188
Arminianism, 40, 41, 42, 110
Arminius, Jacob, 40
Armstrong, James, presiding elder, 87, 104, 106, 176
Army of the Ohio, 211nn6–8 (chap. 18)
Arrington, Alfred, preacher, 98, 99, 100, 101, 204n4 (chap. 9)
Asbury, Francis, 7, 9, 56, 78
Assemblies of God, 54
Atlantic Ocean, 205n13
Attica, 73

Backsliding, 17, 23, 24, 41, 108
Baltimore, 7, 9, 111
Bangs, Nathan, 4, 109, 198n14
Baptism, 136, 172–73, 177, 206n6 (chap. 12), 207n12
Baptists, 4, 9, 10, 24, 38, 39, 41, 45, 50, 51, 61, 99, 111, 114, 130, 135, 137, 154, 155, 169, 172, 179, 183, 206n2, 206n4 (chap. 12); African Americans, 158; Anti-Missionary, 41, 137; Free Will, 41, 137; Hardshell, 137; Missionary, 41, 137; Particular, 137; Primitive, 41, 137; Regular, 41, 137; Separate, 41, 137; and United, 137
Bardstown (KY), 186
Bardstown Pike, 88
Bartholomew County, 210n8
Bascom, Henry B., 36, 38, 49–50
"Battle Hymn of the Republic," 41, 78, 79
Beasontown (PA), 14, 15, 23

Bedford, 60, 71, 124, 125, 189
Benjamin Franklin (steamboat), 159
Bennett, _____ (Quaker), 82
Berry, Col. _____, 144, 145
Big Black Wolfe, The, 81, 82, 83
Big Creek, 75
Big Gayandott, 23
Big Hog Thief Settlement, 123
Big Lick River, 22
Big Salt Creek, 163
Big Salt River, 175
Bigger, Governor Samuel, 138, 141–42, 208n2 (chap. 13)
Bingold (TN), 190
Black Masons, 124
Blade, Damascus, 148
Bloomfield, 61, 62, 65, 67, 69, 94, 95, 97, 201n7 (chap. 5)
Bloomington, 1, 43, 53, 56, 58, 67, 69, 82, 91, 103, 117, 118, 132, 134, 137, 161, 207n10
Bloomington Post, (illus.), 143
Bloomington Religious Times, 157, 169–77, 183, 206n1 (chap. 11); (illus.), 174
"Blow Ye the Trumpet Blow," 40
Bodmer, Karl, 28
Boehm, Henry, 44, 200n4
Book of Common Prayer, 200n6
Book of Revelation, 155, 156, 157, 173
Boreland, Matthew, 58, 59
Boston (MA), 9, 109
Bourbon County (KY), 3
Bowman, _____, 193
Brandon, J., 133
Brandon, Jesse, 169
Brethren, 9, Apostolic Christian, 137; Brethren Church Ashland, 137; Brethren Church (Grace Brethren), 137; Brethren Church Winona Lake, 137; Brethren in Christ, 137; Dunkard Brethren, 137; Old Brethren, 137; Old German Baptists, 137; Old Order German Baptists, 137
Bridges, _____, 167
Bright, Jesse D., 147
Brown County, 123, 173, 175, 205n1, 210n8
Brown, Elijah, 163
Browning, William W., 189, 212n11
Buell, Major General Don Carlos, 187, 211n6
Buell, Reverend Henry, 85, 87, 203n3
Buley, R. Carlyle, 134

Bunger, Phillip, 121, 122, 123, 144
Buskirk, Abraham, 53, 58, 59
Buskirk, Judge George A., 43
Buskirk, Hanah, 43, 47
Buskirk, John B., 58, 59
Buskirk, Samuel H., 43
Buskirk, Thomas, 59
Butler, Charles (NY), 148, 208n5 (chap. 13)
Butler, Squire _____, 123

Calvinists, 8, 24, 39–42, 53, 99, 115, 182
Camp meetings, 3, 4, 5, 10, 13, 14–15, 27, 28, 40, 41, 43, 44, 45, 48–50, 56, 68, 69, 71–72, 81–83, 87–88, 102, 106, 108, 109, 110, 111, 125, 130, 158–59, 202n9 (chap. 5); (illus.), 14
Campbell, Alexander, 41, 169
Campbellites (Christian Church), 38, 41, 61, 99, 111, 114, 133, 136–37, 139, 167, 169, 172, 173, 207n11, 207n13
Cane Ridge (KY) camp meeting, 3, 4, 41, 44, 48, 74, 108, 109, 110, 111, 138, 158, 181, 204n2 (chap. 9)
Carlisle, 149
Cartwright, Peter, 3, 4, 38, 67, 181–82, 202n2 (chap. 6); (illus.), 183
Cary, Jason, 64
"Catholic," 134–35
Catholicism, 45, 46, 47, 68, 134, 136, 153, 154, 172, 173, 175, 199n5, 205n16; prejudices against, 154–57
Chase, _____, Presbyterian preacher, 130, 131
Chattanooga (TN), 185, 190
Chautauqua Movement, 4, 110
Chesapeake Bay, 4, 19, 110, 205n13
Chicago (IL), 87, 115
Chipman, Rev. Draper, 94, 162, 163, 167
Chowden (England), 28
Christadelphians, 169
Christian Union Church, 1, 131, 132, 133, 134, 139, 140, 161–67, 169, 172, 185, 193, 202n14, 205n1, 206nn2–4 (chap. 12), 207n11, 207n13, 209n7
Church of the Nazarene, 54
Cincinnati, 26, 114, 191
Circuit Rider Days in Indiana, 2
Citizens of Zion: The Social Origin of Camp Meeting Revivalism, 48
Civil War, 185–91
Clark, Father Michael J., 153, 154, 208n2 (chap. 14)
Clark's Grant, 38, 181
Clarksburg (VA), 19, 26
Clay County, 149
Cobbing, 18
Columbus (OH), 166
"Come to Jesus," 77, 78
Congregationalists, 8, 9, 24, 39, 47, 70, 111, 114–15, 136, 156, 179, 182, 205n16
Cowger, _____, 101

Crammer, Thomas, 200n6
Crary, _____, 176
Crawfordsville, 85, 87, 207n10
Creek Nation, 75, 76, 78, 80, 81
Croakers, 1
Croherly, Grafton (Terre Haute), 151

Dabney, James, 49
Danville, 129, 130, 205n1
Danville (IL), 120
Daviess County, 65, 149
Davis, Doctor _____, 149, 151, 152
Day, Edmond, 88
Deer Creek, 88
Delaware, 158, 205n13
Delmarva Peninsula, 110, 111, 205n13
Delphi, 88
Democratization of American Christianity, 2, 88
DePauw University, 4, 117, 140, 179, 197n3, 206n5 (chap. 12), 211n7 (chap. 17)
Dew, _____, 172
Disciples of Christ, 41, 61
Dispensationalism, 156
Doctrines and Discipline of the Methodist Episcopal Church (*Discipline*), 8, 37, 60, 67, 68, 73, 162, 176
Dow, Lorenzo, 87–88; (illus.), 89
Dunn, George G., 141, 142, 145, 149, 150, 151, 152
Dunning, Paris C., 141, 142, 144, 145, 208n3 (chap. 13)
Dusand, William, 92
Dutch emigrants, 26
Dutch Reformed, 183

East, James, 163
Eddy, R. M., 181
Edwards, Jonathan, 8, 39, 156, 199n5 (chap. 3), 200n10
Eighty-Second Indiana Volunteer Infantry, 185, 211nn5–8 (chap. 18), 212n11
Elk River, 22
Elston, Isaac, 85, 87
Encyclopedia of Methodism, 4, 36
Enlightenment, 7
Episcopalians, 70, 111, 114, 139, 172, 205n16
Eschatology, 155
Eslinger, Ellen, 9, 48
Evangelical Association, 45, 114, 200n4
Evangelicalism, 44, 45, 111
Ewing, John, 147–48
Excommunication, 161, 209n3

Fairfax, 163
Fairplay, 69, 94, 96, 98, 202n9 (chap. 5)
Farley, William, 163
Farmer, Asberry (Eli's son), 211n2
Farmer, Burton (Eli's son), 211n2

Farmer, Eli, and Andrew Wylie, 139; and anti-Catholic views, 154, 173, 175, 208n4 (chap. 14); attends school in Kentucky, 24; backsliding, 23, 31, 36, 37, 43; birth, 11; and Bloomington business, 117, 118; and *Bloomington Religious Times*, 169–77, 206n1 (chap. 11); and Bloomfield, 61–62, 67, 94, 97; and Brown County, 123; buys land and farms near Bloomington, 56–57; buys salt works, 118; camp meetings, 13, 14–15, 43, 48–50, 54–56, 60, 67, 69, 71–72, 81–83, 87–88, 102, 125–27, 130–31; and Catholic priest, 153, 154, 208n2 (chap. 14); and Chicago, 87, 119; and children, 60, 98, 185–88, 190–91, 211nn2–3, 211nn5–6; and Christian Union Church, 131, 132, 133, 134, 161–67, 205n1; and Civil War, 169, 185–91, 206n2 (chap. 11); and Crawfordsville, 91; and Crawfordsville circuit, 85; and Creek Nation, 75–76, 78, 80, 81; and Danville circuit, 129, 205n1; death, 194; death of first wife, 60; and Delphi, 88; early childhood, 12–13; and Fairplay, 62, 94; father dies, 34; and fighting, 32–34, 59, 121–23; fights Thomas Henley, 146–47; and Franklin circuit, 103, 104, 106, 107, 212n2; funeral, 211n2; grand chaplain of Grand Masonic Lodge of Indiana, 192; and Greencastle circuit, 117, 205n1; and Greene County circuit, 60; ill health, 91–94, 97; and Indiana University being run by Presbyterians, 141–49; and Indians, 90; and Kentucky, 19–24; and Lafayette, 86, 87, 88; and Lawrenceburg conference, 131; and leaving Methodist Church, 162–63, 183–84; licensed by Methodist conference, 56; map showing circuits, cities, and counties he served, xii; opens school, 25, 26–27, 31; marries second wife, 85; and Martinsville, 105, 106, 107; and Michigan City, 87; and Mexican War, 169, 172; and New Albany conference, 123; obituary (illus.), 195; and Paoli circuit, 60; portrait, ii; preaches at Indiana University chapel, 132, 133; preaches to slaves in Natchez (MS), 157–59; and Quakers, 64–65; and riverboats, 31, 34, 35, 36, 38; runs for Congress, 149–52; and Sam Houston, 25–26; serves in War of 1812, 17–19; and Sioux Indians (west of Chicago), 119–20; state senator, 142–48, 192, 205–6n1; studies medicine, 25; talks with Baptist about religion, 39, 42; and temperance, 169, 170, 171; and Texas, 24; and tyranny of Methodist church government, 129; and Vermillion circuit (IL), 73; and Vincennes, 87; and Washington circuit, 94, 97; and White Lick circuit, 103; withdraws from Methodist preaching conference, 131–32, 205n1 (chap. 11)
Farmer, Eli P. (Eli's nephew), 186
Farmer, Eli R. (Eli's son), 211n2
Farmer, Elizabeth McClung (Eli's second wife), 85, 94, 95, 164–66, 203n2, 204n3 (chap. 9), 211nn2–3
Farmer, Harriet (Eli's daughter), 211n3
Farmer, James E. (Eli's son), 185, 190, 191, 204n3 (chap. 9), 211n2, 212n13
Farmer, Joel (Eli's father), 11, 12, 34
Farmer, Joel A. (Eli's son), 185, 187, 188, 191, 211n2, 211n5
Farmer, John A. (Eli's son), 60, 204n3 (chap. 9), 211n2
Farmer, Matilda Allison (Eli's first wife), 56, 60, 204n3 (chap. 9), 211n2
Farmer, Melville (Eli's son), 204n3 (chap. 9)
Farmer, Michael, 60, 71
Farmer, Sarah (Eli's daughter), 211n3
Farmer, Sarah Rice (Eli's mother), 11
Farmer, Thomas (Eli's brother), 50, 60
Farmer, William (Eli's brother), 31, 32
Farmer, William M. (Eli's son), 189, 194, 211n2, 211n5, 212n12
Faux, William, 27
Finley, James, 3
Finney, Charles G., 156, 200n3
First Great Awakening, 8, 39, 44, 70, 137, 156, 200n10
First Prayer Book, The, 200n6
First United Methodist Church (Bloomington), 195
Flack, J. V. B., 166
Flatboats, (illus.), 37
Forbe, _____, 167
Fort Nelson (VA), 18
Fort Norfolk (VA), 18
Fort Poorburg, 18
Fort Wayne Female College. *See* Taylor University
Foster, William, 145
Fox River, 120
Frankfurt (KY), 11
Franklin, Benjamin, 8
Franklin County (KY), 11
Free grace, 200n8
Free will, 200n8
Freedom of the Will, 199n5 (chap. 3)
Frontier Camp Meeting, The, 110
Fry, B. St. James, 77

Genesee conference (NY), 114
Gillbad, 13, 23, 48
Given, J. F., 166
Gorman, Gen. Willis A., 144, 145
Grand Masonic Lodge of Indiana, 192
Granny Island (VA), 18
Greencastle, 117, 205n1
Greene County, 47, 60, 64, 67, 149, 201n7 (chap. 5), 202n3 (chap. 6)
Grimes, _____, 81, 82
Grimes, Stephen, 56
Guide to Holiness, 47

Hamilton, Samuel, 55
Hannigan, _____, 146
Hanover College, 138
Harpers Ferry, 13
Harrison, 180

Harvard University, 70, 98
Hatch, Nathan O., 2, 88, 111, 137, 138
Haven, James, 176
Hawpatch area, 210n6 (chap. 16)
Hendricks County, 130
Henley, Thomas Jefferson, 146, 147, 208n4 (chap. 13)
Herodsburg (KY), 24
Hettonsville, 163
Hillman, Joseph, 78
History of Indianapolis and Marion County, 106
History of Methodism, 109
Holiday, Charles, 81
Holiness Movement, 5, 47, 54, 110
Holiness–Pentecostal Movement, 74
Holland, John, 123
Holliday, F. C., 180
Holy of Holies, 46
Holy Rollers, 54
Hoosier Faiths, 41
Hoosier, Harry, 158, 205n12
Hoover, _____, 187
Houston, Samuel, 17, 25, 26
Howard, General _____, 145, 146, 152
Howard County, 201n7 (chap. 4)
Howe, Joseph, 146
Huffs, David, 47
Hunt, William, 166, 209n11
Hunter, General Morton C., 187, 190, 211n7 (chap. 18)
Huntsville, 166, 209n11

Illinois, 67, 111, 114
Indiana, 138; and evangelical Christianity, 111; growth of Methodist Church in, 179–84
Indiana Asbury. *See* DePauw University
Indiana College. *See* Indiana University
Indiana Magazine of History, 99
Indiana Palladium, 68
Indiana Seminary, (illus.), 132
Indiana State Senate, 142–45, 192, 205–6n1
Indiana University, 117, 138, 139, 140, 141, 142, 208n23; (illus.), 132
Indianapolis, 74, 99, 104, 179, 207n10
Indians, 3, 11, 12, 35, 90
Internal Improvements Act, 142, 144, 170, 208n3, 208n5 (chap. 13)

Jacksonville (OH), 167
Jeffersonville, 167, 207n10
Jeffs, _____, 13, 14
Jerking, (illus.), 89
Jewish synagogues, 183
Jobson, Frederick J., 180–81, 182
Johnson, Rev. Amsa, 125
Johnson, Charles, 4, 110
Johnson, David, 55

Johnson, Findley, 55
Johnson, Lantz, 50
Johnson, William, 110
Johnson, William Courtland, 158

Kanawha River, 23
Kankakee River, 120
Kansiwawa River, 19; salt works, 19
Kansmanawa River, 20
Kentucky, 9, 11, 19–24, 110, 111, 114, 138
King, _____, 118
Kingswood (England), 28
Knox County, 149
Kossuth, sawmill (illus.), 120

LaBerteaux, Asner, 118
Ladies' Home Repository, 155
Lafayette, 85, 86, 87, 88, 153
Lagrange County, 210n6 (chap. 16)
Lasley, _____, 147
Lawrence County, 149
Lawrenceburg, 131, 204n4 (chap. 9)
Leatherwood Camp Ground, 125
Lee, Jesse, 4, 9, 109
Lemon, Doctor William H., 185, 187, 211n9 (chap. 18)
Leonard, _____, 62
Lexington (KY), 24, 74
Liberty Bell, 40
Ligonier, 201n6 (chap. 16)
Limestone (KY), 35
"Limited atonement," 200n7
Lincoln, Abraham, 182, 202n2 (chap. 6), 206n5 (chap. 12)
Little Hog Thief, 123
Logan County (KY), 3, 28
London County (VA), 11
Longlay, _____, 88, 90
Lord, _____, preacher, 13
Lorenz, E. S., 203n9
Lorenz, Ellen Jane, 78, 203n9
Lorenzo Dow and the Jerking Exercise, (illus.), 89
Lossing–Barrett, 89
Louisville, 36, 38, 43, 87, 88, 153, 186, 191
Louisville and Nashville Railroad, 188
Lowe, Gen. _____, 144, 145
Luther, Martin, 45
Lutherans, 136, 205n16
Lynching mobs, 28

Madison, 10, 87, 118, 186, 207n10
Mann, E. B., Universalist preacher, 98, 99, 100, 101
Manogasha River, 35
Marching to Zion, 41
Marietta (OH), 26
Martin, Col. Thomas, 13
Martinsville, 105, 106, 107

Maryland, 158, 205n13
Massachusetts, 207n20
Maxwell, Doctor David, 138, 141, 142, 145
May, Phillip, 132, 133, 207n10, 207n14
Mayfield, Leroy, 58
McClung, Elizabeth. *See* Farmer, Elizabeth McClung
M'Clure, D., 10
McCrea, Col. John, 125, 126
McDonald, Judge David, 101, 151
McNaughton, Reverend Samuel, 186, 211n5
McNemar, Richard, 41
McTyeire, Bishop Holland, 109
Memphis (TN), 98
Mennonites, 9, 135; Amish, 137; Conservative, 137; General Conference, 137; Missionary Church Association, 137; Nonconference Conservative, 137; Old Order Evangelical, 137; Woodland Amish, 137
Merom, 151
Methodism and the Frontier Indiana Proving Ground, 28
Methodists, 1, 2, 7, 9, 10, 23, 24, 154, 155, 169; 1878 hymnal, 205n16; and camp meetings, 60–61; church growth, 108–15, 179–84, 204n5 (chap. 10); and circuit appointments, 86, 207n10; and conferences, 60–61; and credentials, 56, 201n4; General Rules, 37; and marriage, 56; and preachers, 60–61; and protracted meeting, 62, 202n11; and sects: African American Methodist Episcopal Church, 158; African American Methodist Episcopal Church Zion, 158; Christian Methodist Episcopal, 159; Colored Methodist Episcopal Church (CME), 159; Free Methodist, 137; Methodist Episcopal Church, 41, 109; organization of, 67–68; Methodist Episcopal Church South, 36, 109, 159, 205n16; Methodist Protestant, 137, 204n7 (chap. 10); Primitive, 88; Republican Methodist Church, 209n11; United Methodist, 200n4; Wesleyan Methodist, 40, 41, 44, 137, 157; and station appointments, 86, 87, 207n10; and trial, 59, 201n6 (chap. 5); views on dress and church buildings, 37, 38
Mexican War, 17–19, 142, 153, 163, 169, 172
Michigan City, 85, 87
Millennialist, 200n10
Miller, John, presiding elder, 133, 148
Miller, William, 169, 208n5 (chap. 14)
Millerites. *See* Adventists
Milum, Jane, 62, 64
Milum, William, 64
Miners, in England, 199n5 (chap. 2)
Mississippi, 111, 114, 138
Missouri, 67
Monongahela (PA), 17
Monroe County, 1, 101, 149, 166, 211n4; land deed (illus.), 57
Montgomery County, 203n2
Moore, Nelson (Eli's brother-in-law), 74
Moore, Samuel, 189

Mooresville (near Harpers Ferry), 14
Moravians, 9, 136
Morgan, _____, 35
Mormons, 137, 155, 169
Morrow, William, 161, 162, 167, 209n2
Mosler, Henry, 189
Mt. Carmel (IL), 85
Murphy, Harvey, 169
Music, and camp meetings, 76–79

Nashville (TN), 189
Natchez (MS), 153
National Holiness Association, 54, 110
Nebraska, 194
Neeld (Neild), Benjamin, 62, 161, 162
New Albany, 53, 123
New Harmony, 95, 169; Owens settlement, 62
New Jersey, 8, 110
New Spain, 24
New York, 109–10
Newberry, 64, 69
Noble County, 210n6 (chap. 16)
Nonsectarianism, 139–40
Norfolk (VA), 17
Norris, Ira, 166
Northwest Christian Advocate, 114–15
Norvall, Doctor _____, 147
"Noted Infidel," 61, 202n10
Nottingham, Elizabeth K., 28, 29, 198n3

Old Northwest Pioneer Period, 1815–1840, The, 134
O'Neal, John, 64, 65
Ohio, 67, 111, 114, 138
Ohio River, 11, 23, 26, 38, 53
Otwell, Frank, 69
Owen, Rev. Isaac, 134, 148, 149

Palmer House (Indianapolis), 146, 147
Palmer, Phoebe, 47, 110, 201n6 (chap. 4)
Parker, P. C., 172
Parker, Polly, 43, 47
Passmore, Squire, 62
Pattan (Patton) Doctor _____, 61, 62, 95
Penn, William, 8, 156
Pennsylvania, 111, 114
Pentecostalism, 5, 47, 54, 201n7 (chap. 4)
Pering, Cornelius, 132
Perryville, 83
Perryville (KY), battle of, 185, 186, 188, 211n6; (illus.), 189
Philadelphia (OH), 167
Phillips, William, 172
Pine Creek, 73
Pittsburgh, 35
Politics, 141–52
Port Orchard, 18

Posey, Walter, 71
Post-millennialists, 9, 39, 156, 175, 199n5, 200n10
Potomac River, 14
Preaching and preachers, 105–8
Presbyterian Societies of New England, 10
Presbyterians, 3, 4, 9, 10, 24, 39, 41, 45, 47, 70, 86, 99, 111, 114, 130, 136, 137, 138, 141, 154, 155, 156, 172, 179, 182, 183, 205n16, 206n2, 206n4 (chap. 12); divide into Old and New Schools, 41; and Indiana University, 141, 142; New School, 137, 139; Old School, 137, 139; and sects: Associated Reformed (Union), 137; Associated (Seceders), 137; Cumberland, 41, 96, 114, 130, 137, 204n2 (chap. 9); New Lights, 41, 99, 114, 127, 137, 155, 163, 167
Presmore, Squire _____, 61
Princeton, 27
Public Square Religion, 133, 139, 207n13
Puritans, 8, 9, 45, 136, 156
Putnam, _____, 166

Quakers, 9, 64, 65, 111, 135, 136, 137, 155, 167, 172; Central Yearly Meeting, 137; Friends General Conference, 137; Friends World Committee, 137; Hicksites, 137; Indiana Yearly Meeting, 137; Querneyites, 137; Western Conservative Meeting, 137; Western Five Years Meeting, 137

Randolph County, 209n11
Raper, John, 57, 58
Reason River, 24
Redford, A. H., 2
Reed, Isaac, 10
Regulators, 123, 124
Rehobath Chapel (GA), 88
Restorationism, 169–75, 200n10
Revivalism, 4, 5, 27, 28, 39–40, 41, 42, 69–72, 136, 154–57
Revivalist: A Collection of Choice Revival Hymns and Tunes, The, 78
Rice, Richard, 13
Rice, Sarah. *See* Farmer, Sarah Rice
Richey, Russell, 110
Richland Rangers, 211n4
Ritchie, Judge _____, 104, 105, 106, 107, 148
Robertson, James, presiding elder, 163, 167
Robinson, _____, 118
Robinson, Dick, 188
Robinson, Elmo, 99
Rochester (NY), 205n16
Rousseau, General Lovell H., 188, 212n10
Rovenscroft, Captain _____, 188
Rudolph, L. C., 41
Rutter, Calvin, 176

Salem, 87
Salt River, 187

Salt works, 19, 22, 23, 75
Sanctification, 53–54
Sandy Salt Works (KY), 75
"Say, Brother," 78; (illus.), 79
Scott, Captain _____, 26
Scott, James, 176
Second Great Awakening, 2, 3, 6, 27, 54, 108, 137, 156, 158, 194, 200n3
Sectarianism, 5, 132, 134–40, 154–57, 164, 202n14, 206nn2–4, 206n6 (chap. 12), 207n9, 209n7
Sectarianism Is Heresy, 139
Shafer, John, fights with Eli Farmer, 32–34
Shakers, 137, 155
Shaw, _____, 193
"Sheep stealing," 206n2 (chap. 12)
Shelby County (KY), 24, 39
Shelbyville (KY), 48
Shelman, _____, 24
Shepherdsville (KY), 186
Sherman, General William T., 191
Shively, Michael, 17, 18
Simpson, Matthew, 4, 36, 131, 140, 161, 179, 206n5 (chap. 12)
"Sinner's bench," 200n3
Slain in the Spirit, 47, 54, 71, 158, 201n7 (chap. 4)
Slaveholders Rebellion, 98
Slaves, 110, 156, 193
Sluss, John M., 145, 146, 147
Smith, Doctor Abraham, 81, 82, 83
Smith, Joseph, 169
Smith, William, 163
Snake or Serpent Handling, 73, 74
Snethen, Abraham, 61
Socinianism, 182, 211n9 (chap. 17)
Somers, _____, Cumberland Presbyterian preacher, 130, 131
South Bend, 207n10
Southampton (MA), 8
Southern Review, 36
Spencer, 54, 55, 91
Spencer, Spere, 24
Spiritualists, 155
Springfield (KY), 186
Station, Ennis, 11
Stephens, _____, 124
Stevens, Abel, 4, 109, 111, 114
Stone, Barton A., 3, 41
Stowe, Harriett Beecher, 157
Strange, Josiah, presiding elder, 105, 106, 204n3 (chap. 10)
Strawbridge, Richard, 109
Stump speech, (illus.), 150
Sulgrove, Berry, 106
Sullivan, 151
Sullivan County, 149
Sulphur's Creek, 72

Sweeny, _____, 56
Sweet, William Wallace, 2, 4, 197–98n3

Taggart, James, 175
Taggart, William, 175, 210n8
Taylor University, 179
Temperance, 169, 170
Tennent, Gilbert, 8
Tennessee, 110, 111, 114, 138
Terre Haute, 75, 166, 207n10
Testimony of the President, Professors, Tutors, and Hebrew Instructor of Harvard College Against George Whitefield, The, 70, 71
Texas, 24
Third Army Corps, 211n8 (chap. 18)
Thomas, John, 167, 169
Thompson, John, 41
Tilscum, Col. _____, 189
Tippecanoe Battleground, 90
Tolbert, Dr. _____, presiding elder, 123, 124, 125, 126, 127, 129
Trinity United Methodist Church (Lafayette), 87
Troeltsch, Ernst, 44
Tryune (TN), 188, 189

Union Station (Indianapolis), 179
Unitarians, 8, 9, 98, 99, 111, 155, 157, 182, 183, 203n7, 205n16
United Brethren Church, 114, 157, 203n9; and sects: Church of the United Brethren in Christ, 170; Indiana Republican United Brethren, 172; Ohio Republican United Brethren, 172; Republican United Brethren Church, 170, 172, 173, 175, 177
United Theological Seminary (Dayton, OH), 203n9
Universalists, 74, 75, 98, 99, 100, 101, 111, 155, 172, 203n7
"Unlimited atonement," 40

Vanclives, _____, 61
Vermillion Circuit (IL), 7
Vermillion River, 81–83
Vincennes, 27, 85, 87
Virginia, 11, 25, 26, 111, 158, 205n13

Wabash and Erie Canal, 148, 153
Wabash College, 138
Wabash River, 75; (illus.), 28
Wabash Valley, 73
Walker, Col. M. B., 187, 211n8 (chap. 18)
Wallace, David, 103, 104, 204n2 (chap.10)
Wallace's Settlement, 98
War of 1812, 17–19
Ward, Captain _____, 189, 190
Wardle, Annie, 4
Warner, Col. _____, 100
Warren County (GA), 88

Washington, 97, 98, 100, 103
Washington, DC, 205n16
Washington, George, 8
Watts, Isaac, 76
Wayne, General Anthony, 11
Webb, Thomas, 109
Wesley, Charles, 7, 76, 78
Wesley, John, 7, 8, 37, 40, 53, 54, 76, 77, 136, 176, 182, 206n7 (chap. 12)
West, _____ (Eli's brother-in-law), 120
Western Cavaliers: Embracing the History of the Methodist Episcopal Church in Kentucky from 1832 to 1844, 2
Western Christian Advocate, 38, 114, 172, 211n9 (chap. 17)
Western Olive Branch, 99
Western Revival, 2, 3, 5, 6, 15, 54, 108, 109, 111, 114, 137, 138
Western Times, 169
Whig Party, 141, 142, 146, 147, 149, 152, 169
White Cloud (steamboat), 159
White River valley, 64, 102
Whitefield, George, 70, 71, 207n20
Whitehead, Thomas, 126, 127
Whitted, Dr. _____, 163
Wild Cat Creek, 90
Wiley, Allen, 176, 180, 182
Williams, Gayle, 139
Williams, William H., 110
Wilson, _____, 151
Winchester, 130
Winfrey, John, 124
Wood, Aaron, 87
Woodland Indians, (illus.), 119
Worn-out preachers, 1
Wright, Governor Joseph A., 180
Wylie, Captain _____, 187–88
Wylie, Andrew, president of Indiana University, 133, 138, 139, 176
Wylie, John, 186
Wylie, Theophilus Adam, 150
Wynds, Judge _____, 62, 95, 96

Yohegany River, 13

Zion's Herald (Boston), 109